SYSTEMS THINKING FOR INSTRUCTIONAL DESIGNERS

Systems Thinking for Instructional Designers offers real-world cases that highlight how designers foster continuous improvement and manage change efforts across organizational contexts. Using a systems thinking approach, each case describes a holistic process that examines how a set of interdependent elements can be analyzed and coordinated to influence change. Instructional designers, faculty, program directors, digital learning leaders, and other development specialists will learn how systems thinking can solve authentic, real-world challenges. The book's rich narratives cover both successes and failures of meaningful growth, paradigm shifts, and large-scale problem-solving in a variety of settings, including education and industry.

M. Aaron Bond is Senior Director for Learning Services at Virginia Polytechnic Institute and State University, USA.

Suha Rahif Tamim is Clinical Assistant Professor in the Department of Instruction and Teacher Education in the College of Education at University of South Carolina, USA.

Samantha J. Blevins is Instructional Designer & Learning Architect in the Center for Innovative Teaching & Learning at Radford University, USA.

Beth R. Sockman is Professor and Co-Department Chair in the Department of Professional and Secondary Education at East Stroudsburg University of Pennsylvania, USA.

"Readers of this book can draw quickly from these 25 rare and accessible narratives that demonstrate diverse education problem definitions and solutions found by professionals employing principles of systems theory and systems thinking. These cases resonate from diverse institutional settings ranging from K-12 (urban and rural), higher education (college and university), and health care contexts. Written in the voice of instructional designers and others, the editors of this book offer a symphony for education practitioners. This is a must-read for leaders who can benefit from the many lessons learned and shared by systemic change leaders."

Eugene G. Kowch, Associate Professor of Education at the University of Calgary, Canada

"The authors provide a welcome introduction to systems thinking through carefully constructed teaching cases from the world of education and related topics. The cases enable systems thinking faculty and students to explore this growing field through many accessible yet detailed examples which demonstrate the value of a systems approach to addressing chronic, complex problems."

David Peter Stroh, Founding Partner of Bridgeway Partners and Founding Director of AppliedSystemsThinking.com

"I'm so pleased to recommend this book to all change agents. This text is an important addition to the literature in the field, particularly given the strong link to practice and the ability to apply the lessons from these cases to the ongoing activities of those who wish to understand the systemic implications of their own change agentry. Given the diversity of cases, there's something for everyone in this text. This one should be on any practitioner's bookshelf when looking to make system-wide change."

Alison A. Carr-Chellman, Professor and Dean of the School of Education and Health Sciences at the University of Dayton, USA

SYSTEMS THINKING FOR INSTRUCTIONAL DESIGNERS

Catalyzing Organizational Change

Edited by M. Aaron Bond, Suha Rahif Tamim, Samantha J. Blevins, and Beth R. Sockman

Routledge
Taylor & Francis Group
NEW YORK AND LONDON

Cover image: Getty Images

First published 2022
by Routledge
605 Third Avenue, New York, NY 10158

and by Routledge
2 Park Square, Milton Park, Abingdon, Oxon OX14 4RN

Routledge is an imprint of the Taylor & Francis Group, an informa business

Library of Congress Cataloging-in-Publication Data
A catalog record for this title has been requested

ISBN: 978-0-367-90296-4 (hbk)
ISBN: 978-0-367-46441-7 (pbk)
ISBN: 978-1-003-02877-2 (ebk)

DOI: 10.4324/9781003028772

Typeset in Bembo
by Newgen Publishing UK

CONTENTS

NOTES ON CONTRIBUTORS

Todd Adrian is Director of Digital Program Development and Services at Indian River State College. He supervises a team consisting of instructional designers and course developers and works with the IRSC Global staff, faculty, and college administrators to design and develop online programs that support college initiatives. He has worked on several change management projects for the college, including transitions to a new learning management system and enterprise resources planning system. He serves on change management projects while working with teams requiring a systems thinking approach for planning and project management.

Kendal Askins is an administrator at Pleasant Valley Intermediate school. Prior to serving as Assistant Principal at PVI she was a mathematics teacher at various levels and a gifted support teacher for students in grades K-12. She holds both her Bachelor's and Master's degrees from CUNY Queens College and her Educational Leadership Certification from Wilkes University. In her spare time she enjoys spending time with her husband and three children. Mrs. Askins has wanted to teach since she could speak and her love for education continues to develop every day. She believes that one person can make a difference and it is important that our students believe that too!

M. Elizabeth Azukas is Assistant Professor in the Department of Professional and Secondary Education at East Strousburg University. She has been an educator for more than 25 years, with experience teaching at all levels. She has held several leadership roles including curriculum supervisor, principal, curriculum director and assistant superintendent. Her career has focused primarily on education innovation with the goal of increasing equity and access for all students and promoting personalized learning. Research areas include leading educational change; innovation and entrepreneurial skills; design thinking; systems thinking; online and blended learning, and communities of practice.

Dana Powell Baker is Assistant Professor and certified Medical Laboratory Scientist in clinical laboratory science education. Her areas of expertise include interprofessional education and healthcare simulation. Mrs. Baker earned her baccalaureate degree in medical technology from Georgia Southern University. She completed a Master's degree in business administration with an emphasis in human resource management. Subsequently, she obtained a Master of Science degree in healthcare simulation from the University of San Francisco.

Currently, she is pursuing her Doctoral Degree in Curriculum & Instruction at the University of South Carolina.

On a personal note, she enjoys quality time with her family.

Yasha Jones Becton currently serves as a Clinical Assistant Professor with her alma mater, the University of South Carolina. She also serves as a Family Engagement Specialist with the Carolina Family Engagement Center. Her research centers on multicultural education, family engagement and equity pedagogies.

M. Aaron Bond, Ph.D., has worked in the field of instructional technology, distance education and professional development for more than 20 years.

He has served as a corporate trainer, face-to-face classroom instructor, an online instructor and as a secondary principal. Currently he serves as the Senior Director for Learning Services in Technology-enhanced Learning and Online Strategies at Virginia Tech where he oversees faculty professional development, learning technologies and instructional design. He is past president of the Systems Thinking and Change division in AECT and serves on the board of directors for Blue Ridge Literacy. His research includes faculty professional development, authentic learning experiences, communities of practice, socio-cognitive factors on learning and distance learning. He is the co-author of the book *Building Virtual Communities of Practice for Distance Educators*.

Samantha J. Blevins, Ph.D., is currently an Instructional Designer & Learning Architect at Radford University within the Center for Innovative Teaching and Learning. She has broad design and teaching experience in various educational settings, including K-12, higher education and professional development. She has served in various roles for the Systems Thinking and Change division of AECT including Board Representative. Her research focus areas include: diffusion of innovation theory, electronic portfolio implementation; systems thinking and change; integrated learning practices; and faculty development.

Christopher Bogiages teaches courses and supervised doctoral candidates in the doctoral program for Innovation in Education at the University of South Carolina. His research interests include online learning, STEM teacher education and supporting educational activism.

Jeremy W. Bohonos is Assistant Professor in Adult, Professional and Community Education at Texas State University. He earned his Ph.D. in Education Policy, Organization and Leadership with a specialization in Human Resource Development (HRD) from the University of Illinois Urbana-Champaign. He conducts research regarding race and racism in US organizations, history of Adult Education, adult learning through music and mobile learning in Sub-Saharan Africa. He has published in journals that include *Gender, Work and Organization, Adult Education Quarterly, Advances in Developing Human Resources, New Horizons in Adult Education and Human Resource Development* and the *Journal of Adult Learning.*

Julia Bello-Bravo is currently Assistant Professor in the Department of Food Sciences and Human Nutrition at Michigan State University and a co-founder and co-director of Scientific Animations Without Borders (SAWBO). Dr. Bello-Bravo's research interests lie at the intersection of effective communication and education, specializing in informal education and communication strategies to reach low- or non-literate learners in developing and developed countries. Areas of research include identifying, developing and deploying scalable strategies for effective educational knowledge transfer and solution uptake to the 800 million low- and non-literate learners globally. Much of her research involves rural areas of Sub-Saharan Africa—over a dozen countries to date—investigating the appeal and learning gains delivered by animated educational videos viewed on mobile phones.

Todd Breiner is Principal at Pleasant Valley Intermediate School in Kunkletown, PA and has nine years of administrative experience. Prior to his time at PVIS, he served as an assistant principal at Emmaus High School in Emmaus, PA. He served one year as an assistant to the principal, two years as a grade level principal, and three years as the Assistant Principal for Academic Affairs. Mr. Breiner has taught health, physical education and driver education. He holds two Bachelor degrees in Health Education and Physical Education from East Stroudsburg University, earned a Master's of Education from Kutztown University in Curriculum and Instruction, and his Principal's Certification from Penn State University.

Janet K. Brishke is Project Director at the University of Florida. In this role, she leads all activities for the annual evaluation of the Florida KidCare program. Ms. Brishke also manages the Citizen Scientist Curriculum program, a joint collaboration between the OneFlorida Clinical Research Consortium and the University of Florida Clinical and Translational Science Institute. The curriculum is an open educational resource available to assist program managers who face challenges in operationalizing the education of community stakeholders. Ms. Brishke holds a Master of Public Health in Social and Behavioral Sciences from the University of Florida.

Russell D. Clark currently is Interim Director of Curriculum and Instruction for Anderson School District Two in Anderson, South Carolina. He teaches as an Adjunct Instructor of Literacy at Anderson University's College of Education. He has a Literacy Coach endorsement from the South Carolina Department of Education and is a doctoral candidate in Curriculum and Instruction at the University of South Carolina.

Michelle A. Cole, DNP, MSN, RN, CPN, is an innovative education leader with expertise in pediatric and public health nursing. With over a decade of teaching in higher education, Michelle takes a primary role in mentoring the next generation of nurses. Her areas of interest include pediatric clinical practice, global clinical immersions, and supporting students in their developmental journey of cultural awareness and sensitivity.

Michele Connors has been teaching Language Arts in grades 8–12 for the past 15 years in public schools in both Pennsylvania and Maryland. In 2006 she received a Bachelor's Degree in Literature from Lycoming College in Williamsport, Pennsylvania, and in 2020 she earned her Master's Degree in Professional and Secondary Education from East Stroudsburg University, East Stroudsburg, Pennsylvania. She is currently enrolled in the doctoral program in Educational Leadership and Administration at East Stroudsburg University.

Ariana Eichelberger is Associate Specialist and Instructional Designer in the College of Education at the University of Hawaii at Manoa. Ari manages the Instructional Support Group of the College and coordinates the College's faculty professional development program. As a faculty member of the Department of Learning Design and Technology, Ari teaches graduate and undergraduate courses in instructional design and technology integration. She is also an instructional designer with the COE's Distance Course Design and Consulting group (DCDC).

Christy Evans graduated from the University of Florida with a Master of Science in Accounting and is a tax accountant for a regional public accounting firm. Christy has been a Citizen Scientist for six years. She serves as a member the OneFlorida Clinical Research Consortium Steering and Executive Committees and works with researchers to help improve community health. Christy has also contributed to the making of the Citizen Scientist Curriculum, as well as several presentations and publications that have come from that work.

Khary Fletcher is Director of Humanities for Hartford Public Schools in Connecticut. Khary has taught at both the secondary and elementary levels in various roles such as social studies teacher, reading/language arts consultant, and reading interventionist. Khary is currently pursuing his doctorate in Curriculum and Instruction at the University of South Carolina. He earned a Sixth Year in Reading and a BA in History from the Southern CT State University and a masters in Secondary Education with a focus in literacy. His current action research interests involve cultural sustaining reading practices as part of instruction for middle and high school English Language Arts students.

Rick Gardner serves as the Chief Medical Officer (CMO) for CURE International and the Medical Director at CURE Ethiopia. He completed his surgical training in the UK and spent his Fellowship at the Hospital for Sick Children, in Toronto, Canada. His first introduction to CURE was in 2009 as a Surgical Fellow at CURE Malawi. Seeing the burden of childhood disability firsthand in Sub-Saharan Africa and the impact that CURE was having in the country were instrumental in his move to Ethiopia. He has served at CURE Ethiopia since September 2013, both as a Consultant Orthopedic Surgeon and as the Medical Director.

Christina Gunther, EdD, is Clinical Assistant Professor and Director of the Health Science Program and Global Health Programs at Sacred Heart University. Dr. Gunther's expertise lies within the field of cultural competence, diversity, equity, and inclusion in the healthcare arena. She presents and consults nationally on topics that include diversity, power and privilege, implicit bias, and stereotype representations. Dr. Gunther's current research focuses on students' self-awareness of their own cultural habits and implicit biases, best practices for creating culturally appropriate healthcare curricula, and reducing gender discrimination through empowerment of the individual.

Sri Andini Handayani is Project Coordinator at St. Jude Global Asia Pacific, St. Jude Children's Research Hospital. She works to bridge the gaps between evidence generation and program implementation. Andini applies health systems and policy perspectives to foster collaboration in the Asia Pacific region in improving health outcomes for children with cancer sustainably. She obtained a Master of Public Health degree with a concentration in Global Health from Boston University and a Master of Arts in International Development and Policy from the University of Chicago under the Obama Foundation Scholars Program. She was PUSKAPA's Associate for Research, Monitoring, and Evaluation for a full year of its CRVS program implementation in 2017–2018.

Eileen M. Handberg is Research Professor of Medicine, Director of the Cardiovascular Clinical Trials Program in the Division of Cardiovascular Medicine and Program Co-Director, OneFlorida Clinical Research Consortium. She is an active clinical trialist in the areas of ischemic heart disease with a focus on women, hypertension, cardiovascular cell therapy, prevention, and exercise interventions. She is an Adult Nurse Practitioner, working in interventional cardiology, general cardiology outpatient, and manages research patient care. She has contributed to over 300 peer-reviewed articles and abstracts, featured in *JACC*, *JAMA*, *Circulation*, the *Journal of Women's Health*, among others.

Kendall St. Hilaire is Campus President of IRSC Global at Indian River State College. She holds a Master of Science in Instructional Systems and Design from Florida State University and a Doctor of Education degree at the University of Florida in higher education administration and policy. She has served on the Board of Directors for the University of Central Florida's TOPkit program since 2016. She serves on the Executive Committee of the Florida Virtual Campus. Her interests include researching the field of online education in order to serve online students and support the completion of their credentials.

Riad Homsi, MD and Fellow of the American College of Obstetricians and Gynecologists (FACOG), has been in private practice since 1994. He chaired many committees in quality improvement and perinatal quality care at Baptist Memorial Hospital for Women in Memphis, TN. He received multiple quality awards related to his work in improving perinatal quality care of women. He is also a past chairman of the Department of Obstetrics and Gynecology, a past president of the medical staff at Baptist Memorial Hospital for Women and Children Hospital, and on the teaching clinical faculty of the University of Tennessee OB-GYN residency program.

Gina Horne, MSN, RNC-OB, is Practice Specialist for Perinatal Services at Baptist Memorial Healthcare Corporation in Memphis TN. She has participated in a number of practice improvement initiatives through the Institute for Healthcare Improvement and the Tennessee Initiative for Perinatal Quality Care, and has presented some of this work for the Council of Women & Infants' Specialty Hospitals, the Tennessee Hospital Association, the Association for Women's Health, Obstetric, and Neonatal Nurses and the TIPQC. In her current role, Gina provides education and facilitates the incorporation of evidence-based practices for nine system healthcare facilities providing perinatal services.

Rhonda Jeffries is Professor and Program Coordinator for Curriculum Studies and her scholarship focuses on curriculum inquiry and equity pedagogies informed by critical race and Black feminist theories. She is a Professional Development Liaison with Richland School District Two; a governing council member of the

National Network for Educational Renewal; co-editor of *Impacting Education*, the Carnegie Project on the Education Doctorate journal; and editor of *Queen Mothers: Articulating the Spirit of Black Women Teacher-Leaders*.

Santi Kusumaningrum is Director of PUSKAPA (Center on Child Protection and Wellbeing)—a think-tank based at Universitas Indonesia. She is also an Adjunct Assistant Professor for Population and Family Health at Mailman School of Public Health, Columbia University. She works to make systems and services equate safety and wellbeing, and enables social inclusion and resilience of children and marginalized individuals. She does research to inform actions, advocacy to get buy-in, and program management to realize solutions. She was trained in Criminology and Social Policy in Universitas Indonesia and got her Doctorate in Public Health from Columbia University.

Peter Leong is Associate Professor with the Department of Learning Design & Technology at the University of Hawaii at Manoa. He has extensive experience in the development and delivery of online courses and distance education. Dr. Leong currently serves on the Executive Board of the International Council of Educational Media and the Teaching, Colleges & Community conference advisory panel. His research interests include student satisfaction with online learning, computer science education, faculty's belief about online teaching, and teaching and learning in 3-dimensional virtual worlds.

Lynne Lieux, Ph.D., received her BS in Mathematics from Maryville University, her M.A. in Physics from Washington University, and her doctorate in Educational Administration from the University of New Orleans. The focus of her research was on the capacity of educators, individually and collectively, to embrace educational change. She has worked in PK-12 schools across the US as a teacher and administrator and has served as a trustee of several schools, including Maryville University. Dr. Lieux was instrumental in establishing one of the first 1:1 computing programs in Louisiana. Currently, Dr. Lieux is working with The Jacobs Institute on Innovation in Education and as Adjunct Professor at the University of New Orleans.

Meng-Fen Grace Lin is Associate Professor in the Department of Learning Design and Technology (LTEC) in the College of Education at the University of Hawaii at Manoa. She teaches graduate-level courses on mobile learning, design thinking, and research and evaluation of LTEC. Her recent research interests center on applying design thinking, creativity, and problem-solving in real-world education contexts.

Barbara B. Lockee is Professor of Instructional Design and Technology in the School of Education at Virginia Tech. Her research and teaching are centered at the intersection of instructional design and distance learning, exploring strategies to support the creation of effective online education based on the principles of human learning. For more than 25 years, she has consulted with workplace learning professionals in healthcare, military, government, and nonprofit organizations to support their training and instructional design efforts. Dr. Lockee is Past President of the Association for Educational Communications and Technology and serves on the CMR Institute's board of directors.

Anne Namatsi Lutomia is currently Postdoctoral Research Associate at Purdue University with SAWBO. She holds a Doctoral Degree in Human Resource Education with a minor in Gender and Women's Studies from the University of Illinois at Urbana-Champaign. Her research interests span international scientific collaboration, learning technologies, adult learning, gender, and communities of practice. She is currently working on the SAWBO-RAPID scaling program that uses educational animations to mitigate Covid-19 secondary challenges in Ghana, Kenya, Nigeria, and Bangladesh.

Christina McDonald directs sponsored research and is Assistant to the Provost for research at East Stroudsburg University of Pennsylvania. She holds a BA in Comparative Literature from U.C. Berkeley, an MA in Education Administration and Policy Studies from the University of Pittsburgh, and is pursuing her Doctorate in Educational Leadership from East Stroudsburg University of PA. Prior to working in higher education, she was employed by the Open Society Institute from 1997–2010 where she was a program officer in the Education Support Program, working to transform educational systems in Central and Eastern Europe, the Caucuses, and former Soviet Republics.

John Medendorp holds a Ph.D. in Higher, Adult, and Lifelong Education with a specialization in international development from Michigan State University. He currently serves as Director of the Borlaug Higher Education for Agricultural Research and Development (BHEARD) program as well as Deputy Director of the Legumes Systems Research Innovation Lab, and Co-PI for the SAWBO-RAPID scaling program at Michigan State University with a special emphasis on human and institutional capacity development programs. He is currently conducting research on biotechnology capacity development in Indonesia and Bangladesh as well as agricultural research capacity development through the BHEARD program and adult learning systems using educational animations in the SAWBO-RAPID scaling program. He has also authored a report on human and institutional capacity development and gender practices in the Feed the Future Innovation Labs for USAID.

Sheila E. Murphy, Ph.D., serves on the faculty of the School of Public Affairs at Arizona State University, where she co-designed and instructs the Certified

Public Manager program, serving federal, tribal, state, county, and municipal government professionals. She has served as consultant to government, private sector, and nonprofit organizations for 27 years. Sheila's research interests include social systems design, systems-based education, distance education, and organizational communication.

Barry Pittendrigh is currently the Osmun Endowed Chair in Urbana Entomology at Purdue University. Previously he was the Michigan State University Foundation Professor (2016–2020), and, before that, held the C.W. Kearns, C.L. Metcalf and W.P. Flint Endowed Chair at the University of Illinois at Urbana-Champaign (2008–2016). He is also a co-founder and co-director of SAWBO, and he has worked in the area of international development for the past two decades, primarily in Africa.

N. Peter Reeves is Founder and President of Sumaq Life LLC, a life sciences start-up company. Sumaq Life LLC was formed to create technological innovations and increase translation of scientific discoveries into real-world applications. Prior to Sumaq Life LLC, Dr. Reeves was an Associate Professor in the College of Osteopathic Medicine at Michigan State University. He has authored/coauthored over 50 peer-reviewed publications and has been a PI/co-PI on approximately $5M in federally-funded research. Dr. Reeves has a doctorate in biomedical engineering from Yale University.

Tracey A. Regenold, Ph.D., earned her degree in education with a concentration in Occupational and Technical Studies from Old Dominion University. She holds the Master of Public Administration degree from Arizona State University. Tracey is an independent scholar and consultant, developing education for boards of directors, elected officials, and leaders in government workplaces to guide them in designing and implementing more effective and inclusive organizational and social systems. Tracey's research interests include systems-based education, social systems design, and the use of visualization in systems planning.

Ahoo Salem is the Executive Director of Blue Ridge Literacy (BRL), a non-profit organization that offers English literacy services to foreign and native-born residents of Roanoke Valley. With a background in sustainability sciences and international migration, her work and research explore the ways in which differential access to resources shapes and impacts experiences of everyday life for immigrants and refugees in different host settings. Originally from Iran, Ahoo holds a Ph.D. in sociology from Universita Degli Studi di Milano, in Milan, Italy.

Gail Samdperil, EdD, is Clinical Associate Professor and the Associate Dean of the College of Health Profession at Sacred Heart University. In addition, Dr. Samdperil services as Program Director of the graduate athletic training program. Her area of contemporary experience is in the field of cultural competence, leadership. and professional development. Dr. Samdperil's current scholarship focuses on students' leadership qualities as well as continued maintenance of competence in the area of athletic training. Dr. Samdperil serves on several national committees for the Commission on Accreditation of Athletic Training Education and the Board of Certification.

Widi Laras Sari leads the Research, Monitoring, and Evaluation arm of PUSKAPA (Center on Child Protection and Wellbeing) Universitas Indonesia. Her work combines managing research, synthesizing evidence, evaluating programs, and disseminating social and health studies results. Widi has a range of research experience, including inclusive growth and evaluation of universal health insurance schemes in Indonesia. She was trained in Economics at Universitas Indonesia and The Australian National University. She provides a quality assurance oversight to the evidence and knowledge building component in PUSKAPA's CRVS work, and ensures that knowledge informs policy reform in Indonesia.

Domenic Screnci retired recently from Boston University. Domenic is the former Senior Advisor for Digital Learning and Innovation and Executive Director for Educational Technology, Training, and Outreach in Information Services and Technology at Boston University. Dr. Screnci served the university as an educational technologist, instructional systems designer and integrator, instructional designer, curriculum developer, and producer of curriculum materials for traditional and new media-based educational projects. He has a Master's Degree in Educational Media and Technology and a Doctorate in Curriculum and Teaching from Boston University. His career spans over 40 years of experience in the field of educational technology.

Elizabeth A. Shenkman, Ph.D., is the Chair of the Department of Health Outcomes and Biomedical Informatics and also is the Co-Director of the University of Florida Clinical and Translational Science Institute and the Associate Director for Community Outreach and Engagement for the UF Health Cancer Center. Dr. Shenkman is a health outcomes researcher with a research focus on: 1) determining which combinations of health care delivery, community, and patient factors influence quality and outcomes of care; and 2) developing and testing corresponding evidence-based strategies to reduce disparities in health outcomes among underserved populations.

Beth Rajan Sockman, Ph.D., is Professor of Education at East Stroudsburg University. Beth works to untangle the complexities that drive disparities to maintain the status quo. Systems thinking and learning design serve as the primary tool to increase meaningful learning. Her background includes experience as a tenured classroom teacher, international/national youth peace director, instructional design and learning technology consultant, and a professor since 2007.

Spending time in nature aids endeavors, Beth ponders the beauty, disparity, and the interconnectedness of thriving environments as a metaphor to create learning that enables stakeholder voice through design. She is an active member of the Association for Educational Communications and Technology and the division of Systems Thinking and Change.

Jay Starnes, EdD, is a K-12 public school administrator and university Adjunct Instructor in Northeastern Pennsylvania. His areas of research and practice are in human consciousness, motivation, and educational systems. Prior to his work as a school district administrator, he taught early childhood and elementary school students, coached wrestling, tennis, and football, and worked as a school principal at various grade levels. Jay serves in leadership positions on a nonprofit community foundation that works to sustain and advance equality, and on a statewide interscholastic athletic association. He is an avid hiker and can often be found on the Appalachian Trail.

Jill Stefaniak is Associate Professor in the Learning, Design, and Technology program in the Department of Career and Information Studies at the University of Georgia, USA. Her research interests focus on the professional development of instructional designers, designer decision-making processes, and contextual factors influencing design in situated environments.

Mónica Sulecio de Alvarez works as an independent designer of distance education experiences for complex learning in Guatemala, Central America. She holds a Master's degree in Instructional Design from Virginia Tech State University and in her designs, she focuses on the integration of knowledge, skills and attitudes to help learners develop performance that is meaningfully useful in everyday life. She has worked with diverse subject matter experts in the public and private sectors, and currently serves on the Board of the Systems Thinking and Change Division of the Association for Educational Communications and Technology.

Suha Rahif Tamim, EdD, MPH, is Clinical Assistant Professor in the Curriculum Studies program in the Department of Instruction and Teacher Education at the University of South Carolina. She earned her Doctor of Education in Instructional Design and Technology from the University of Memphis and her Master of Public Health from the American University of Beirut. Her research interests revolve around systems thinking and the design of learning environments, with a focus on constructivist, online, and health-related environments. She currently serves as Co-editor in Chief for Impacting Education: Journal of Transforming Professional Practice. She is an active member of the Association for Educational Communications and Technology and the Carnegie Project on the Education Doctorate.

Rahmadi Usman is the Lead for Legal Identity and CRVS Pillar in PUSKAPA (Center on Child Protection and Wellbeing) Universitas Indonesia. He started his career volunteering for NGO work in Aceh, Indonesia, and got professionally active in the development sector since he contributed to the Aceh Tsunami relief and recovery in 2005. He joined PUSKAPA full time in 2013, and since 2019, he has been leading its work in improving the civil registration system. He dedicates his faculty to ensure all individuals' (especially children and vulnerable ones) have possession of legal identity documents, that they facilitate their access to basic services, and their vital data is appropriately managed, used, and protected. He obtained a Master's degree in Criminology with a concentration on Child Protection from Universitas Indonesia.

1

INTEGRATING SYSTEMS

A Practical Guide

M. Aaron Bond, Suha Rahif Tamim, Samantha J. Blevins, and Beth R. Sockman

Challenges can arise in all workplace environments. No matter the profession, situation, or need for change, systems thinking offers a powerful approach for addressing complicated issues by providing tools for thinking, organizing, and action. Drawing upon the expertise of professionals across many disciplines, this book provides detailed narratives on how systems thinking was used to approach real-world problems. The stories detail success and failure, to help professionals develop a systems thinking approach to problem-solving and change management for sustainable solutions that meet the evolving needs of stakeholders.

Systems are intrinsic to human behavior and organizational development and can be found everywhere, in both micro and macro forms. Systems thinking is a set of synergistic analytic skills used to improve the capability of identifying and understanding the interrelated systems, predicting their behaviors, and devising modifications to them in order to produce desired effects (Arnold & Wade, 2015). Though organizations try to simplify causal relationships into linear actions, this is only part of reality. Organizations have complex needs because organizations are just that, organismic. Decisions and consequences to those decisions made within organizations do not fit nicely into a hierarchical chart. Instead, systems thinking can help organizations address complex problems which are inherently nonlinear by examining the parts and the whole simultaneously (Cabrera & Cabrera, 2015). When planning change initiatives it is essential to understand the system in which the problem exists before developing a plan to influence change. Every action can impact other areas of the system (Gibons, 2014), and if not careful, a "solution" can generate greater problems elsewhere. Systems thinking employs thoughtful problem-solving, as components are analyzed within the context, examining the interrelationships between each component and how these components affect the

DOI: 10.4324/9781003028772-1

whole (Arnold & Wade, 2105; Senge, 2012). The process can be a challenge since generating change involves fluidity while continuously analyzing interactions (Cabrera & Cabrera, 2015; Senge, 2012).

Brief History

As theories go, systems theory and systemic thinking are fairly new in academic and popular writing. Their complex and fluid nature makes concepts challenging to grasp; as soon one mentally pins the theory down, a new concept "jumps in," so it feels like comprehension is wiggling away. To help us understand the evolution, Midgley (2000) describes three historical waves where each addresses a different aspect of systems that enriches and expands the field.

The first wave provides grounding in general systems theory by articulating what systems are, and how systems operate. The description of systems compared how organizations were defined by others contrasted to how they actually operated. Organizations were often discussed in isolated parts, but systems emphasized the interconnected parts with the whole (Banathy, 1973; Bertalanffy, 1968; Capra, 1996; Reigeluth, 1993). From the beginning, systems theory was characterized by modeling hard systems and borrowing metaphors from biological and ecological systems that visualized interconnections and computational metaphors of networking. These metaphors helped describe the complexity of social systems (Banathy, 1973; Bertalanffy, 1968), while still providing a functional approach to operations.

The theories highlighted the interactive flows in and out of the systems while aiming to maintain equilibrium. Since equilibrium was an organic-explicit aspiration, systems theory was one of the first theories to emphasize "why" change to any system was difficult to sustain since a destabilizing force challenged the system; the system strived to revert back to the "old" way of working (Banathy, 1973; Bertalanffy, 1968; Capra, 1996; Hutchins, 1996; Reigeluth, 1993). Substantial change could not be piecemeal, but meaningful change would happen when the whole system transformed.

The second way is often known as soft systems. Less reliant on the hard metaphors of the physical world, soft systems were interpretative, intentional, and more in search of building understandings between stakeholder groups with processes to support the intentions. The focus was solving problems within an organization (Wilson & van Haperen, 2015). With greater emphasis on different stakeholders groups and the perspectives that they supplied, various models emerged that could help solve the problems by comparing people's mental models to the real world (Checkland, 1981; Senge, 1990). Leaders championed a systems understanding as an imperative for sustainable-meaningful change. To make the process accessible, various steps were parsed with linear – interactive and iterative steps on the way to achieve solutions.

The third wave focused on critical systems thinking by addressing power relationships. Systems became a set of thinking tools for emancipation (Stroh, 2015) and expanding empowerment of people (Brown, 2017). The pluralistic ideas of systems were embraced with emphasis on stakeholder involvement, nonlinear movement, and embracing the feedback loops to make change for sustainable solutions (Meadows, 2008). Newly emerging is an extension of the third wave or perhaps a fourth wave. System thinking embraces complexity as an organic-adaptive-responsive movement (Brown, 2017; Kowch, 2019) that also includes focus on the individual (Carr-Chellman & Carr-Chellman, 2020), and, simultaneously, seeks to simplify the system's elements (Cabrera & Cabrera, 2015). Unlike the first wave, it is accepted that the enormity of the whole system change may not be realistic for most circumstances. The focus is to improve performance by providing a new way of thinking about relationships and acknowledging the challenges and the characteristics of the systems.

Because of its broad appeal, systems theories that can be applied to education, science, business, society, and personal development (Kowch, 2019; Senge, 1990). Regardless of the system theory used or the context, there are common concepts that can be applied. The making of bread is a complex process with many inputs (ingredients), processes (kneading, baking, etc.), and many possible outputs (varieties of bread, disastrous results, mediocre success, or a perfect loaf). We will use this analogy of bread making to make explicit the commonalities to visualize each concept.

- *The whole is bigger than the sum of the parts* (Hutchins, 1996). We need to parse organizations to describe them, but with systems, there is an understanding that the reduction will never equal the whole. (Bread is more than the ingredients of flour, yeast, and water.)
- *We have models in our mind that represent how the world works* (Cabrera & Cabrera, 2015). Sometimes those mental models match reality and sometimes they do not. We always have to check the mental model. Feedback from other stakeholders helps to check the model of reality. (Bread: what is the best way to make bread?)
- *Systems are messy* (Kwoch, 2019). Systems are complex, nonlinear, in constant-flux, adaptive, and interconnected. As a result of the dynamism, systems are hard to describe. They are understood best with rich descriptions of the context, parts, and images (Bread: the process of making bread can also be messy, between the flour, sugar, water, and yeast, you must eventually get your hands dirty in order to knead the bread into loaves.)
- *Embrace the messiness and conceptualize the interconnectedness* (Hutchinson, 1996). Making a hierarchical organizational structure may support responsibilities, but not reality. Organizations are networks where innovations flow. Each part makes a difference and it doesn't matter where it resides on the organization

chart. (Bread: all the ingredients make a difference. One is not better than the other.)

- *Each stakeholder and stakeholder group will have a different perspective on the process* (Rogers, 2003; Senge, 1990). The stakeholders in different parts of the system, have their networks, their flow and will perceive the goal(s) based on their investments. (Bread: all the different parts that come together to create bread … farmers, transporters, baker.)
- *Each stakeholder or stakeholder group will have a different definition of success* (Senge, 1990). The stakeholders will have opinions about what is "best" based on their positioning, and therefore will have a different idea about what "success" looks like. (Bread: what kind of bread is best Italian, nan, pita, puri, mochi, pão de queijo?)
- *Oftentimes solutions do not reside in "either/or" thinking but in "and/both" thinking* (Brown, 2017; Stroh, 2015). Multiple perspectives are not necessarily competing ideas. Multiple explanations can support solutions that often acknowledge reality by meeting more stakeholder needs. (Bread: there are different ways to make bread. You can often use the ingredients of one and cook it differently and it will make a different kind. Italian bread, nan, or pão de queijo can all make a hot dog bun.)

Book Organization

This book seeks to simplify the complexity by providing a collection of real-life narratives that describe how systems thinking can be employed to influence change to ensure adoption, implementation, and sustainability. There has been much published on the importance of systems thinking for successful change, but very few through the perspective of the practitioner. Most of the published work explores theoretical foundations and mechanisms of systems thinking. Actual cases of systems thinking for change are rare. Through an instructional design perspective, these narratives will highlight an interactive and systematic process of analysis and decision-making to address both problems and actions. This collection of cases provides relevant examples to practitioners in the field. Cases are drawn from a broad spectrum of settings. This broad approach portrays the many variations of systems thinking and innovative approaches taken for change. As such, the aim is to present a book that is a useful resource for scholars and professionals alike. Though the array of cases represents a variety of settings, it only scratches the surface of the many instances in which a systems thinking approach can be applied.

Each chapter in this volume addresses a case analysis of a complex problem from a systems thinking and change perspective. Each case is purposely short to allow for quick reference and to be accessible by many audiences. While many of the cases exemplify holistic views, they have been grouped according to their emphasis: visionary change, strategic planning, implementing change, managing change, and evaluating change. As systems are complex, so are the associated change efforts. By grouping cases by process stage, the editors hope to make it easy for readers to locate cases most relevant to their own change efforts. In each grouping there are cases from K-12 education, high education, industry, and health care.

Storytelling is a great way to break the complex into understandable chunks. Authors in this edited volume were encouraged to write their cases by describing all parts of the system and the problem being addressed. Systems are messy and the complexity of the situations included in each case offers a rich look at how systems thinking can be used to identify and address problems. By giving the reader the full picture and describing efforts to make change, each case provides valuable insight that is transferable.

To make this content more approachable, each case is consistent and presented using a templated structure. As you read each case, take time to reflect on the story told, the strategies employed, and what strategies might work in your own system. Authors begin each chapter with an overview of the problem and the setting in which it exists. The overview is followed by a description of the roles of the key players involved in the problem or affected by it and the dynamics of interactions between them in order to highlight the system in which the problem resides. Then, an analysis of the case presents challenges, complexities, and the underlying causes of the problem. Next, authors discuss how the problem was resolved, addressing process, outcomes, and options suggested. Finally, the authors discuss lessons learned, including successes and failures, and ending with a conclusion. This structure is meant to help readers process the information presented in each chapter. Each case includes:

1. *Introduction*: Overview of the problem or innovation, setting, context;
2. *System and Key Players*: Stakeholders and their roles in the system;
3. *Case Analysis*: Challenges, complexities and the underlying causes of the problem;
4. *Problem Resolution*: Strategies, outcomes, options considered;
5. *Lessons Learned*: Successes and failures;
6. *Conclusion*;
7. *Reflective Questions*: Self-examination and the connection of various experiences of past, present and future;
8. *References*;
9. *Appendices*: If applicable.

Conclusion

Systems thinking and change crosses all disciplines. Incorporating systems thinking into change efforts can help solve complex problems. This volume of case studies is written to help the everyday practitioner apply systems thinking and change process principles. This text should serve as a practical guide to facilitate change efforts and to provide advice on how to do that within different contexts. Using real stories and cases from a wide variety of contexts, this book offers a realistic approach to help influence change. It is not comprehensive in its approach, but there are many lessons to be learned from the expertise gathered here. The editors hope that this book provides a fresh perspective on the real work happening in the field of systems thinking and change.

This edited volume relies upon the expertise of a collective membership of a professional organization. Representing systems thinking and change scholars and practitioners, members of the Systems Thinking and Change (STC) Division of the Association for Educational Communication and Technology (AECT) served as authors and editors for this volume. STC seeks to increase awareness, both within and outside of AECT, of the body of knowledge about the change process and to facilitate guidance for implementing these processes. All proceeds from this volume are directed to STC to further these efforts.

References

Arnold, R. D. & Wade, J. P. (2015). A definition of systems thinking: A systems approach. *Procedia Computer Science*, 44(C), 669–678. https://doi.org/10.1016/j.procs.2015.03.050

Banathy, B. H. (1973). *Developing a systems view of education: The systems model approach.* Siegler/Fearon Publishers.

Bertalanffly, L.V. (1968). *General systems theory: Foundations, development, application.* George Braziller Inc.

Brown, A. M. (2017). *Emergent strategy: Shaping change, changing worlds.* AK Press.

Cabrera, D. & Cabrera, L. (2015). *Thinking made simple: New hope for solving wicked problems.* Odyssean.

Capra, F. (1996). *The web of life: A new scientific understanding of living systems.* Anchor Books.

Carr-Chellman, D. J. & Carr-Chellman, A. (2020). Integrating Systems: The History of Systems from von Bertalanffy to Profound Learning. *TechTrends*, 64(5), 704–709. https://doi.org/10.1007/s11528-020-00540-1

Checkland P. B. (1981). *Systems thinking, systems practice.* Wiley.

Gibbons, A. S. (2014). *An architectural approach to instructional design.* Routledge.

Hutchins, L. C. (1996). *Systemic thinking: Solving complex problems.* Professional Development Systems.

Kowch, E. (2019). Introduction to systems thinking and change. In M. J. Spector, B. B. Lockee, & M. D. Childress (Eds.), *Learning, design, and technology* (pp. 1–14). Cham: Springer. https://doi.org/10.1007/978-3-319-17727-4

Meadows, D. (2008). *Thinking in systems.* Chelsea Green Publishing.

Midgley, G. (2000). *Systemic intervention: Philosophy, methodology, and practice.* Kluwer Academic.

Reigeluth, C. M. (1993). Principles of educational systems design. In C. M. Reigeluth, B. H. Banathy, & J. R. Olson (Eds.), *Comprehensive systems design: A new educational technology* (pp. 50–66). Springer-Verlag.

Rogers, E. (2003). *Diffusions of innovations* (5 ed.). Free Press.

Senge, P. M. (1990). *The fifth discipline: The art & practice of the learning organization.* Bantam Double Day Dell Publishing.

Senge, P. M. (2012). *Schools that learn: A fifth discipline fieldbook for educators, parents, and everyone who cares about education.* Crown Business.

Stroh, D. P. (2015). *Systems thinking for social change: A practical guide to solving complex problems, avoiding unintended consequences, and achieving lasting results*. Chelsea Green Publishing.

Wilson, B. & van Haperen, K. (2015). *Soft Systems Thinking, Methodology and the Management of Change (including the history of the systems engineering department at Lancaster University)*. Palgrave MacMillan.

PART I

Visionary Change

2

SYSTEM THINKING THE VISION FOR CHANGE IN THE READING INTERVENTION SYSTEM (K-12)

Russell D. Clark

Introduction

The need for change is found in the constant desire to provide the best for students. Reading intervention is a complex process that requires a team of effective educators to work collaboratively together to meet the diverse needs of students. Without the active collaboration of all who are involved in teaching reading, students will continue to struggle. Classroom teachers must work collaboratively with reading interventionists.

Imagine a student working desperately in his classroom to learn to read using strategies his classroom teacher introduced. Then, the same student goes to his reading intervention classroom and is presented with a completely different set of strategies. The student has not had time to grasp either set of strategies fully. He leaves both classrooms confused. The deficiency in communication between teachers working with students is a problem within the school system. Many times, classroom teachers and reading interventionists never communicate about or collaborate on the instructional strategies being used to meet the needs of students. Using communication tools will better serve the students and help them meet their reading goals.

In this case, the elementary school is part of a Rural School District, serving 573 students in the 2018–2019 school year from grades pre-Kindergarten to 5th grade. This small town has a population of 3,504 people.

During grade-level planning, teachers and interventionists discussed the progress of the students they shared. However, when problem areas related to student growth were discussed, the teachers and interventionists were unable to find solutions that worked. Understanding the need for collaborative reflection and

DOI: 10.4324/9781003028772-3

progress monitoring was challenging for some teachers. In the school's intervention programs, as in many pullout intervention programs, the time for weekly planning with the classroom teacher was neglected even though the team knew that collaboration directly impacted reading interventions.

To address the problem of a lack of supportive reading strategies, an innovative systems approach to collaboration was facilitated to address the issues within the reading intervention system. When teachers met collaboratively to solve student problems, they utilized various background experiences and specific skills to meet students' needs. Teachers who failed to plan together to meet the needs of students missed valuable insight from other professionals that may have directly impacted student growth (Tucker, 2015).

A literacy coach at the research site helped teachers and interventionists design instructional strategies to meet student needs. Literacy coaches are not evaluators of instructional practices; however, they provide feedback for instructional practices. An increase in communication between the reading interventionist and the classroom teacher was the vision for change within the reading intervention system. The literacy coach wanted the teachers and interventionists to use a shared document to communicate the planned instructional strategies. All teachers involved would discuss the student's strengths and weaknesses through the shared document. Through this discussion, the teachers and interventionists would decide on any changes to the instructional plan. Change during this case study took place within the planning and administration of reading interventions. The goal was for teachers to be problem solvers when dealing with student achievement.

Teachers and interventionists benefited from investigating the needs and developing a plan to support the education of at-risk students. Looking at the overall system in place that allows teachers to plan and collaborate brought about a solution that provided the resource and structure to help students meet reading goals.

The causal loop (see Figure 2.1) describes the structure of the problem within the reading intervention system (Senge, 2012). The human structure (see Figure 2.2) reveals the interconnectedness of the key players and the point at which the connections fail. Evans (2001) states: "System theory, rooted in cybernetics, emphasizes the multiplicity and complexity of factors that affect the functioning of any person or group over time" (p. 11). The problem being investigated deals with the lack of collaboration between classroom teachers and the reading interventionists. The literacy coach discovered new avenues to possible solutions by using the systems thinking approach. Senge (2012) states: "From a systems perspective, focusing on a specific event the tip of the iceberg will prevent you from seeing the complexity of the school organization" (p. 126). Stepping back from the specifics of a problem allowed one to see the patterns and structures involved. Looking at mental models of the issue gave a more in-depth understanding of the overall processes at work in the specific event (Senge, 2012). The causality of the

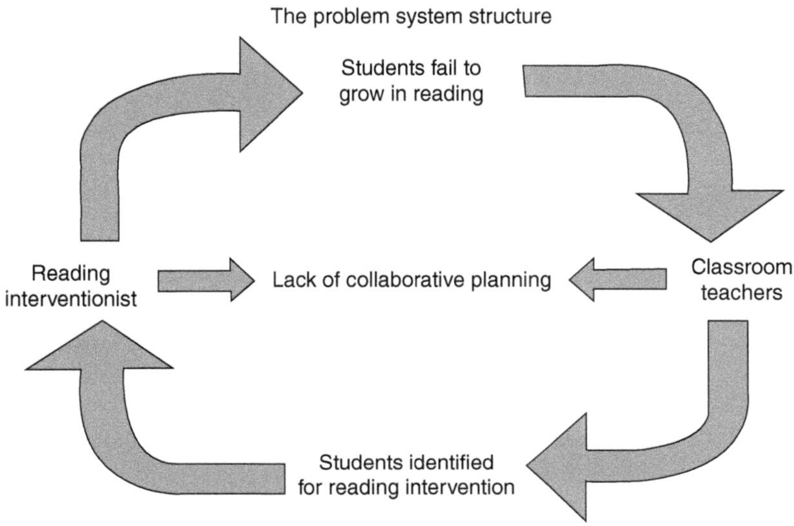

FIGURE 2.1 The Causal Loop

Note: The system structure of the problem centers on the lack of collaboration between the reading interventionist and classroom teacher.

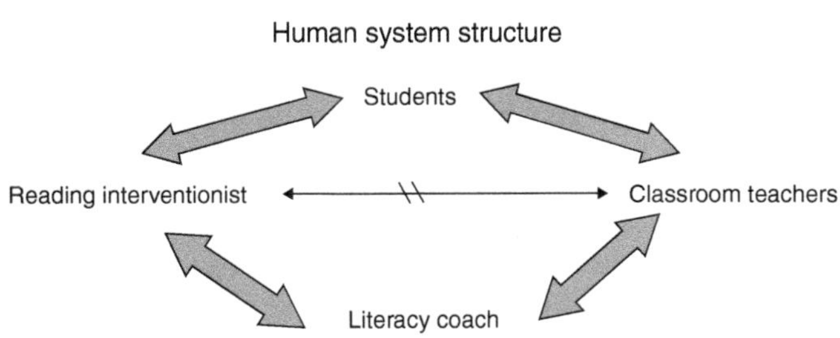

FIGURE 2.2 The Human Structure

Note: The human system structure diagram illustrates the lack of communication between the reading interventionists and the classroom teachers.

problem became apparent when components of the causality loop were identified as seen in Figure 2.1.

System and Key Players

Key players in this system include students, the classroom teacher, the reading interventionist, and the literacy coach. The classroom teacher identified students that required reading intervention then referred these students to the reading interventionist. However, reading interventionists and classroom teachers did not meet to discuss student results or progress. See Table 2.1.

TABLE 2.1 System Key Players

System Key Players		
Key Players	*Role*	*Descriptors*
Students	• multiplier	• low achieving readers (at least one grade level below their current grade) • other factors exacerbating the problem: poverty, lack of prenatal support, developmental delays
The Reading Interventionist	• plan and implement specific instructional strategies	• highly trained in instructional strategies that help struggling readers overcome their deficits in reading skills
The Classroom Teacher	• identify students who required reading intervention	• responsible for teaching grade-level reading skills and strategies for the entire class
Literacy Coach	• facilitated data meetings	• develop an intervention plan for students who showed reading deficiencies

Note: This table characterizes the key players within the system of reading intervention.

Case Analysis

The Interconnected System Between Human Components

Senge (2012) states: "Sometimes if you want to change behavior, it's enough to raise awareness of the structures at play" (p. 134). The interconnectedness of the reading intervention system had many human components as seen in Figure 2.1 and Figure 2.2. A solution to the problem resided in allowing others to see these interconnected relationships. In describing these human interconnective system dynamics, Senge (2012) states that "When you understand them and how they operate separately and together, you gain a great awareness of the system around you" (p. 135). Reading interventionists and classroom teachers who fail to collaboratively plan reading interventions seldom see the results that would have been possible if they had taken the time to plan the reading interventions.

Problem Analysis – Collaboration

First, students in need of reading intervention were identified. Next, the students were referred to the reading interventionist, who then pulls the students for more intense instruction. The problem occurred when the reading interventionist and the classroom teacher did not communicate about how they are teaching the students. With this lack of communication and collaboration, students had one teacher using a strategy that is different from the approach the other teacher used. The student became confused and unable to achieve proficiency at either method. Within the system, the lack of communication multiplied the number of students in the intervention. Students who did not master reading strategies could not make the growth needed to be taken out of the reading intervention.

Meanwhile, more students were identified as below reading level and in need of remediation by an interventionist. Therefore, more students were added to the reading interventionists class throughout the year. This increase in students exacerbated the problem even more; the number of students being served reduced the amount of time that classroom teachers and interventionists had to collaborate.

Complexity – Reluctant Faculty

Evans (2001) states: "One's openness to innovation depends on a combination of factors, chief among them one's personality, life experience, and career experience" (p. 92). The main element in the failure to collaborate between the reading interventionist and the classroom teacher was found in veteran teachers' reluctance. Teachers within the system were, as Evans (2001) describes, "closer to dejection that deflates energy than to anger that inspires action" (p. 94). The classroom teachers and the reading interventionists are all considered as midlife and midcareer (Evans, 2001). The classroom teachers and reading interventionists are stable in their careers, have a less optimistic view about human behavior, and have become attached to their burdens (Evans, 2001). Two of the teachers involved in this system for reading intervention were considered to be in the "exit period of several years of progressive disengagement in which one prepares to leave or retire" (Evans, 2001, p. 103). Below is the reinforcing loop (Meadows & Wright, 2015) depicting the process found within the reading system as seen in Figure 2.3.

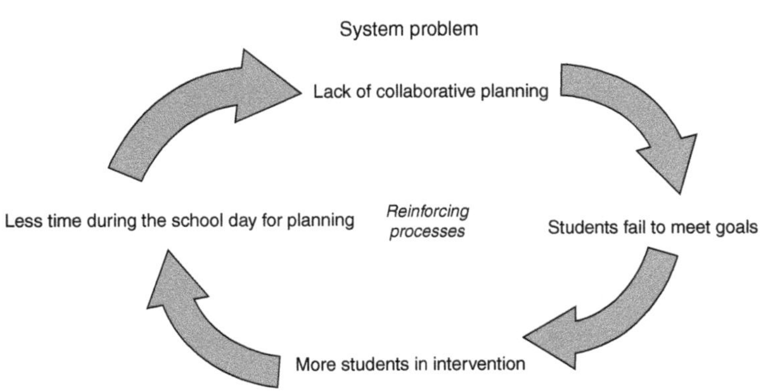

FIGURE 2.3 The Reinforcing Process

Note: The reinforcing process of the system problem is the continual influx of students into the intervention system.

The more students identified for intervention, the more stress is placed on the teachers.

Problem Resolution

The problem resolution was divided into two categories, the team learning design and the communication and collaboration tool.

Team Learning Design

Building a "we are in this together" attitude was difficult, especially when finding the time to collaborate seemed impossible. According to Senge (2012): "At its core, team learning is a discipline of practices designed, over time, to get the people on a team thinking and acting together" (p. 115). Team learning was a way to overcome the challenges teachers faced. Team learning promoted the attitude that everyone is working together to solve problems. Senge (2012) describes this as: "It means continuously talking, with respect and deliberation, about the issues that must be understood and resolved" (p. 115). Teachers needed to remember and refuel their passion for teaching.

A collaborative team approach was implemented between the classroom teacher and the Interventionist. Weekly data team meetings were held to determine shared goals. During the meetings, teachers and interventionists brought student reading data that included running records, answers to comprehension questions, and other anecdotal notes. The team used the data to determine the instructional strategies that would be best for the student. Each participant felt involved in the process of developing the collaboration process. To create agency, each teacher needed to have input and feel as if they had been heard within the training. Communication was the foundation of the learning team. Within this process, the teachers developed a deeper understanding of each other's position. Communication between the classroom teacher and Interventionist was necessary if they were going to implement the plan.

Communication and Collaboration Tool

Classroom teachers and reading interventionists worked together to develop a tool to help with communication and collaboration. The tool developed was a simple chart on a Google document that included the student's strengths, weaknesses, and possible strategies for reading instruction to be used in the classroom and during the intervention. The document was shared, so all of the parties involved had access to it. This chart enabled the student to receive the same instructional practices in the classroom and during the intervention. This synchronization of reading strategies greatly decreased student confusion and allowed for successful interventions. The ability to strategically plan instructional strategies and reflect on student data

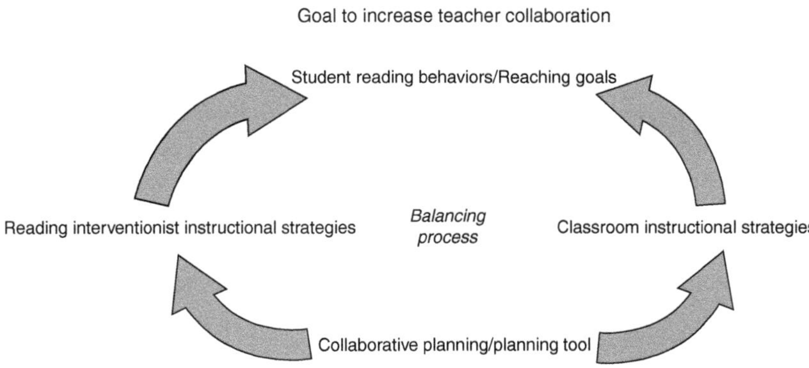

FIGURE 2.4 The Balancing Process

Note: The balancing process to increase student achievement is contingent on the collaborative efforts between the interventionists and the teachers.

increased student achievement and facilitated more collaboration. Teachers became less resistant to using the collaborative tool once they began to see growth in student achievement. Improving communications lead to a more efficient transfer of strategies between the intervention and in the classroom. Developing dialogue was the first step in creating a real team mindset where one did not exist. Even though the goal to increase achievement is balanced by collaborative planning between the reading interventionist and classroom teacher (see Figure 2.4), they were still reluctant to the idea of collaboration. Senge (2012) uses a palette of inquiry to facilitate such discussions: "Balancing advocacy and inquiry, genuinely curious, makes reasoning explicit, ask others about assumptions without being critical or accusing" (p. 107). Asking the reading interventionist about her current view of the level of collaboration with the classroom teacher helped facilitate the discussion. Asking the classroom teacher about strategies that could be beneficial for the interventionist also facilitated a discussion. Opening a dialogue between the two led to an opportunity for the literacy coach to share his point of view without seeming condescending to the current state of collaboration. In this situation, advocating for each perspective as a neutral party helped facilitate a deeper dialogue into the collaboration efforts. Although the teachers and interventionists seemed willing to participate in the discussion, the literacy coach still sensed some apprehension. Teachers and interventionists appeared passively resistant. Strategies to address this resistance and apprehension to change will be the subject of future research.

Lessons Learned

Change within any school can be difficult, and the need for change can be a matter of perspective. Moving into a phase of implementing change within the reading intervention program of our school required the reading interventionist and the classroom teacher to see the need for change. This change went against the natural desire to stay the same. Evans (2001) describes unfreezing as an approach that "recognizes the tendency of people and systems to maintain homeostasis innovation requires learning of something new, usually in place of something old, which unavoidably makes people anxious" (p. 56). Proposing a change in the way teachers collaborate in providing reading intervention to students produced resistance through expected factors. Teachers and interventionists were supported in many ways. The literacy coach helped lessen their fear of trying new approaches, ignited a commitment to the processes, and provided a structure for consensus and change.

Lessening the Fear of Trying

As Evans (2001) states, "Unfreezing is a matter of lessening one kind of anxiety, the fear of trying, but first of mobilizing another kind of anxiety, the fear of not trying" (p. 56). In order to motivate change within the reading intervention system, the discomfort was placed within the system. Discomfort requires a confrontation in such a way to avoid any personal implications of failure (Evan, 2001, p. 57). Pointing out the discrepancies within the reading instruction by performing observations of strategies being used by students in both situations revealed the discrepancies with planning for the students. Noting the differences helped motivate change by proving, as Evan (2001) describes, "The risks of inaction are very real, and we must change" (p. 58). Once teachers saw the lack of cohesiveness in their instructional practices, they understood why students are not growing. They realized the risk to students with unaligned instructional practices. This discovery motivated teachers to change practices.

Ignite Commitment

"Letting go of the old and embrace the new" (Evans, 2001, p. 58). After reviewing and analyzing student data matched with instructional strategies, the classroom teacher and the reading interventionist realized that the strategies they were using were not supporting each other in the goal of helping students reach their reading goals. This revelation led to a commitment to collaborate. Overcoming the resistance to change and developing a commitment was an "integral part of adaptation" (Evans, 2001, p. 59). Bypassing any egos that might have been in play and developing a cohesive, collaborative structure was required for commitment to creating a collaborative plan. Avoiding teachers seeing change as a personal attack against their teaching abilities and keeping a perspective that collaboration was to improve their practice was essential to move into a commitment stage for implementation. This was accomplished through open dialogue, support, and the cultivation of personal relationships throughout the process. An "I'm on your side" relationship was developed.

Change and Consensus

Change always produces conflict within any organization. "It creates winners and losers and upsets existing power arrangements" (Evans, 2001, p. 68). Attempting to bring about a system change between the reading interventionist and the classroom teacher developed a power struggle between the two teachers. As the classroom teacher and reading interventionist developed collaborative planning strategies, more classroom teachers noticed the success and began to "buy-in" to the proposed change. This "buy-in" was fueled by the increase of student mastery of reading goals. This was made evident through a careful review of the data. For example, during one collaborative meeting teachers and interventionists agreed that a particular student had grown and that growth was directly due to the use of the collaboration tool that aligned their instructional strategies. As collaborative planning continued to be successful, a schoolwide consensus for the change was reached.

Setting up a new norm within the area of collaborative reading intervention was essential. As Evan (2001) describes, "Change redefines proficiency" (p. 63). Providing both the classroom teacher and the reading Interventionist with professional development on best practices and collaborative planning was imperative to ensure the success of the proposed change in the reading intervention planning.

To help carry out the new collaborative structure, all parties had to cohere to its implementation. Working with both the reading interventionist and the classroom teacher allowed the literacy coach to observe and facilitate a better understanding of these essential parts of the proposed change.

Conclusion

Providing a supportive culture to ensure the successful implementation of the change to the reading intervention system was undeniable. Evans (2001) understands that encouraging teachers to focus on the positive results of the collaboration will help them overcome discouragement. By providing teachers with a positive culture to implement the initiatives, teachers were empowered to overcome the difficulties and the naysayers that were found within the school. A school culture that is built upon adaptability will be thriving (Evans, 2001, p. 142). The experience suggests that teachers realize the benefits of collaborative planning when they are supported. If resources are made available that foster a collaborative environment, the culture will be one of positive reflection on the process.

Reflective Questions

During this study, several questions arose that need further consideration.

- How could asking the reading Interventionist about her current view of collaboration with the classroom teacher help facilitate the discussion?

- In this situation, how could using inquiry and advocating for each perspective, as a neutral party, help facilitate a more profound dialogue into the collaboration efforts without seeming condescending to the current state of collaboration?
- How could having each person involved create his own ladder of inference while asking questions throughout the process help facilitate advocacy within each system member?
- How did understanding the components involved in the reading intervention system develop an understanding of their interconnectedness that impacted student learning?

Additional Resources

Dufour, R. (2009). *Professional learning communities at work: Plan book*. Hawker Brownlow Education.

Dufour, R., Eaker, R. E., & Dufour, R. (2006). *Professional learning communities at work: 2005 institutes; best practices for enhancing student achievement*. Solution Tree.

Mattos, M. (2016). *Concise answers to frequently asked questions about professional learning communities at work*. Solution Tree Press, a division of Solution Tree.

Sammon, G. M. (2008). *Creating and sustaining small learning communities: Strategies and tools for transforming high schools*. Corwin Press.

References

Evans, R. (2001). *The human side of school change: Reform, resistance, and the real-life problems of school change*. Jossey-Bass.

Goddard, Y. L., Goddard, R. D., & Tschannen-Moran, M. (2007). A theoretical and empirical investigation of teacher collaboration for school improvement and student achievement in public elementary schools. *Teachers College Record*, 109(4), 877–896.

Meadows, D. H., & Wright, D. (2015). *Thinking in systems: A primer*. Chelsea Green Publishing.

Senge, P. (2012). *Schools that learn: A fifth discipline fieldbook for educators, parents, and everyone who cares about education*. Crown Business. ISBN 978-0-385-51822-2

Tucker, C. (2015). Can you hear me now? A study of communication among teachers of at-risk students through response to intervention (Order No. 3714755). Available from ProQuest Dissertations & Theses Global. (1707675471). Retrieved from https://login.pallas2.tcl.sc.edu/login?url=https://search-proquest-com.pallas2.tcl.sc.edu/docview/1707675471?accountid=13965

3

ADVANCING A MARGINALIZED EUROPEAN GROUP (EDUCATION/ INTERNATIONAL)

Christina McDonald

Introduction

In the years following the collapse of the Berlin Wall,[1] and the subsequent collapse of communist political regimes in the region of Central and Eastern Europe,[2] societies were in a state of flux. As governments lost their total grip on society, an opportunity unfolded to seize the moment to enact change; civil society was emerging with many groups self-organizing and naming themselves nongovernmental agencies (NGOs) in the name of a cause. What this meant to the activist was the possibility to make societal changes while things were still pliable and change-worthy; civil society and populations' ability to self-organize was in and of itself a huge societal shift, and one that could impact the course of countries' futures. Some argue that the fruition of NGOs was "the single most distinctive aspect of the revolutions of 1989" (Starr, 1991, p. 1).

One of the early civil society issues to emerge at this time was human rights, which were neither robust nor even existed under communism. Although all human rights were emerging and in need of defense, the rights of Roma[3] in particular heeded particular attention; under communism, the Gypsies were considered neither an ethnic group nor a nation. The Roma are an oppressed group that historically has not had an effective voice in, or access to, systems of justice in the countries of the region. With an estimated population of between 8 and 12 million across Europe, the Roma are one of its largest and most vulnerable minorities. The problems Roma face are long-standing, complex, multi-faceted, and sectoral; international organizations and university researchers have provided extensive documentation of the continuing persecution facing Roma throughout the region (Barany, 1994; 2002; Save the Children, 2001).

DOI: 10.4324/9781003028772-4

The focus of this case is the education sector because it is the field in which I work, in which I have had first-hand experience, and for which I know the context best. Researchers have also documented and recognized the barriers to accessing quality educational opportunities for Roma (Cahn et al., 1998; Ringold, Orenstein, & Wilkens, 2003; Open Society Institute, 2007). Roma children and youth have traditionally been among the most marginalized students in the public schools of Central and Eastern Europe and make up the largest number of children who do not finish or never attend school. That barriers exist is problematic, not only from a human rights point of view,[4] but because education determines future life chances and is critical for finding stable and well-paid employment. A seminal report released in the early 2000s revealed that:

> Gaps in education persist in the transition period and are most evident in an analysis of the educational levels of the population … the educational attainment of Roma lagged significantly behind the non-Roma population, with Roma much less likely to continue on to secondary and post-secondary education.
>
> *Ringold, Orenstein, & Wilkens, 2003, p. 41*

The problem was documented in black and white. This report was published and publicly available for governments to see and to account for, just as countries of the region were just entering, or queuing to enter, into the European Union.[5] The pressure was on for governments who wanted to be part of the EU to be accountable to their citizens and to enact policies that benefited their citizens; concurrently, citizens were demanding their rights. Countries of the region, which had acted individually for long stretches of time, most as individual silos, were at once called to attention to see themselves vis-à-vis one another. There was a common point of reference, Roma rights, and a common goal: to join the EU and to bring Central and Eastern Europe up to modern, European standards. Could the deplorable situation of the Roma within their borders be tolerated any longer?

I had been researching, writing, and advocating for educational equity and change for Roma in collaboration with other NGOs and international agencies and addressing national education officials and ministries of education on behalf of the Open Society Institute (now the Open Society Foundations) since 1997 when I was first hired by the foundation.[6] I was passionate about equity and poured myself into exposing the issue. However, there was seemingly no impact. Others, perhaps, felt the same. It seemed as if individually we were all giving 100 percent, but collectively, we saw no change.

System and Key Players

At the center of this case analysis were the Roma communities of the region whose situation had not changed and who were, for the first time possibly ever allowed to self-organize and have a voice for themselves. At the micro level (Werhane, 2008), Roma communities were responsible for ensuring their children attend school and for advocating on behalf of themselves to local and sometimes the national government. On the meso level (Werhane, 2008), the local education authorities and schools situated in Roma communities were responsible for enrollment of Roma children and youth. At the macro level (Werhane, 2008), national governments represented by ministries of education were responsible for national policy and guidelines to provide direction to local school districts for education. Representatives of national governments were responsible to represent their countries in intergovernmental and international efforts to improve educational outcomes for Roma.

These three levels repeated themselves in each of the countries of the region and worked, by and large, independently of each other. They faced the same problems and were emerging from similar political legacies, but were acting independently and not cooperating. Place onto this vertical framework the new players of civil society, which were first introduced post-1989. These NGOs inserted themselves into the meso and macro levels because there were NGOs that were very local and embedded in communities and others that had greater scope and worked on the national level.

Finally, intergovernmental agencies, private foundations, and international organizations were found on the supra level (Moos, 2006). They brought visibility to issues and had a level of influence on governments that smaller, nationally based NGOs did not. The supra level became increasingly important in this international dialogue to provide objective, external information and monitoring to governments, to advocate to governments, and often to formulate possible policy recommendations for governments; this level played a watchdog role keeping governments accountable to their citizens.

Some of the key, nationally based, macro-level NGO players at that time were: One for All, All for One Foundation (Hungary), Romani CRISS (Romania), Amalipe and Drom (Bulgaria), ETP, Young Roma Association, and the Wide Open School Foundation (Slovakia).[7] On the supra level intergovernmental agencies and foundations involved were: The European Roma Rights Center (ERRC), the World Bank, the Open Society Institute (OSI), the United Nations Development Program (UNDP), UNICEF, the European Community, the Council of Europe, Minority Rights Group International, among others.

Case Analysis

At the turn of the decade (1990–2000), bringing together multiple system players and actors on the national level to address systemic racism, including educational inequality, was a foundling and burgeoning practice. Countries that had been under Soviet-influenced rule, and who had endured very strict regulations of freedom, did not have experience with dialogue within their own borders. Intellectual freedoms were limited under previous regimes, there was a culture of mistrust, and access to outside knowledge was not abundant. Bringing different system levels together on the national level to recognize, address, and confront issues involved overcoming long-standing differences between the target group, the Roma, and majority population. Historically, there had been great mistrust between minority and majority populations.

The dynamics between these players, nationally, was often contentious, but sometimes cooperative. The push-and-pull between civic organizations demanding rights, and governments responding to those demands, was vociferous and at times tense. Beyond this reality, there was no practice of reaching outward, seeking help, and looking beyond one's borders. Moreover, where was a country to look for positive examples? When looking to your neighbor for an example, in this situation, your neighbor was not one step ahead of you but at the same pace as you. Accessing relevant information to assist with societies moving forward takes time, raising awareness to issues and problems within a society takes time, and change takes time.

This moment in time was a wake-up call to countries that heretofore had not considered human rights nor worried about access to education for all. As they emerged from previous regimes, countries faced the question: to whom were they accountable? Yes, they were accountable to their citizens but were there repercussions to not taking action? Governments and citizens may have had the best intentions to change but without a larger momentum or impetus for that change, it was happening at a snail's pace or not at all.

In the early 2000s, the European Union had begun the process of accession for countries from the region. The pre-process of what governments had to do, and the criteria of what they had to meet to gain entrance, was already in motion. The Copenhagen Criteria was the larger framework to guide a country's entrance. To be included, a country needed to have institutions that preserve democratic governance and human rights, have a functioning market economy, and accept the EU's obligations (European Parliament, 1998). The obligation that countries had to ensure the rights of their citizens was a big intervening variable in the play to address the inequalities experienced by Roma citizens.

Then came a tipping point. Various voices had been speaking loudly for so long; singly as nations, from community leaders to local government representatives, to macro-national voices. Pressure had been building up for years, from 1989 to the present day. Most wanted change and to see movement but working individually did not budge the issue. In 2003 eight governments of Central and South Eastern Europe took an historic step by agreeing to a common framework for action toward improving the situation of Roma communities. That initiative was called the Decade of Roma Inclusion 2005–2015.

Problem Resolution

On February 2, 2005 in Sofia, Bulgaria, Prime Ministers representing their governments from Bulgaria, Croatia, the Czech Republic, Hungary, Montenegro,

Romania, Serbia, Slovakia and the former Yugoslav Republic of Macedonia signed the Decade Declaration, which committed governments to "work toward eliminating discrimination and closing the unacceptable gaps between Roma and the rest of society" (Kirova, n.d.). The Decade Declaration itself is one sheet of paper with country leader signatures. However, it was accompanied by other obligations. To achieve the Decade goal, governments signed a terms of reference (TOR) and were obliged to create action plans. In signing the TOR they obliged themselves to: financially commit to their action plans, involve Romani partners as equal partners, serve in the presidency role one time, among other obligations. The National Action Plans summarize the goals, targets, and indicators that each country planned to achieve during the Decade. These plans – which included education, employment, health, and housing – were intended to complement and reinforce existing national strategies for Roma that had already been in place in nearly all of the countries. The plans also included three cross-cutting themes: discrimination, gender, and income poverty.

A high-level regional conference that publicly and officially launched the Decade followed the formal Declaration. That conference was called *Roma in an Expanding Europe: Challenges for the Future*, hosted by Hungary and took place June 30–July 1, 2003 in Budapest, Hungary. From the vantage point of 2020, such a conference and meeting may not seem unusual. At that time, however, it truly was unprecedented. This event was a high-stakes, high-profile conference. Media was very present. The energy of expectation filled the air. Many prominent and visible leaders from participating countries, and also from intergovernmental organizations, were there. Roma presence was visible, large, and prominent. For those who had been working to end discrimination, both Roma and non-Roma, it was a visible recognition of being heard, of finally having action to so many years of advocating. One could feel that this was the beginning of change. There was hope and anticipation for something new, for a better way forward.

The sought change was equality in all sectors for Roma. Convening governments, intergovernmental and nongovernmental organizations, Roma civil society, and non-Roma allies built a strong foundation for that change and demonstrates a principal of the systems approach: It engaged multiple stakeholders to "identify an initial vision and picture of current reality" (Stroh, 2009, p. 118). The ensuing action plans within the Decade, national and international steering committees, domestic and international meetings, round tables, policy forums, and media events demonstrated other principles of systems thinking such as engaging stakeholders to explain their competing views and affirming a compelling vision for the future (Stroh, 2009). These efforts served the purpose of allowing competing views of why the chronic problems facing Roma exist and integrated "diverse perspectives into a map that provides a multipartial and more complete picture of the system and root causes of the problem" (Stroh, 2009, p. 118).

The conference was the face of the unprecedented event, that of European governments coming together to commit to change. Although I was not privy to the high-level meetings and conversations that took place for the Declaration signing to happen, nor for the launch conference to take place, it undoubtedly did. That those behind-the-scenes conversations occurred and that the movement was launched, I believe, was a critical key to change.

It took a large, multi-institutional and multi-system-level conversation to have movement and progress in this extremely important area, combating discrimination, closing the gap in welfare and living conditions between the Roma and the non-Roma, and breaking the cycle of poverty and exclusion. That this conversation resulted in European, governmental commitment to change is evidence of the power of advocacy for social issues. Not unimportant to this movement was the presence of the nongovernmental organization and the external voice to government, which added an objective and pressuring presence to ignite action and commitment.

Lessons Learned

That the Decade happened at all and served an important role in sparking the process of positive change for Roma was in and of itself a success and was recognized by the Decade (Roma Integration 2020 Regional Cooperation Council, n.d.). At the same time, the Roma Cooperation Council (RCC) recognizes that the Decade "left significant unfinished business in the actual achievement of its ambitious aim" (Roma Integration 2020 Regional Cooperation Council, n.d.).

Of the four Decade areas of focus, education is the one that made the most progress within the Decade and since the end of the Decade (Rorke, Matache, & Friedman, 2015). This is true despite the small and often unreliable body of statistical data which allow careful comparisons over time (McDonald & Negrin, 2010). At the end of the Decade, the continued unavailability of comparative, reliable data remained and made systemic outcomes monitoring very difficult. This systemic problem is one that in itself warrants advocacy in order to make future progress. External, reliable data on key education indicators was and is key to helping improve practice.

Perhaps the success story of education within the Decade, and beyond, was due to the creation of the Roma Education Fund (REF), established in 2005 in the frame of the Decade. The REF received generous monetary contributions on the part of participating government, private foundations and multilateral agency donors, and dedicated itself to closing the gap in educational outcomes between Roma and non-Roma. The REF continues to operate to this day, is one enduring legacy of the Decade, and continues to provide financing to incentivize educational change in the form of research, advocacy, grants, and scholarships.

Last, this experience demonstrated that it is possible to have a conversation on various system levels to bring about change and improvement and that it is possible to bring to the forefront a policy issue that is not always top priority for the government. A vital component for this to happen is good leadership for momentum and change.

Conclusion

Despite successes and failures, the Decade of Roma Inclusion was in itself an unprecedented event that launched a movement and progress toward citizen equality in a large portion of Europe. It demonstrated real dialogue between national voices as well as international ones. Without the varying systems cooperating together on multiple levels, progress would not have been made. Post-Decade, the lessons learned throughout were imparted to and recognized by the European Union, which was seen as the continuing best platform to "take over the legacy of the Roma Decade, using its existing tools to throw new light on the challenges of Roma integration" (Roma Integration 2020 Roma Regional Council, n.d.). Any further progress rests on the participating countries and the new systems dialogue between the European Union framework, and them.

Reflective Questions

- Five years after the end of the Decade, how much momentum for educational equality has continued in participating countries?
- Is the leadership and momentum from a cross-system initiative necessary to sustain progress?
- Would there be real dedication to continuing to improve equality in education for Roma on the national level alone?

Notes

1 The Berlin Wall was brought down on November 9, 1989.
2 Countries included in this region include: Albania, Bulgaria, Croatia, the Czech Republic, Hungary, Poland, Romania, the Slovak Republic, Slovenia, and the Baltic countries of Estonia, Latvia and Lithuania (OECD, 2001). My use of the term also includes the former Yugoslavian states of: Bosnia & Herzegovina, Montenegro, North Macedonia, Montenegro, Serbia and Kosovo.
3 The Roma are an Indo-Aryan ethnic group also referred to as Romany or Gypsies. This ethnic group originated in India, but migrated and currently primarily reside in Europe.
4 The right to education is a fundamental human right protected under Article 28 of the United Nations (UN) Convention on the Rights of the Child (CRC) ratified by all EU Member States and under Article 14 of the European Union Charter of Fundamental Rights.
5 On May 1, 2004 eight countries of Central and Eastern Europe jointed the European Union: The Czech Republic, Estonia, Hungary, Latvia, Lithuania, Poland, Slovakia, and Slovenia. Bulgaria and Romania joined later on January 1, 2007, and Croatia joined on July 1, 2013.
6 Although I was hired by the Open Society Institute in 1997, I had been aware of and working on this issue since 1995 when I was in graduate school and had made contact with NGOs in Hungary due to my thesis focus.

7 This list is not meant to be exhaustive. I am giving examples from select countries to demonstrate. Each country had its own NGOs that were active and participating. The same is true for intergovernmental agencies.

Additional Resources

Brearley, M. (1996). *The Roma/Gypsies of Europe: A persecuted people.* Institute for Jewish Policy Research.

Decade of Roma Inclusion. (n.d.). *Roma Integration 2020 Regional Cooperation Council.* www.rcc.int/romaintegration2020/romadecade_p/18/roma-decade-and-roma-integration-2020

European Parliament. (1998). Briefing No 20. *Democracy and respect for human rights in the enlargement process of the European Union.* www.europarl.europa.eu/enlargement/briefings/20a2_en.htm

Lame, E. (2014). Segregation, an alarming problem that Roma face in the education system. *Mediterranean Journal of Social Sciences* 5(27), 1385.

Liégeois, J. P. (1994). *Roma, gypsies, travellers.* Council of Europe.

The Roma Education Fund. (n.d.). www.romaeducationfund.org/

Romani Early Years Network. (n.d.). https://reyn.eu/

References

Barany, Z.D. (1994). Living on the edge: The East European Roma in post-communist politics and societies. *Slavic Review* 53, 321.

Barany, Z.D. (2002). *The East European gypsies: Regime change, marginality, and ethnopolitics.* Cambridge University Press.

Cahn, C., Chirico, D., McDonald, C., Mohacsi, V., Peric, T., & Szekely, A. (1998). *Roma and the right to education: Roma in the educational systems of central and eastern Europe.* European Roma Rights Centre. www.errc.org/roma-rights-journal/roma-and-the-right-to-education--roma-in-the-educational-systems-of-central-and-eastern-europe

Kirova, I. (n.d.) *The Decade of Roma Inclusion: Addressing racial discrimination through development.* UN Chronicle. www.un.org/en/chronicle/article/decade-roma-inclusion-addressing-racial-discrimination-through-development#:~:text=The%20initiative%20was%20launched%20on,with%20the%20commitment%20to%20%22work

McDonald, C. & Negrin, K. (2010). *No data, no progress: Data collections on countries participating in the Decade of Roma Inclusion, 2005–2015.* Open Society Institute. www.opensocietyfoundations.org/publications/no-data-no-progress-country-findings

Moos, L. (2006). What kinds of democracy in education are facilitated by supra-and transnational agencies? *European Educational Research Journal* 5(3), 160–168. https://journals.sagepub.com/doi/pdf/10.2304/eerj.2006.5.3.160

OECD (2001). https://stats.oecd.org/glossary/detail.asp?ID=303

Open Society Institute. (2007). *Equal access to quality education for Roma. Volume 1 and 2.* www.opensocietyfoundations.org/publications/equal-access-quality-education-roma-vol-www.opensocietyfoundations.org/publications/equal-access-quality-education-roma-vol-2

Ringold, D., Orenstein, M., & Wilkens, E. (2003). *Roma in an expanding Europe: Breaking the poverty cycle*. The World Bank. https://documents.worldbank.org/en/publication/documents-reports/documentdetail/600541468771052774/roma-in-an-expanding-europe-breaking-the-poverty-cycle

Roma Integration 2020 Regional Cooperation Council. (n.d.). *Decade of Roma Inclusion 2005–2015*. www.rcc.int/romaintegration2020/romadecade_p/18/roma-decade-and-roma-integration-2020

Rorke, B., Matache, M., & Friedman, E. (2015). *A lost decade? Reflections on Roma inclusion 2005–2015*. Decade of Roma Inclusion Secretariat Foundation. www.esem.org.mk/en/pdf/Najznachajni%20vesti/2015/11.2015/A%20Lost%20Decade.pdf#page=16

Save the Children. (2001). *Denied a Future: The right to education of Roma/Gypsy & Traveler children in Europe*. www.ungei.org/resources/files/SaveTheChildren_dafvol1.pdf

Starr, F. (1991). The third sector in the second world. *World Development* 19(1), 65–71.

Stroh, D.P. (2009). Leveraging grantmaking: Understanding the dynamics of complex social systems. *The Foundation Review* 1(3), 9. https://scholarworks.gvsu.edu/cgi/viewcontent.cgi?article=1128&context=tfr

Werhane, P. H. (2008). Mental models, moral imagination and system thinking in the age of globalization. *Journal of Business Ethics* 78(3), 463–474. www.jstor.org/stable/pdf/25075623.pdf?casa_token=-6zXqLcOkQYAAAAA:s9AIVf3I56fCUgeMPSCFtBZh5Rjam7Qcj1bLMrSYqS_m2p2JWUUUm6grtY_v8xnxSCShDv5DRc3Oi2ncXU6m7TsiyQ6qddGSjZ25COVT-Xws3sJQigVb

4

RETHINKING MANAGEMENT STRUCTURES IN HIGHER EDUCATION

Domenic Screnci

Introduction

This case study shows how support groups within higher education responsible for delivering "instructional support services" can be organized to represent all stakeholders, if done in a thoughtful, critical, and systematic way. Through systems thinking (Forrester, 1994), this case study provides steps and guidance to analyze and assess similar systems and proposes an alternative organizational model based on system thinking strategies. The efforts behind this case study used some systems thinking ideas and concepts found within the literature (Forrester, 1994; Cabrera, Colosi, & Lobdell, 2008; Cabrera & Cabrera, 2018), which offers ways to analyze and conceptualize a new model for classroom instructional support in higher education institutions. The case presented shows that any system conceptualized and proposed, and any changes suggested will need to transcend the traditional business hierarchal organizational models and departmental structures that have historically persisted for managers and leaders in higher education.

System and Key Players

In my 34 years working in academia, I have found through personal experiences and working with colleagues from other institutions that the organizational structures we have worked in leans more toward a traditional hierarchical organization as seen in the online search for existing university's organizational structure represented in Figure 4.1. Traditional higher education organizations are organized this way mostly due to how funding mechanisms and political boundaries are designated. When attempting to address issues holistically, involving different departments within the organizational structure to address complex problems can

DOI: 10.4324/9781003028772-5

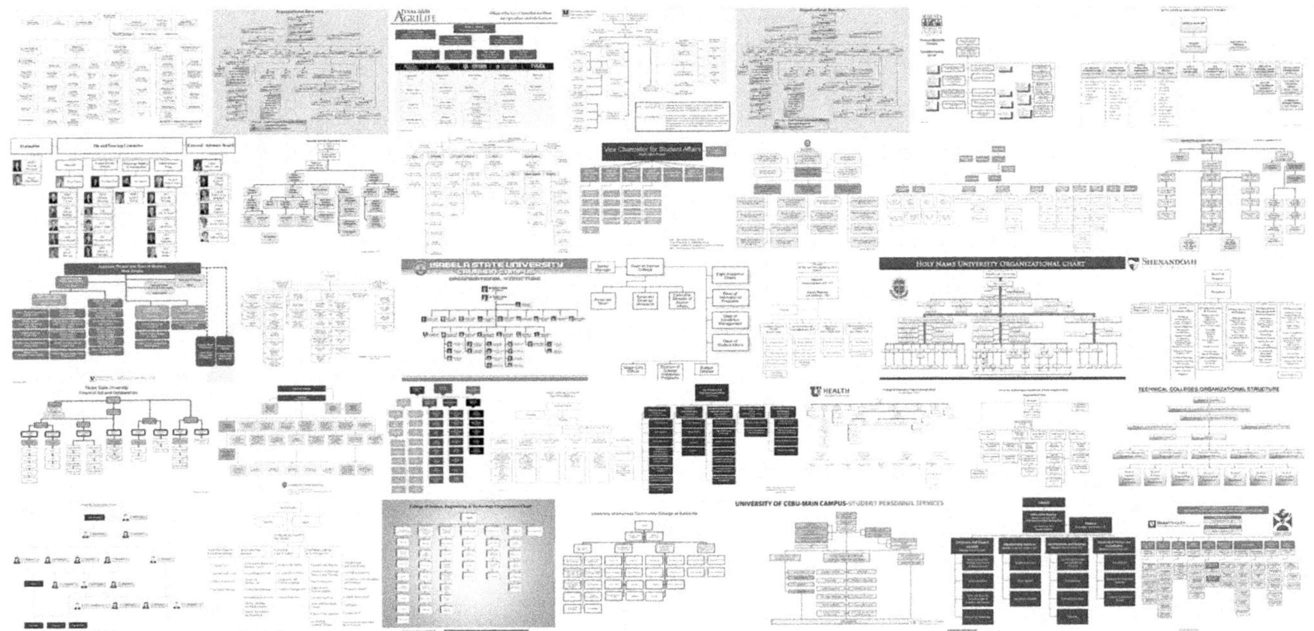

FIGURE 4.1 An Example of an Online Search for University Organizational Charts

Note: An online search for university organizational charts, although not legible, graphically shows how common higher organization structures exist in higher education.

be challenging. Some departments may have a scope of responsibilities that overlap or conflict with other units providing mission-critical instructional support services. This overlap creates a challenge to getting the work done in an expedient and comprehensive way. In addition, this traditional compartmentalized organizational model makes organizations focus staff and resources on addressing a department's perspective of priorities instead of suspending their operational values and priorities to serve the institution's core instructional needs. As a result, departments across the organization may struggle to collaborate on core mission-critical objectives resulting in less-than-optimal project outcomes.

Case Analysis

Can organizations be organized differently to enhance the quality of services provided to its teaching and learning community?

This case study uses a systems thinking approach to explore ways to modify an institution's organizational structure to overcome the hindrance derived from an organization's compartmentalization of effort. This work followed a process of gathering information and identifying hidden structures to support a mental model as suggested in "System Thinking Made Simple" (Cabrera & Cabrera, 2018). By analyzing a university's current organizational structure and processes, the challenges can be better understood. Observing and documenting the dynamics in place, opportunities for systemic change can be identified. The insights gained can help innovators find prospects to forge new pathways of cooperation and collaboration between institutional service groups. Once relationships and interdependencies are understood, it may be possible to introduce an alternative management model for supporting an institution's core mission of instructional classroom facilities' development and support while also creating a mechanism for continuous service improvement.

Taking a practitioner's perspective, the approach, in part, used for this case study and suggested to be used in other higher educational organizations was based on Forrester's (1994) research on system dynamics, systems thinking, and soft Operational Research (OR), which clearly articulates a procedure that includes reviewing case studies, practicing soft OR, using systems thinking, analyzing system dynamics, and engaging in a conceptualization phase. A logical sequence of steps to approach this effort begins with identifying all an organization's systems and support components required to aid and facilitate classroom instruction. Next, the relationship of these service departments to each other should be evaluated (Forrester, 1994). In doing so, you are likely to find that instructional support at many universities is often organized in a traditional management structure. This hierarchical approach can create a fragmented effort to holistically service the community's instructional needs.

When assessing an institution, whether it be to focus on daily operational needs or the renovation of existing facilities and services, or the development of new instructional spaces, organizational units that might be considered in this process are support services departments such as: information technology, educational technology, audiovisual support, space management, facilities construction, and building maintenance. While this list may vary on an organization's structure, a common finding is that each department may have a different system in place, as well as protocols to follow when delivering its expertise and services. As a result, support services can evolve into a complicated and fragmented array of overlapping activities, which can inhibit transparency to its intended patrons – faculty and students using the teaching and learning environment. Having an awareness of the meaning and dimensions of transparency should allow managers to maximize information quality given the specific nature of the organization's relationship with its stakeholders (Schnackenberg & Tomlinson, 2014). With the lack of transparency, managers responsible for contributing services and the processes involving the support of instructional environments, academic administrators, faculty, and support staff who rely on these services to deliver instruction can become confused and frustrated.

Organizations in higher education are designed and organized to focus attention on discrete operational objectives and goals. Similar to large manufacturing and service organizations, universities are often structured in a hierarchical or pyramid structure.

Human resource efforts in large organizations are commonly grouped among units based on established vertical boundaries and management structures. These units generally engage in common activities that are essential to an organization. Within each individual unit's culture, staff develop distinct ways of thinking and working to address common tasks that support the overall mission of the organization. The relationships of these units may vary based on their task and perceived value to the organization at large (Davis & Lawrence, 1977).

This description is probably accurate for most universities. One result of such an organizational structure is that the institutional power and control of the decision process will often center on groups that possess political, financial, strategic influence or technical proficiencies. Figure 4.2, a common organizational chart for many of the units and services supporting instruction, shows that the organizational distribution of many functional departments and divisions within the university, excluding academic departments responsible for supporting the delivery of instruction, is distributed across an organization's vertical hierarchical structure. It is important to note that names of different units, their functions, and their organizational distribution on their organizational chart may vary based on the institution's organizational and operational past.

Because of the nature of the vertical structure and the way responsibilities, budgeting and planning are distributed, and formal and informal communication flows in hierarchical organizations, the barriers of horizontal access and the perceived level of accountability of units involved can inhibit collaboration and communications on essential operations and projects.

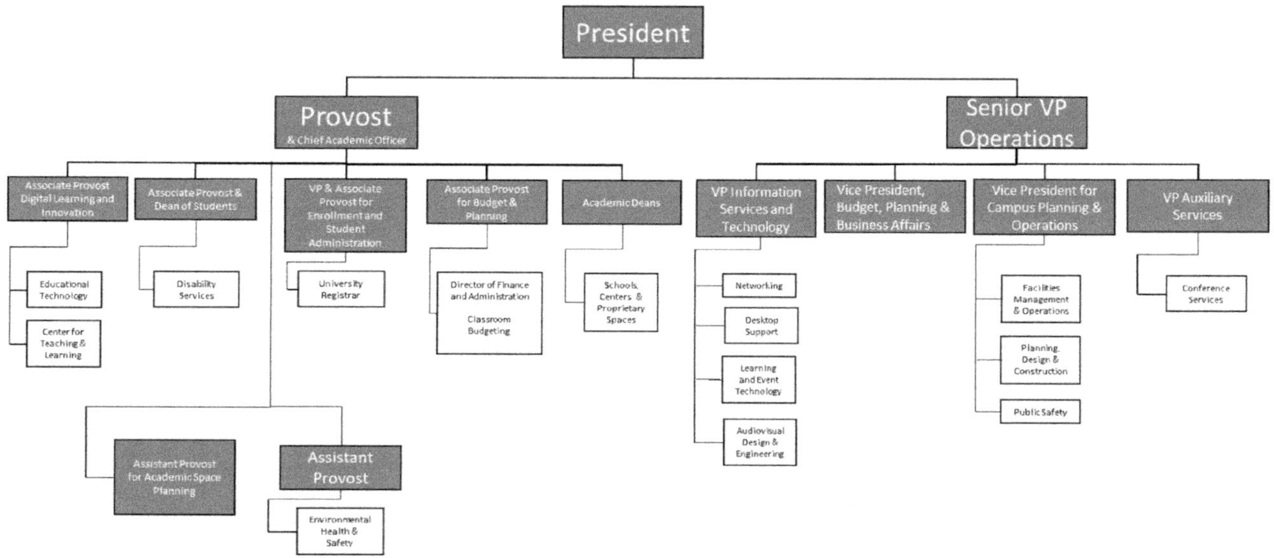

The distribution of support for classroom development or management may vary based on how your organization is structured, but as in many higher educational hierarchal organizations those responsible for classroom planning, budgeting, development and operations are usually distributed across an organization as shown in this org chart. The budgets, skills and responsibilities they represent are accountable first to their vertical organizational leadership and then secondly to any working group or committee working on an organization's classroom efforts.

FIGURE 4.2 A Representation of the Distribution of Responsibility for Classroom Development and Support in Higher Educational Organizations

Note: What is not represented here is Occupational and Student Health team members, key in health crises such as the COVID-19 pandemic. Their involvement will ensure that safety measures are being considered and implemented to protect both faculty and students in a classroom.

Organizations often struggle to adapt their management methods to respond to increased complexity (Lepore, Montgomery, & Siepe, 2016). In considering a matrix management model approach to solve this challenge, the organization would need more than one dimension for its operations management. Historically, committees and project teams created to address instructional needs are created on-demand and dissolved when the "project" is considered complete. Some committees can become permanent to respond to a persistent need. Unfortunately, project teams or committees can be created without adequate autonomy, budget, authority, or organizational agility to act as needed. As a result, they can become ineffective at solving complex instructional support challenges.

In existing hierarchical structures, one question you should ask is: How constructive are the interactions between departments in your traditional management model at solving complex problems around instruction support services? After reflecting on either experience or through a more formal inquiry, findings suggest the level of collaboration is not very constructive and a more formal and persistent model should be put in place to create a more supportive system to tackle the complexity that needs to be addressed. One alternative to consider is implementing a matrix management model to address this challenge.

Thoughtfully organized, a matrix management structure placed over an existing vertically structured organization could include the representation of all departments, units, and groups needing to be involved and working to address the same instructional support goal. As suggested, in the most straightforward matrix configuration, the organization should have two dimensions: one vertical, as reflected in the existing hierarchical organizational chart structure, and a new horizontal structure, which addresses the unique support needs of an organization. Through this horizontal structure, a cross-functional operation could be an effective way to address the multidimensional needs of instructional support. Matrix organizations are accomplished by grouping relevant units in the organization together to provide comprehensive representation of expertise and services essential to support their teaching and learning constituency. Cross-functional staff reporting must be established and standard business processes for this new organization will need to be implemented. Once a horizontal operational management model is created and implemented, it needs to be communicated and explained to all institutional leadership, as well as the teaching and learning community for transparency.

In any higher educational organization, a few efforts in which this approach could be applied are in developing new instructional space, the day-to-day support of classroom instructional needs, and the maintenance of instructional areas. From a tactical perspective, one comprehensive matrix organization can address all complex classroom support needs.

Figure 4.3 is a case example of the complex involvement required to develop new instructional space at a university. From a technical perspective, creating a new instructional facility is usually managed on a project basis using a project

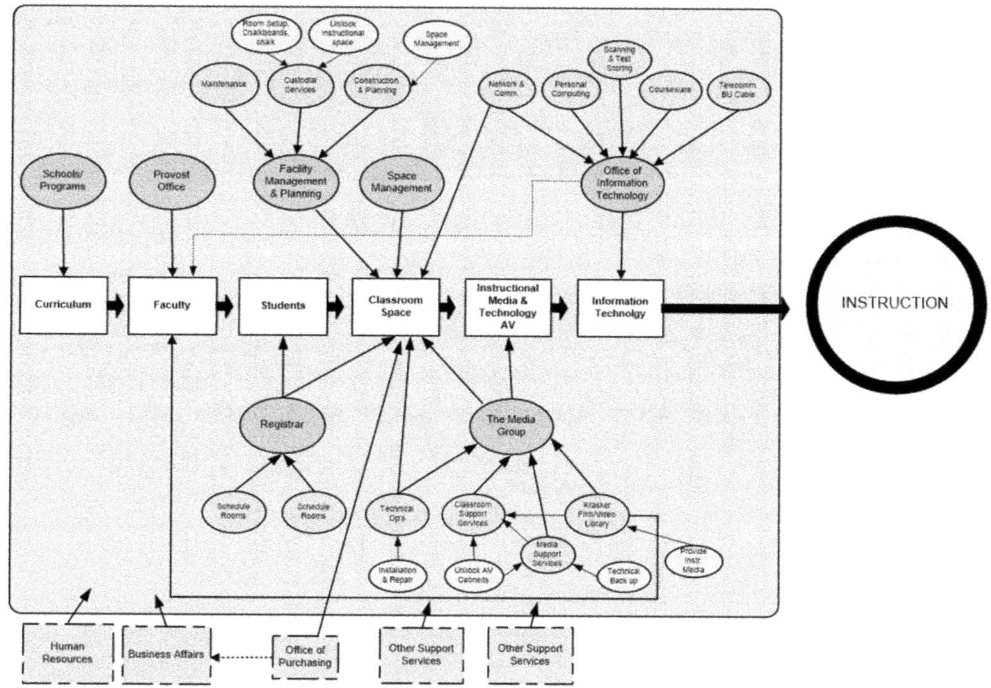

FIGURE 4.3 Horizontal Map for Instructional Delivery Support Cross-Functional Processes

Note: The diagram illustrates the dynamics involved in the development of classrooms and the delivery of support services required to assist instruction in many higher educational institutions. Departments and interactions may vary in different environments. The intent of this diagram is to illustrate the complexity of effort required that may not be obvious to others in administration working outside of this process.

leader approach. Deciding what space should be developed, how it should be developed, and establishing an appropriate budget for such projects is often made without all stakeholders' representation. With the renovation or upgrade of an existing facility or instructional technology system, no formal process is in place to manage these projects holistically. To ensure that the instructional facility development and maintenance process is optimized, a system approach should be in place to ensure that all stakeholders are represented in the decision process. A matrix management model can help achieve this goal. A model which promotes system optimization and user satisfaction should be considered.

Traditionally, organizational transformation is often implemented by altering assignments or rearranging boxes on a hierarchical organizational chart. This type of change has little impact on how complex, cross-functional mission-based services or support mechanisms are provided. To optimize an organization's efforts, all instructional support needs within an organization must be better aligned. Creating and managing the support organization in a vertical and horizontal dimension, resulting in a cross-functional matrix approach, will help address most of the organization's complex instructional needs.

How can a university create a structure that will manage the people, resources, and budgets available across functions to support instructional delivery? Managing across a vertical structure requires the adoption of a matrix organizational structure. For this to work, horizontal structures need to take precedence over vertically orientated management. In Figure 4.4, you can see an example of how this can be accomplished is by identifying and managing operational efforts and a portfolio of projects within a matrix structure. The new matrix organizational structure ideally should report to a provost level position responsible for teaching and learning.

Why use this management approach to solve this problem? Vertical organizational units often operate independently. Matrix organizations use structures that make these units more dependent and supportive of other units' efforts. Large organizations have complex problems. As a result, the scope and breadth of the problem should be dealt with by numerous individuals within the organization. (Martin, 2005).

Martin (2005) also states that ramifications are different for individuals and groups, and because of this, a multidisciplinary team will make a more effective decision and hopefully provide better support and service to an organization.

Martin (2005) points out that there are disadvantages to the concept. One of the more daunting issues is the complexity and pace of the decision process employing this model. There is also a diffusing of responsibility or "a lack of accountability" that also needs to be realized (Martin, 2005). With good leadership and management, this "lack of accountability" can be addressed (Ray & Elder, 2007).

This is an example of how someone looking to solve a similar problem might organize their thoughts and conceptualize a model. Any model created will evolve

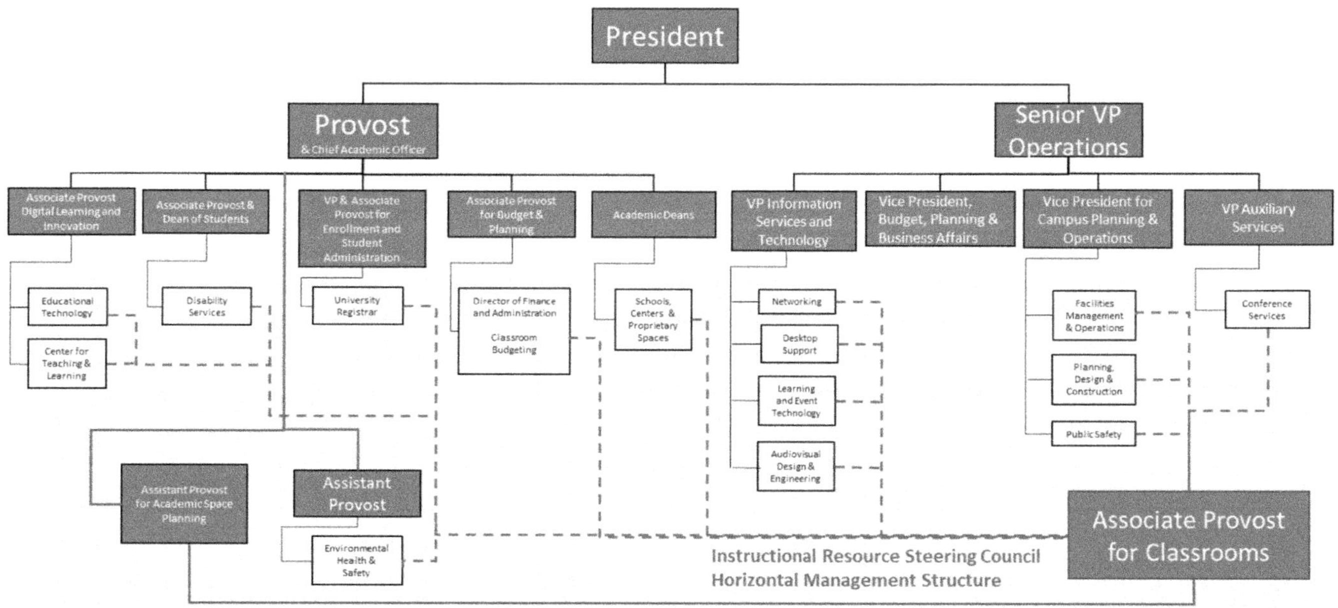

In a Matrix, mission-based approach to management, the distribution of support for classroom development or management should not be based on how your institution is hierarchically organized but on a mission-based approach that groups those responsible for classroom planning, budgeting, development and operations are grouped under one department or unit functionally and perpetually responsible for the development and operations of classrooms for the organization. This approach will ensure that resources for classroom support are not competing for attention and resources within a multipurpose vertical organizational unit but are consolidated in a matrix organization so that strategic planning, funding and development for classroom resources are structured to meet the organizations needs in a consistent and continuous way across time, budget and leadership changes.

FIGURE 4.4 A Horizontal (Matrix) Management Structure Laid Over a Traditional Hierarchical Organization

with additional input and guidance from the organization's leadership team and other stakeholders.

Soft OR, speaking to stakeholders about the current or baseline management structures and processes to help identify problems and work to break them down into their basic components, should also be undertaken. Once the needed information is collected on the existing system, processes, and mechanisms, this information can be communicated to senior management. It is essential to show how efforts can be disorganized and inefficient, making them ineffective at providing the space, as well as the orchestrated and timely services, needed to teach students. Delivering services needed daily might be successful under current systems but are probably the product of the sheer determination of individuals or departments responding to the professional commitment and personal dedication that fills an operational void.

By concentrating on instruction, a core operation of a university, a possible outcome of efforts is to refocus the administration's attention on this issue and also prioritize the curriculum's instructional environment and technological needs. This focus might help the institution consider making a progressive move in a more system-based direction. The resulting schema, if structured correctly and fully adopted, will create coherence of effort while enhancing accountability and communications throughout the organization (Hilliard, 2019). Bridging relations across an administrative and academic divide can also help with this effort (Marr, 2009).

When the project used in this case study was undertaken, qualitative data was collected using surveys, interviews, and the evaluation of primary source resource materials. The primary source resource materials included department organizational charts and an identified list of participants in project teams and committees that were currently working on instructional support related projects across the university. Key business and academic administrators, as well as users throughout the institution, were also interviewed to probe for more information and insight into current support successes in order to identify existing shortcomings.

After the assessment and analysis of the current organizational processes were completed and a new management model conceptualized, a written report was prepared, and presentation materials were created to summarize and articulate findings and recommendations proposed. To respect the organization's politics, project findings were submitted to an immediate supervisor. The research and corresponding proposal were then shared with the business and academic leadership in the organization that could help advocate for change.

Problem Resolution

Administrators in this situation did not consider systems thinking in the adoption of the proposed change which led to the continuation of inefficient and ineffective approaches to managing instructional support in their organization. As with any change, there will be skepticism that a different system can work and make a significant difference in service quality or support. Also, the idea of changing "business as usual" may lead to resistance from the systems key players who are needed to cooperate on the initiative.

Inevitably, departmental territorialism will also occur. In vertical organizations, direct reporting lines and department structures give managers the autonomy, budget, and power they enjoy. Changing that structure will not be looked upon favorably. From a change management perspective, it will take time and perseverance to change a traditional organization (Murthy, 2007). In this case, implementing a true matrix approach will blur lines between roles and functions in administrative and academic facets of the organization. Because of the proposed matrix model and the proposal's disruptive nature, the proposition was not accepted by leadership.

Lessons Learned

Using systems thinking to take on a project of this magnitude and complexity offers an opportunity to enhance leadership capacity. The process of assessing the problem, exploring new operational structures, and developing viable alternatives to solve an organizational problem through the lens of systems thinking offers an opportunity to actualize personal learning goals along with professional and institutional growth. There are times and places when proposing and adopting bold and progressive ideas are more readily accepted. Smaller institutions may be more receptive and possess the agility to implement a proposed matrix management system opposed to larger institutions like the one used in this case that needs to expand its awareness of how systems thinking might solve complex problems in the future.

Conclusion

Higher education, with its different stakeholders, its diverse academic and scientific pursuits, along with its complex organizational structures are challenging organizations to manage. I have always described our work environment to others unfamiliar with the field as controlled anarchy. It can be a difficult environment in which to survive, let alone thrive. Darwin has shown us that evolving is required for survival. When undertaking a project that proposes a disruptive outcome, especially around an organization's structure, it is important to first assess your organization's receptiveness and tolerance for change. Some organizations are more willing to innovate than others. Some organizations see innovation taking place only around technology.

More progressive organizations may be more insightful and see organizational challenges as multidimensional. They are willing to confront and update management systems as well as technology to help their organizations become more efficient, effective, and responsive to community needs.

Innovative system-based ideas, especially those involving departmental structures and the assignment of staff resources within an organization, will flounder if progressive and bold leadership is absent.

So, what can be accomplished in environments that may be reluctant to change? Incremental steps can be taken by organizing communities of practice and governance structures to lay the foundations of matrix-based management ideas (Screnci, 2017). This may help to develop momentum by showing the effectiveness of these efforts to address and solve complex organizational challenges.

Eventually efforts might be recognized by leadership and be formally adopted to serve the organization. This advocacy for change can come at some professional cost and systemic change takes time. If you are committed to an organization's values and principles and are resolute on working for some time to serve its mission, then time and patience are key. Individuals in leadership positions do change over time and with new leadership new prospects for shared values and collective advocacy may emerge, which will seed new opportunities for continued systemic change.

Reflective Questions

- What is your organization's history when it comes to systemic change? Has it been dormant or active? If dormant, is it worth the undertaking? If it is active, has it been managed well? Was there a positive outcome? If so, how can you mirror that effort? If not, why?
- Has your organization been receptive to the adoption and diffusion of new ideas in the past? If it has, has it been in technology, curriculum, organizational structures?
- Is your current leadership receptive to change in your organization?
- Do you consider yourself a change agent? Is there a change agent(s) already in your organization that you can use as a resource to assist you in your effort?
- What opportunities exist in your organization that you can use to start laying down the foundation of a matrix form of management? Are there advocates you can engage in your efforts?
- Are there examples of higher educational organizations that have implemented matrix organizational structures? In what areas? To address what problem? Were they successful? If so, what was their implementation plan?
- What are the negative aspects of implementing a matrix organizational system? Is your organization nimble or strong enough to overcome their drawbacks?

References

Cabrera, D., & Cabrera, L. (2018). *Systems Thinking Made Simple: New Hope for Solving Wicked Problems (2nd ed.)*. Plectica Publishing.

Cabrera, D, Colosi, L., & Lobdell, C. (2008). Systems thinking. *Evaluation and Program Planning* 31(3) (2008): 299–310.

Davis, S. M., & Lawrence, P. R. (1977). *Matrix*. Addison-Wesley Publishing Company.

Forrester, J. W. (1994). System dynamics, systems thinking, and soft OR. *System Dynamics Review* 10(2–3): 245–256.

Hilliard, I. (2019). *Coherency Management an Alternative to CSR in a Changing World (1st ed.)*. Springer International and Palgrave Macmillan.

Lepore, D., Montgomery, A., & Siepe, G. (2016). Managing complexity in organizations through a systemic network of projects. In A. J. Masys (Ed.), *Applications of Systems Thinking and Soft Operations Research in Managing Complexity* (p. 35). Springer International Publishing.

Marr, J. D. (2009). *Interpersonal Communication and Professional Relationships between Faculty and Administrators in Higher Education*, PhD thesis. Spalding University.

Martin, P. K. (2005). *Quick Guide Management Series: The New Matrix Management*. Martin Training Associates. Renaissance Educational Services, Inc.

Murthy, C. S. V. (2017). Organizational Culture (Ch. 6). In *Change Management (1st ed.)*. Himalaya House.

Ray, D., and Elder, D. (2007) Managing horizontal accountability. *The Journal for Quality and Participation* 30(4): 24.

Schnackenberg, A. K., & Tomlinson, E. C. (2016). Organizational transparency: A new perspective on managing trust in organization-stakeholder relationships. *Journal of Management* 42(7): 1784–1810.

Screnci, D. (2017, April 24, Monday) Building communities of practice to support EdTech. *Educause Review*. https://er.educause.edu/articles/2017/4/building-communities-of-practice-to-support-edtech

5

SUPPORTING STUDENT VOICE TO PROTEST AND THE IMPETUS FOR CHANGE (K-12)

Jay Starnes and Beth R. Sockman

Introduction

This case chronicles a persistent student and supportive administrators dedicated to social justice in their school system. To protect entities, little is disclosed regarding the discussion and emotions surrounding events.

System and Key Players

In 2016, a 4th-grade student of color wrote a letter to the school board requesting that the district consider observing Dr. Martin Luther King, Jr. Day as a holiday, but the board took no formal action on the request. In 5th grade, the student met with the principal of his school, who heard his concerns. The student explained that little happened in school related to Dr. Martin Luther King, Jr. and that there was little done related to Black History education in general. Hearing the student's concern, the principal and student collaborated to develop several school-wide activities to augment Black History education in the particular school.

The student persisted. When the student was in 6th and 7th grade, he expanded collaboration with the school's student council, building principal and district curriculum director to develop Black History Month activities. From the more extensive work, awareness grew about the dearth of curriculum materials and resources that inform children about Black leaders and the historical and current experiences of people of color.

The student's activism included writing an annual letter to the school board. He wrote about the need to acknowledge the value of Dr. Martin Luther King's work, make the celebration a school holiday, and include Black History. Year after year, he wrote the same letter of request with the same result; no action was taken.

DOI: 10.4324/9781003028772-6

The district's informal response to the student's letter was that it was better for students to be in school, where students could be exposed to Dr. Martin Luther King, Jr. content rather than to be out of school on holiday. The rationale could seem logical since schooling aims to form character and knowledge, but looking closer, the policy rests on unchecked racist ideas. Why? Most USA school calendars include holidays to honor Presidents and Columbus. Yet, in this case, there was no holiday to celebrate the people brought to the USA as slaves over 400 years ago, and a significant leader that helped raise the moral consciousness of the entire nation.

The remainder of this case attempts something dangerous; that is, it addresses a complex issue with few words. To guide thoughts, we explain how systems biases influence a school district's thinking and the way a few students – supported by a few school leaders – were able to use the unfortunate events that caused traumatic shame to make beginning policy changes.

Current policies are supported by systemic racism, even if non-intentional (Kendi, 2019). How can one district honor the call to move toward antiracist policies with a predominantly White population? (See Table 5.1 for the School Districts Demographics.)

Innovation – Students Organized and Facilitated a Community's Peaceful Protest

In June of 2020, during the wake of the George Floyd murder (Taylor, 2021), the student asked for a virtual meeting with the middle school principal and curriculum director. In the meeting, he revealed his plan for a march, promoting awareness concerns for people of color and solidarity with the Black Lives Matter movement. He requested the school facility as a beginning point for the march, and the district's help with communication and advertising.

June of 2020 was during the COVID-19 pandemic, and the school district was closed to all in-person activities. The state had restricted indoor and outdoor

TABLE 5.1 School District Student Demographics

Student Race	*Percentage %*
Native American	0.2
Asian	1.2
Black	1.2
Native Hawaiian or Pacific Islander	0.1
Hispanic	9.7
White	84.5
Two or more Races	2.7

Note: 54.4% of the students are considered economically disadvantaged.

gathering sizes as well and imposed strict masking and social-distancing orders. When presented with obstacles associated with the pandemic, the student had a plan to comply with district and state restrictions.

In mid-June, 2020, approximately 500 people marched in support of the students and Black Lives Matter following all masking and social-distancing regulations. The march was peaceful. Counter-protesters were encountered with peace and invited into the conversation. The march was a unifying event for the community and catalyzed to build capacity for policy shifts.

Case Analysis

To understand the complexity of change, culture will be explained in terms of systems, and then traumatic shame as an impetus for change. Our cultures are mapped onto who we are as people and how we interact with the world. Culture influences who we are – our identity and beliefs, going far beyond the nuclear family but through layers of systems in which we are interconnected (Wikerson, 2020). One definition of culture intuits the vastness: Culture "refers to a dynamic system of social values, cognitive codes, behavioral standards, worldviews, and beliefs used to give order and meeting to our own lives as well as the lives of others" (Delgado-Gaitain & Trueba, 1991 in Gay, 2018). Multilayered culture stands durable, influencing our individual and collective consciousness through generations (Harro, 2018) and becomes normalized, whether empowering or oppressive.

Using a systems level model, schools can be visualized within society, receiving from the broad, large society systems overlapping levels that affect the other. The systems levels can be referred to as the supra system, macro, meso, and micro (Sockman et al., 2019). The supra system represents the greater society with the national norms and stereotypes (Harro, 2018). Macro systems refer to the groups and organizations in which individuals participate. In this case, the school district serves as a macro system. Children are initiated into various groups, one of which is school. The meso level represents the still smaller part, which holds the classroom. Last, the individual is considered the micro system which encompasses personal identity (see Figure 5.1) and the way the individual views the world.

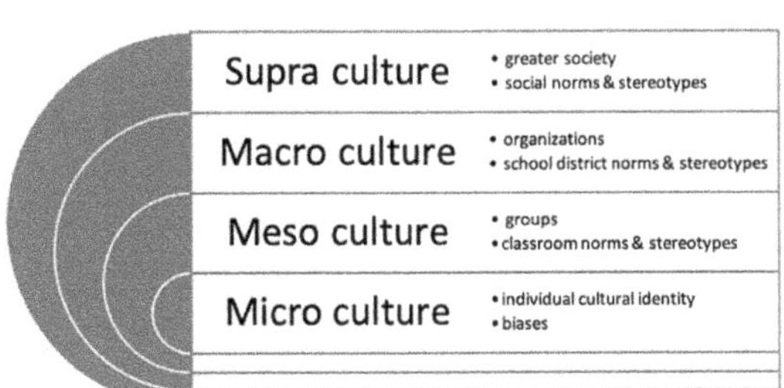

FIGURE 5.1 Example Systems Level Model

From this model, the school exists within a system that is not value neutral but an extension of the larger system of values. The purpose of today's schools can be debated, but primarily school is an organization to prepare students to thrive in our democracy (Dewey, 1916; Krishnamurti, 1974; Sant, 2019), embodying the structure, hierarchy of power, and pedagogy to reflect adult hopes for the future generations. Those same curricular hopes reflect the people in control so that society can repeat itself.

In a societal critique of the system, Critical Race Theory (CRT) explains how racism has been transmitted throughout the systems (Ladson-Billings, 1998). CRT purports the following basic systemic principles: racism is normalized in USA society; narratives about Black and other unrepresented people keep them "one-down"; legal and policy practices fail to be the catalyst for social change; and people who are White are the main beneficiaries of Affirmative Action (Wilkerson, 2020).

These principles have been practiced for 400 years with proven resilience to change though oppressive. The USA has enacted some policies to support equitable systems, yet racism persists within the conscious and unconscious minds, finding legal ways to assert implicit biases. A few things can interrupt this formidable cycle, but traumatic shame is one of those things.

Complexity – Traumatic Shame at the Supra Level Influenced the District

It is hard to stop a societal system cycle that perpetuates itself (Harro, 2018). The interconnectedness demands power and influence to unlock all levels to make a culture shift toward all racial equality. Zembylas (2020) notes that traumatic shame can interrupt the cycle because of its nature. Traumatic events share a commonality. They "cannot be transformed into knowledge … because it is the sign of a catastrophic cycle wound and a devastating rupture of the social bond" (Woodward, 2000 in Zembylas, p. 55). Something or some events happen that are so horrid, typical analysis can barely describe it. We have had many such events in USA history (Wilkerson, 2020), from the shame of slavery's beginning to lynching. Still, little has been as visually available to the general population as the events from the summer of 2021 through live video documentation and distribution.

The vivid murder of George Floyd and others (Taylor, 2021) caused larger society to look in the mirror, questioning our ethics and entrenched racial bias is embedded in our cultural norms. The event caused critical reflection the way traumatic shame does, having an ethical and political affect; we are "always bound to an ethical orientation and relationality to 'the other' that is inescapable" (Zembylas, p. 55). Zembylas views the "other" as the marginalized population that may be perceived differently than people in power view themselves. When experiencing traumatic shame, officials at the school were open to recognizing the perspectives of students of color differently than in the past.

Complexity – Power and Influence of the Community

The middle school principal and curriculum director did not have the district system's authority to approve the student's plan but asked questions and suggested some possible solutions to overcome obstacles. The next step was to support the student in presenting his idea to the next system's level with individuals who did possess the authority to approve his plan. A meeting was scheduled where others in the system could hear the student's program, ask questions, and grant approval. Afterwards, they scheduled an appointment with the district superintendent.

Before the meeting with the superintendent, the student asked for an interim meeting. The meeting's purpose was to expand the planning team to two additional students of color and two additional district administrators. The three students and four administrators met virtually to discuss logistics, potential obstacles, including political and safety concerns. A local rally in a neighboring borough resulted in threats of violence, counter-protesters, and various groups of armed bystanders.

District leaders were scared for students' safety and were aware of the political and social ramifications of supporting this protest. Like many communities, some residents held a strong sentiment equating support for the Black Lives Matter's movement meant not supporting police, which would promote lawless looting and vandalism. Ironically, the students and families involved in the protest faced threats of violence against them.

Planning for the physical and emotional safety of students was paramount. Previous antiracist work in this community resulted in students and families feeling isolated, ostracized, and viewed as disruptive. Aside from the planning for physical safety, students needed support from school leaders to communicate a partnership. It was important for the community to understand that the students and families were not alone.

In the next virtual meeting, the three students and four administrators were joined by the district assistant superintendent and the superintendent. The students presented their plans: They would march from the local borough park, through town, to another park; guest speakers would orate at the conclusion. They needed to secure permits from the borough council and already had secured support from the town mayor and police chief. Then the students asked the school district for their alliance: encourage the march by communicating support in the form of a statement on the district's website and social media, communicate educational resources through a list on the website, and show encouragement for the students on the day of the march.

Additional requests from the student activists included a review of policies, budgets, and programs to eradicate systemic racism, to revisit the observation of Dr. Martin Luther King, Jr. Day as a district holiday, and to engage in an ongoing conversation about school culture and environment. The district agreed to support all the students' requests.

Problem Resolution

Even at the supra level, when traumatic shame is experienced, those in power can often recognize the suffering of others that are unlike themselves (Zembylas, 2020), and the doors can be open for the "critical conversations that expose the complexities of shame and its transformation possibilities" (p. 62) at the macro, meso, and micro levels. Likewise, the district saw the need for change.

In mid-June, 2020, approximately 500 people marched in support of the students and Black Lives Matter. District students, alumni, teachers, and administrators accounted for a large portion of those attending the protest. Local law enforcement supported logistics and distributed water to the protesters. Local politicians and community members marched in solidarity. There was a small number of counter-protesters, and they were encountered with peace and invited into the conversation. The march was a unifying event for the community and built capacity for policy shifts in the district.

After four years of requests, the board finally approved to designate Dr. Martin Luther King, Jr. Day. In August 2020, the board amended the 2020–2021 school calendar, which included the observance of Monday, January 18, 2021, Dr. Martin Luther King, Jr. Day as a school holiday.

The progress persisted. After a conversation with a district literacy partner, the three students who organized the march were offered, and participated in, paid summer internships. During the internship experience, students were apprenticed by leaders in literacy as a social justice movement.

The district began and continues to audit its budgets, policies, handbooks, and curriculum. The result of the audits has resulted in language changes in district documents, changes in instructional materials and curriculum, and new courses focusing on human rights. Conversations and actions about improving culture, environment, and experiences in the district continue.

Lessons Learned

Education leaders can persistently support the student voice even if oppressed, and with preparation, collective voices can lead to collaborative activities that begin the transformation to more significant equity. Our experience is interconnected. The supra system of societal events can affect the community and serve as leverage to shift the structured school system. Failure can be nested in our collective societal consciousness that may go unnoticed when unchecked.

Conclusion

Schools shape the next generation to build the society, but schooling is also the byproduct of society (Wilkerson, 2020), entangled in a web of systems that make the curriculum (Gay, 2018) and structures durable against change. Traumatic shame affects society, and therefore the school system, making way for "social transformations" that can create space for shame to operate pedagogically (Zembylas, 2020, p. 55). In this case, school officials saw what was not seen previously from a perspective that was not their own. The students and prepared school leaders gave the school district a way to begin acting, to see reality from another perspective – the students of color.

The authors implore the readers to guard against the oversimplification of a complex issue that deserves personal interrogation. This case was one example of how student activists and the school leaders that supported them fostered transformation amid crises. Traumatic shame is, in fact, a "shameful" instigator of social change because it demonstrates the way humanity's heart finally breaks – only after a horrendous act. The reader likely feels a lack of depth, but it is hoped that the readers will deepen their knowledge with further work. Kendi (2019) wrote: "Racial equity is when two or more racial groups are standing of relatively equal footing" (p. 18). We have a long way to go. Our school systems should dedicate themselves to this truism by investigating and implementing actions and curriculum that uphold students of color's narratives through curriculum and experiences. A diversified curriculum would better enable all students to be global citizens. However, since we influence the system, only when we individually delve into who we are can our institutions collaboratively build toward a more equitable world.

Reflective Questions

- When you read this case, what stands out to you?
- What are you going to do to learn more about yourself or your affiliated organizations?
- "To get beyond racism, we must first take account of race. There is no other way. And to treat some persons equally, we must treat them differently" (Court Justice Harry Blackmun in Kendi, 2019, p. 19). Keeping that in mind, how do we construct our schools to be antiracist?

Additional Resources

Adams, M., Blumenfeld, W. J., Catalano, D. C. J., DeJong, K. S., Hackman, H. W., Hopkins, L. E., Love. B. J., Peters, M. L., Shalasko, D., & Zúñiga, X. (Eds.). (2018). *Readings for diversity and social justice* (4th ed.). Routledge.

Implicit Bias – Take various self-test to check your implicit bias https://implicit.harvard.edu/implicit/takeatest.html

Social Justice Toolbox: www.socialjusticetoolbox.com/ This should only be visited after reading and engaging in critical conversations with skilled facilitators on culture and race.

Wilkerson, I. (2020). *Caste: The origins of our discontents*. Random House. https://doi.org/10.1080/00497878.2020.1862844

References

DeJong, K. S., Hackman, H. W., Hopkins, L. E., Love. B. J., Peters, M. L., Shalasko, D., & Zúñiga, X. (Eds.), *Readings for diversity and social justice* (4th ed., pp. 27–34). Routledge.

Delgado-Gaitan, C., & Trueba, H. (1991). *Crossing cultural borders: Education for immigrant families in America*. Falmer.

Dewey, J. (1916). *Democracy and education: An introduction to the philosophy of education*. Macmillan.

Gay, G. (2018). *Culturally responsive teaching: Theory, research, and practice*. Teachers College Press.

Harro, B. (2018). The cycle of socialization. In Adams, M., Blumenfeld, W. J., Catalano, D. C. J., Kendi, I. X. (2019). *How to be antiracist*. One World. https://doi.org/10.1177/0196859920961032

Kendi, I. X. (2019). *How to be an antiracist*. Random House Publishing Group.

Krishnamurti, J. (1974). *On education*. Nagar, Chennai: Krishnamurti Foundation Trust Ltd.

Ladson-Billings, G. (1998). Just what is critical race theory and what's it doing in a nice field like education? *International Journal of Qualitative Studies in Education*, 11(1), 7–24. https://doi.org/10.1080/095183998236863

Sant, E. (2019). Democratic education: A theoretical review 2006–2017. *Educational Researcher*, 89(5), 655–696. https://doi.org/10.3102/0034654319862493

Sockman, B. R., Clossey, L., Carducci, O. M., Batson-Magnuson, L., Mazure, D., White, G., Wehmeyer, A., Green, B., & Wells, H. (2019). Systems thinking as a heuristic for the implementation of service-learning in a university In M. Spector, B. Lockee, & M. Childress (Eds.), *Learning, design, and technology*. Springer. https://doi.org/10.1007/978-3-319-17727-4_91-1

Taylor, D. B. (2021, January 6). George Floyd protests: A timeline. *New York Times*. Retrieved from www.nytimes.com/article/george-floyd-protests-timeline.html

Wilkerson, I. (2020). *Caste: The origins of our discontents*. Random House. https://doi.org/10.1080/00497878.2020.1862844

Woodward, K. (2000). Traumatic shame: Toni Morrison, televisual culture, and the cultural politics of the emotions. *Cultural Critique*, 46, 210–240.

Zembylas, M. (2020). The ethnics and politics of traumatic shame: Pedagogical insights. In Dernikos, B. P., Lesko, N., McCall, S. D., & Niccolini, A. D. (Eds.), *Mapping the affective turn in education: Theory, research and pedagogies* (pp. 54–68). Routledge.

PART II

Strategic Planning

6

IMPROVING SCHOOL CULTURE THROUGH SYSTEMATIC CHANGES (K-12)

Kendal Askins and Todd Breiner

Introduction

This case summarizes how systemic thinking was employed to transform an intermediate public-school culture. Through the development of a shared leadership system, social emotional support system, and an instructional empowerment system, teachers and administration were able to develop a learning community where faculty and staff: regularly collaborate, participate, and contribute to an environment that enhances instructional practices, encourages respect and rapport, and promotes the success of the whole student.

System and Key Players

The Pleasant Valley School district, located in Kunkletown, Pennsylvania, is one of the school districts located in the Pocono Area of Monroe County. The school district has four schools: an elementary school that services grades kindergarten through third grade; an intermediate school that services grades four through six; a middle school that services grades seven and eight; and a high school that services grades nine through 12. The intermediate school will be the focus of this study.

The intermediate school was built in the year 2000 in order to accommodate the fast-growing community and the then overpopulated schools in the Pleasant Valley School district. Since its opening, Pleasant Valley Intermediate School (PVIS) has experienced a total of 23 administrators. This includes the roles of both the principal and assistant principal positions. On average, administrators were staying only one to two years. With each administrator came new procedures,

DOI: 10.4324/9781003028772-8

systems, leadership styles, cultures, and visions. However, no leader stayed long enough for their visions to be carried out.

Constant administrator turnover created a culture of rejection, resentment, and disappointment among the PVIS staff. They felt that no one listened, and had a hard time understanding why the Intermediate building was the only building to experience such a high turnover rate. In June 2018, two new administrators were hired, Todd Breiner, principal, and Kendal Askins, assistant principal. Understanding the history and the current climate, they knew that change was needed. They began speaking to staff members, giving surveys, and seeking to understand how students felt. In addition, they sought to understand the current culture of the building, the history of how that culture developed, and what was needed to begin moving the staff forward.

After collecting and analyzing data throughout the course of the first year, a goal for changing the culture of the school was created. Specifically, the goal was to create an atmosphere and culture where everyone who walked through the PVIS doors knew and could feel that they wanted to be a part of the culture of the school. "No school leader can ignore school ethos and school culture very long and succeed" (NCEE, 2016). A sustainable system of change and leadership that would continue in the absence of individual people and would continue if there is ever a change in leadership, needed to be created to meet this goal. To succeed in this, the change initiative was approached by implementing systems that incorporate relationship and trust building, shared decision making, collaboration, open communication and caring constructive feedback.

How can administration break down faculty, staff, and community fears by building an environment that promotes relationship building, trust, collaboration, communication, and shared leadership?

Case Analysis

PVIS had a history of making building-based decisions that led to tremendous inconsistencies in the district. There was a history of administrative turn over and micromanaging. Due to administrative turnover, there were tremendous inconsistencies in the process from one administrative leadership team to the next. Each administrative team had to make decisions independently and with very little guidance from district driven process or procedure and consequently, this led to poor staff morale and upset community stakeholders. Changes were made to school stakeholders rather than with school stakeholders. Due to the frequent change and turnover, a repetitive change syndrome was created. Abrahamson (2004) refers to a repetitive change syndrome as

> Initiative overload, change-related chaos, and widespread employee anxiety, cynicism, and burnout. The results? Not only do relentless tidal shifts of change create pain at almost every level of the company and make

> organizational change harder to manage, more costly to implement, and more likely to fail, but they also impinge on routine operations, and render firms inwardly focused on managing change.
>
> *Fullen, Hill, & Crevola, 2006, p. 16*

This historical environment added to the cultural negativity and lack of successful lasting change.

Due to poor morale and a past history of lack of trust, the faculty and staff approached new leadership coming from outside the district by putting up walls, barriers, and resistance because they felt that all administrators would treat them the same or that all administrators would come and go. "Trust, in any relationship–organizational or individual – is absolutely indispensable to success" (Stronge, Richard, & Catano, 2008). The administrative team hired in 2018 had to develop systems that would help to eliminate this fear, break down the walls and build back the trust and rapport with all members of the school community.

Stakeholders

The stakeholders in this study included all of the students, parents, teachers, support staff, and the administration team. Each stakeholder provided different information needed for the study. (See Table 6.1.)

Students

Currently, PVIS has 887 students enrolled. This includes 265 fourth graders, 292 fifth graders, and 330 sixth graders. There are a variety of clubs and committees that

TABLE 6.1 Stakeholders and Their Roles

Position	*Role*
Students	Representatives from each class, meet once a month to discuss school culture from a student's perspective, give suggestions for improvements that students want to see.
Parents	Advisory, share concerns and successes from a parent's perspective. Offers suggestions for improvement.
Teachers	Determine what students will be on the Principal's Student Council, completes surveys providing successes and failures from a teacher's perspective, offers suggestions for improvement, shares needs for continued success, volunteer on building level committees.
Administration	Provide dates for Principal Student Advisory Council and Principal Parent Advisory Council, create and distribute surveys to the staff, final decision on programming changes, lead committees for teacher input.

have been created to help involve students in the school. One of the committees that was created is the Student Advisory Committee. The committee is composed of 31 students. It includes representatives from each fourth, fifth and sixth grade homeroom in the school. Students are referred to the committee by their homeroom teacher. The committee meets bi-monthly and the agenda of these meetings mimic that of the parent meetings. Students share their perspectives and provide feedback to the principal and assistant principal. Another group that was created is the Student Ambassadors. This group meets with school counselors and helps to implement student initiatives in the building.

Parent-Teacher Organization

PVIS has an active Parent-Teacher Organization with monthly meetings open to all parents of all students who attend PVIS and all teachers who work at PVIS. This organization helps with bridging the communication between parents, teachers, and the community to help provide a successful learning environment for the students. The board, responsible for the overall operations of the organization, consists of a president, vice-president, secretary, and treasurer. The meetings are held to provide the members with updates of decisions and all decisions are discussed at the meetings.

Title I Funding

The school is a Title I school and receives Title I funds to help supplement educational programming. As part of the school's Title I plan, there are multiple family engagement nights and activities that are planned and implemented by the faculty. Attendance at these events is usually high and positive feedback from students and families is consistently received. Additionally, the school holds three Title I family meetings each year: one in the fall, one in the spring, and one for assistance in planning the Title I goals.

There are 74 teachers at PVIS. The teachers are organized in a teaming structure. Each grade level is made up of three-member teams with a teacher for English Language Arts, Mathematics, and Science/Social Studies. In addition, there are some two-man teams made up of one teacher in Mathematics/Science and the other in English Language Arts/Social Studies. There are also learning support teachers, math specialists, and reading specialists in all three grades. The building also has four school counselors and an instructional support teacher.

The administrative team at PVIS consists of the principal, assistant principal, and dean of students. These three team members have worked together since the beginning of the 2018–2019 school year.

Problem Resolution

Three systems were created within the school structure to help break down fears and promote relationship building, trust, collaboration communication, and shared leadership. These systems were: Shared Leadership System, Social Emotional System, and Instructional Empowerment System. "When staff members collaborate and take ownership of tasks in these areas, ownership of problem solving and decision making resides with a team rather than remaining solely the responsibility of the school leaders" (Stronge, Richard, & Catano, 2008).

When approaching building a system of shared leadership, multiple leadership committees were established, and a collaborative process of open communication was implemented. Each committee that was established used a combination of problem solving and shared decision making. The committees that were created include, but were not limited to: Building Leadership, Scheduling, CREATE Lab,[1] and the SERT Team.

Shared Leadership System

Most of the committees meet monthly and the agenda was developed by sharing a Google Doc with all of the members and asking these members to add any items to the document they would like to discuss. There were committees that did not meet monthly but more on an as needed basis. An example of this would be the scheduling committee. Halfway through the 2018–2019 school year, a meeting with the committee was called to discuss some of the issues with the current schedule. The committee was composed of representatives from each grade and content area in the building. In addition, the administration did not choose specific people to be on the committee. Anyone who wanted to be on the committee had the opportunity to join. There were a series of meetings to collect data from the faculty and staff, compare it with state requirements and district goals, and develop a new schedule and teaming structure. After the committee developed a proposal, it was shared among the rest of the faculty, with central office administrators, and the board of school directors. This process allowed everyone to have a say in the new schedule and teaming structure that was going to be implemented.

Social Emotional System

To build a system of social emotional support, a Mindfulness Room for teachers was developed and a space for teachers was created for teachers to feel safe by listening and encouraging teachers to share their worries and concerns while simultaneously addressing patterned behavior. Additionally, providing supportive processes in times of need increased the level of trust and comfort in addressing all issues (ex. transition to distance learning and support provided during death of faculty members).

Instructional Empowerment System

To build a system of instructional empowerment Professional Learning Communities were restructured to support collaborative professional growth. "School improvement must focus on specific structures of teacher professional learning" (Jenson et al., 2016). Data was collected and examined, and goals were created to develop and align common forms of assessments that effectively evaluated intended student learning outcomes and monitored the effectiveness of classroom instruction. Additionally, these communities were another opportunity to continue to develop a learning community where faculty and staff regularly collaborate, participate, and contribute to an environment that enhances instructional practices, encourages respect and rapport, and promotes the success of the whole student. In addition, a CREATE Lab was developed and implemented as an extension to the classroom. The CREATE Lab is a classroom that was designed to be an extension of the classroom. It integrates art and classroom content through a variety of stations. Students are encouraged to explore the room without being guided to a specific task by the teacher. These two implementations have given teachers a different perspective about instructional practices and what learning looks like.

Lessons Learned

There have been a number of lessons that have been learned through this process. The relationships that teachers have with one another and with administration are very powerful. These relations have been used to help move the vision along. More teachers have begun to volunteer and look for opportunities to contribute to the building and the school community. Teachers are beginning to share a variety of emotions with the administration, not just the emotions that they think the administration wants to see. Teachers have begun to trust the administration to make decisions that are in the best interest of students, faculty, staff, and the school organization. Teachers have begun to speak up against those that continue to complain about the past. The silent majority is beginning to become more vocal about the loud minority resistance.

Teachers are responsive to change when they are a part of the process, see a plan being implemented with fidelity and see the administration follow through and keep their word. This demonstrated a respect for their time and expertise. The process is just as important as the end product. Despite being difficult at times, honest and open communication helped to build a transparent relationship and trust in a short period of time. These difficult conversations that provide direct feedback without trying to address issues through evaluation will only help quickly build an understanding and appreciation of support with your faculty and staff.

Conclusion

A shared leadership approach helped to make staff feel more included not only in decision making but in their value as a professional. "Most significantly, development of multiple leaders promotes sustainability, allowing the established belief system and practices of the school to endure beyond the tenure of one leader" (Stronge, Richard, & Catano, 2008). While teachers have indicated that they now feel that leadership is shared and supported, they still have indicated that data is not always used to make decisions and that they are not comfortable taking risks.

Currently discipline referrals have remained the same and no significant decrease has been found. This might have contributed to current beliefs on discipline. Those beliefs have not yet been addressed in the shared leadership systems that have been implemented throughout the building.

Each year the committees that are in place are evaluated to determine if that committee is still necessary. Teachers know what to expect and know that if they join these committees that their voice can and will have an impact. The school culture has begun to change into what they want it to be. "Culture changes only after you have successfully altered people's actions, after the new behavior produces some group benefit for a period of time, and after people see connection between the new actions and the performance improvement" (Kotter, 2012). In addition, teachers value the input of their colleagues. They were more willing to be a part of change if they felt that their colleagues supported the change. See Table 6.2 for additional information.

School culture has an impact on instructional practices, social emotional well-being and shared leadership opportunities. By approaching school culture through a systemic lens, three systems were able to be developed (shared leadership, social emotional and instructional empowerment) to help break down fears and promote relationship building, trust, collaboration communication and shared leadership among the faculty, parents, students, and administrators.

Reflective Questions

- How do we keep these implemented systems running despite a change in administration?
- How do we create an environment where teachers feel taking risks and making mistakes is accepted?
- How do we develop an environment where teachers are comfortable learning from one another and positively debating with each other?
- How do we continue to foster an atmosphere where the quiet majority feels comfortable standing up to the loud minority when they are negatively resisting positive change and growth?

TABLE 6.2 Survey Results from Staff Survey Given on School Culture

Question	*2018–2019 Percent Agreed*	*2018–2019 Percent Neutral*	*2019–2020 Percent Agreed*
Shared and Supportive Leadership			
Staff members are consistently involved in discussing and making decisions about most school issues	43.40%	32.90%	77.80%
Staff members have accessibility to key information	46.10%	32.90%	75.60%
The administrative team is proactive and addresses areas where support is needed	52.60%	27.60%	88.90%
Opportunities are provided for staff to initiate change	48.70%	28.90%	75.60%
Leadership is promoted and nurtured among staff members	42.10%	35.50%	82.20%
Decision making takes place through committees and communication across grade and subject areas	50%	27.60%	84.50%
Staff uses multiple sources of data to make decisions about teaching and learning	51.30%	31.60%	80%
Shared Values and Vision			
Staff members share visions for school improvement that have an undeviating focus on student learning	40.80%	40.80%	80%
Decisions are made in alignment with the school's values and vision	51.30%	32.90%	82.20%
A collaborative process exists for developing a shared vision among staff	39.50%	43.40%	77.80%
School goals focus on student learning beyond test scores and grades	40.80%	36.80%	66.70%
Parents are actively involved in creating high expectations that serve to increase student achievement	30.20%	43.40%	35.60%
Data are used to prioritize actions to reach a shared vision	39.50%	43.40%	68.90%
Collective Learning and Application			
Staff members work together to seek knowledge, skills, and strategies and apply this new learning to their work	59.20%	23.70%	88.90%

TABLE 6.2 Cont.

Question	*2018–2019 Percent Agreed*	*2018–2019 Percent Neutral*	*2019–2020 Percent Agreed*
A variety of opportunities and structures exist for collective learning through open dialogue	47.30%	30.30%	82.20%
Staff members engage in dialogue that reflects a respect for diverse ideas that lead to continued inquiry	48.60%	36.80%	80%
School staff members collaboratively analyze multiple sources of data to assess the effectiveness of instructional practices	44.70%	34.20%	75.50%
Staff members regularly share student work to guide overall school improvement	42.10%	42.10%	73.30%
Opportunities exist for coaching and mentoring	42.10%	30.30%	73.40%
Staff members collaboratively review student work to share and improve instructional practices	42.10%	32.90%	75.60%
Supportive Conditions			
A culture of trust and respect exists for taking risks	39.50%	44.70%	62.20%
Outstanding achievement is recognized and celebrated regularly in our school	44.70%	38.20%	53.40%
School staff and parents exhibit a sustained and unified effort to embed change into the culture of the school	25%	53.90%	42.30%
Communication systems promote a flow of information between the administrative team and staff members	48.60%	26.30%	75.50%
Data is made available to provide easy access to staff members	43.40%	31.60%	71.10%
Appropriate technology and instructional materials are available to staff	42.10%	34.20%	68.90%
The administrative team takes an active role in educational programs offered in our school	51.40%	30.30%	73.30%
Professional Staff	69.70%		75.60%
Supportive Staff	30.30%		24.40%

Note

1 The CREATE (**C**onnect **R**ealize **E**ngage **A**ttend **T**ransform **E**xpand) Lab is a place for creative inquiry and documented discoveries about teaching and learning.

References

Abrahamson, E. (2004). *Change without pain: How managers can overcome initiative overload, organizational chaos, and employee burnout.* Harvard Business School Press.

Fullan, M., Hill, P., & Crevola, C. (2006). *Breakthrough.* Corwin Press.

Jensen, B., Sonnemann, J., Roberts-Hull, K., & Hunter, A. (2016). *Beyond PD: Teacher professional learning in high-performing systems.* National Center on Education and the Economy.

Kotter, J. P. (2012). *Leading Change.* Harvard Business Review Press.

Stronge, J. H., Richard, H. B., & Catano, N. (2008). *Qualities of Effective Principals.* Association for Supervision and Curriculum Development.

7

COMMUNITY HEALTH ASSESSMENT

Best Practices through a Systems Thinking Approach (Health Care/International)

Christina Gunther and Michelle A. Cole

Introduction

Healthcare needs assessments are a critical part to any well-functioning healthcare system. The needs of the community and the availability of local healthcare must intersect. Using a systems thinking approach allows for a collaborative community partnership, which is a critical element in conducting rich healthcare assessments that influence any needed change. Lazanski (2012) suggests that a systems approach can provide an opportunity to identify "patterns and structures" that lie below the surface. This is particularly true for deeply ingrained cultural patterns and system structures that operate in an implicit nature. In deeply impoverished communities, systems may operate on a "survival" level rather than operating in an interrelated, holistic nature with the good of the entire system as the goal. Left unchecked, this practice will disrupt the system at a number of levels (Caldwell, 2012). The healthcare needs assessment described in this case study follows a systems approach model, yet met with several overarching failures due to a breakdown within implicit systems patterns.

Strategies to overcome these challenges follow the systems thinking approach. Senge (1990) emphasized viewing the system as a whole and focusing on interrelationships of the parts. Further, Arnold and Wade (2015) describe understanding interrelationships and how they create "dynamic behavior" (p. 9). The interconnections in the relationships serve as "feedback loops" that inform key players and also help to explain nonlinear relationships that influence the dynamic behavior in a system (p. 9).

DOI: 10.4324/9781003028772-9

System and Key Players

The target population for this case study was located in a rural community of the Dominican Republic (DR), one hour from a public hospital and four hours from the nation's capital. The key players were this case study's authors, a local clinic, community members, a non-governmental organization, and a U.S. regional health network that all served to collect data on the health of the population and recommend changes in order to meet community needs.

The identification of systems and key players was an essential first step. Considering who was invested in the health and outcomes of the community was imperative to promote success for the community assessment. The local non-governmental organization (NGO) identified needs within the local community and sought to systematically identify, develop, and prioritize a plan to help improve the lives of those in need by addressing the community's challenges. With similar initiatives the NGO connected with a partner, a U.S.-based healthcare system with a vested interest in global health programs and education. The healthcare system had an established Global Health Initiative team that consistently reached beyond the local borders to deliver care to low-resource communities with identified barriers to healthcare. The commitment and strengths of the healthcare system provided a strong platform of support for the initiative. Supporting communities of need was the goal of the project and were well matched with the work and mission of the primary researchers, who were faculty at a U.S.-based university (the authors of this case study) that educates healthcare professionals, the NGO, and the healthcare system.

The most vital player in the system was the community itself. The identified community is located in a remote area of the DR with just over 16,000 persons having a median age in the early 20s. The terrain is mountainous with crystal blue waters edging the coast. In stark contrast to the lush vegetation and the picturesque beaches lies a community that has unmet social and healthcare needs.

Previous attempts to meet the needs of the community resulted in the creation of an expansive hospital infrastructure that was intended to address the most pressing health needs of the community. The hospital infrastructure remains largely inoperative, due to financial and personnel constraints, rendering only a small section of the structure operational as an outpatient clinic. Limited resources, including human capital and supplies, are available to support the clinic's operations.

Case Analysis

The opportunity to make a sustainable impact on a community through a health needs assessment involves a systems thinking framework that is well planned and well executed to create collaborative relationships with key players in the community, as well as the community as a whole. All players create the dynamic behavior patterns that must interconnect to provide successful feedback loops. For example, trust is a behavior that must be present in order for community members to provide honest and open responses to the healthcare needs questions. The answers provide the feedback loop to the researchers who then loop in the funding organizations and management team.

In an effort to determine the healthcare needs of the community, a Dominican-based NGO that focuses on the socioeconomic transformation of individuals, families, and communities partnered with the U.S. based healthcare system to execute a community needs assessment. This collaboration was created to assist in the identification of the needs of the community and to develop a sustainable plan to address the areas of concern. The healthcare system sought a collaborative partner, a U.S. local university, with expertise in public health, global health, and education of healthcare professionals to support the development and execution of the community assessment. Two key players from the university, in addition to a U.S. graduate student, local community leaders, and the NGO, were committed to the plan.

With the key players identified and in agreement to work together, goals were established. A data collection instrument was constructed by university team members who served as the research project leaders. The university team members were leaders in public and global health initiatives. Semi-structured interview questions, using a survey that was adapted from the World Health Survey by the World Health Organization (WHO), were created and translated to Spanish, the language spoken in the community.

Prior to arriving in the community, the key players from the U.S. conducted an inquiry to obtain additional background information to promote understanding of the community of interest. Previous work from members of the healthcare system who spent time in the community was reviewed and used to modify and adapt the community assessment survey. Although not plentiful, data and statistics from the community were reviewed to expand understanding of priority health needs and cultural habits. Prior to departing the U.S., the research project leaders were informed of an innovative and collaborative plan to hire a local DR physician to support the execution of the community assessment and to serve as a liaison between the identified players, including the identified community. The addition of this key player was an important contributor to the understanding of the culture, values, and ideals of the identified community. Members of the local community, viewed as informal community leaders, embraced the identified project and volunteers, were committed to working with the team. Their presence, in addition to the physician, brought credibility and acceptance to the community assessment team. The result of interrelating these parts of the system was establishment of trust in the community.

To conduct the interviews, three distinct groups were created all consisting of a community volunteer who lived locally who also served as a translator. Two groups were led by a member of the U.S. university team and the third group was led by the local physician. A goal was set to interview 100 randomly selected families in seven distinct neighborhoods of the community representing a sample of 504 participants.

The primary informants were female heads of the household. Several areas of needs and community concern emerged from the data including high unemployment rate of 26 percent, limited education, with 30 percent without formal education while another 30 percent completed primary years of education. The inability to meet the needs of their family was expressed by 76 percent of the respondents, with 72 percent demonstrating food insecurity. More than half responded that their health was good (58 percent), with the remaining reporting moderate or poor health. Community members expressed the need to have medical services available to them, with a focus on women's and children's health.

Through observation and interviews, the research team identified that inconsistent and unreliable access to healthcare was a threat to the community. Funds and resources that were previously allocated to improve the local hospital infrastructure were unaccounted. The hospital infrastructure was limited and lacked basic necessities including sanitation and medical supplies. In addition, access to full healthcare services was over one hour's driving distance and the community's ambulance was inoperable.

Problem Resolution

The system requiring change in this case was the healthcare access system in a rural community in the DR. Each player involved within the system was required to play a collaborative role in the success of this project. The local hospital structure had experienced multiple iterations of operation without significant success over the past several years. With the systems thinking framework that included members of the local community and the U.S.-based hospital system, a relationship was formed with the healthcare facility, previously constructed but only partially functioning.

The careful planning to complete a community assessment to provide data to support a plan for increasing the availability of healthcare resources was thoughtful and included key players and processes. A robust and comprehensive community assessment provided the NGO and local community with data to support a plan to improve the availability of healthcare services within the local community. The research project leaders, based on the community assessment findings, provided recommendations and strategies for the NGO and community's consideration. Several options were suggested to make the system functional: develop a strategic plan for the incorporation of additional services, including inpatient services; include expert consultants as key players (e.g., a gynecologist or nurse midwife if birthing at the local hospital is a goal); complete a comprehensive inventory of available equipment and supplies if not already available – determine what supplies are necessary for particular services based on consults with key players, that is, expert consultants; consider including community members in the planning/

implementation process, such as a mayor or other elected official, a prominent church leader or other respected community member for total community inclusion in the system; and increase training for nursing staff to boost the quality of care. Implementing these steps to ready the hospital for acceptable and safe care and full hospital service were necessary for strengthening the system as a whole.

Strategies for system support implementation were provided to the NGO director and U.S.-based hospital director. Strategies included conducting a complete assessment of the strengths and educational/professional needs of the nursing staff followed with the development of a plan to train nurses based on the area of care and role for each hospital unit. A key suggestion was to hire a professionally trained nurse(s) who can serve as the nursing leader to guide the education and training of the nurses for an inpatient setting. Adding the board of directors of the NGO as key players in the system was suggested in order to avoid a breakdown in the system based on implicit cultural patterns. For example, what happened to the previously awarded funds for hospital improvement? Another strategy suggested canvasing the community for interested members to join any implementation strategy discussions. An additional strategy was to include the government health ministry in the system as a vital key player. Reimbursement for health services was at a breakdown level because billing was not followed through on after a patient visit. Bills were not submitted to the ministry for processing. Finally, the main hospital an hour away from the community should become a key player to assist in serving the rural community by rotating healthcare professionals to the clinic. Community members were receptive to the initiative and hopeful toward future initiatives.

Lessons Learned

Overcoming barriers to conducting health needs assessments include relationship building and establishing trust through identifying common goals and objectives with key players of the system to be assessed. Democratic leadership, the presence of a community organizer, involvement of support staff, a history of positive working relationships and including key community members (Israel et al., 1998) are required. Challenges and barriers that can impact the development of a partnership in a community include many interrelated parts. A lack of trust and respect; inequitable distribution of power and control; conflicts with differences in perspectives, priorities, assumptions, values, beliefs, and language; conflicts over funding; conflicts with different emphases on tasks are all parts that must be reconciled to achieve a well-functioning system. It is a time-consuming process, albeit a critical one.

Conclusion

A systems thinking approach to conducting rich and fruitful healthcare assessments can provide a model for success. This is particularly true for impoverished communities where patterns and structures operate at a level that lies below the surface and focuses more on the need for individual survival. These patterns will eventually disrupt the system due to fragmentation based on interrupted feedback loops.

Although the critical data collection process in this case was successful, the overall goal of the project failed. Key players could not repair the break in the feedback loop. Additional key players in the system needed to be included, and several processes needed adjustment. Unfortunately, adjustment of the processes (locating missing funding; billing the health ministry) may have highlighted implicit processes that individuals did not want to be discovered. Sadly, the clinic in this rural community remains inoperative due to these breakdowns.

Reflective Questions

- When discovering a system component does not "fit," what strategies should be used/implemented?
- What parts of the system could have been better developed prior to the U.S. team initiating the project?
- Where and how does accountability fit into the system? Individual/organization?
- How does feedback/communication fit into a system with implicit patterns of operation? What areas/methods of communication should be developed/enhanced?

References

Arnold, R. D., & Wade, J. P. (2015). A definition of systems thinking: A systems approach. *Procedia Computer Science, 44*(2015), 669–678.

Caldwell, R. (2012). Systems thinking, organizational change and agency: A practice theory critique of Senge's learning organization. *Journal of Change Management, 12*(2), 145–164.

Israel, B. A., Schulz, A. J., Parker, E. A., & Becker, A. B. (1998). Review of community-based research: Assessing partnership approaches to improve public health. *Annual Review of Public Health, 19*, 73–202.

Lazanski, T. J. (2012). Systems thinking = thinking out of the box = reaching quality of life. *6th IQC, 6*, 3–7.

Senge, P. (1990). *The Fifth Discipline, the Art and Practice of the Learning Organization.* Doubleday.

8

A SYSTEMS APPROACH TO DESIGNING INSTRUCTIONAL CREDENTIALING PROTOCOLS

Addressing Chaos, Transparency, and Performance (Health Care)

Jill Stefaniak

Introduction

Historically, healthcare professionals have been taught how to perform a variety of medical procedures through the "see one, do one, teach one" approach (Beck, 2004). Of course, prescribing this type of training philosophy can pose several problems for the learner and trainer. Instructional designers will often come across instructors and program directors who defer to these types of learning strategies because they were trained similarly.

Traditionally, most healthcare professions train their students in silos. Many healthcare professionals will find themselves working within teams to deliver patient care. While the expectation is that individuals, of varying disciplines, work together, the disciplines train separately. While research in medical education is promoting more interprofessional educational training opportunities earlier in programs (Reeves et al., 2013; West et al., 2016), the instructional designer can provide a pivotal role when designing instruction that poses implications across the healthcare system.

Training practices of healthcare professionals have a significant impact on patient safety. The role of the instructional designer in a healthcare setting is to help medical, nursing, and allied health educators identify opportunities to emphasize the systemic implications of medical practices. There is increased pressure to design viable and sustainable solutions as they often have a direct impact on patient safety. The instructional designer needs to demonstrate an understanding of the inputs and outputs pertinent to the healthcare environment they are designing within. Failure to do so will result in design solutions that will fall short and will be unsustainable.

DOI: 10.4324/9781003028772-10

Many trainees in healthcare-related fields learn and perform under a significantly higher level of cognitive load due to the amount of subject matter content that needs to be covered within a restricted amount of time. Instructional designers working with program directors and instructors for medical, nursing, and allied health programs need to be more cognizant of the use of instructional strategies to mitigate the effects that cognitive load can pose on the learner. They must also take into account the need for healthcare professionals to make decisions promptly and work in highly stressful situations.

This case study explores how a large metropolitan healthcare system embraced a systems view to develop a credentialing program to train junior physicians on how to insert central lines in the intensive care unit. The impetus for this case was the aftermath that took place when a junior physician performed a medical procedure on a patient that they were not trained or qualified to perform. This ultimately resulted in the death of a patient. To prevent similar events from occurring, the hospital organized a team, led by an instructional designer, to design and develop a training program that would serve as a means for credentialing junior physicians after they had completed various stages of training and demonstration of competency.

System and Key Players

Central line placement is a procedure that is performed by several different medical specialties (i.e., general surgery, emergency medicine, internal medicine, and anesthesiology). Resident physicians are provided with opportunities to learn and practice central line placement throughout several of their clinical rotations.

A committee was formed with representatives from each discipline that performed central line placements to develop protocols and procedures to be followed when training residents on central line placements. The committee was responsible for dissecting the problem and developing a solution to prevent future occurrences. The structure of the committee included the residency directors for the general surgery, emergency medicine, internal medicine, and anesthesia programs. As residency directors, they provided direct oversight into the clinical rotations and training programs that each residency was responsible for completing at the hospital in their respective field. The clinical director of the intensive care unit (ICU) and a nursing manager were also members of the committee to provide insight into the types of procedures that required oversight during rotations in the ICU.

An instructional designer with experience in organizational performance improvement also assisted the committee to determine appropriate training and performance indicators. Last, a director of quality improvement and patient safety provided input to ensure that the committee's recommendations adhered to accreditation policies and procedures that were implemented in the hospital. The committee was responsible for dissecting the problem and developing a solution to prevent future occurrences.

Upon further review of the situation, the lack of training on central line placement was the most prevalent contributing factor. The committee also discovered that each medical discipline has its informal protocols in place regarding preferred central line placement techniques. These discipline-specific protocols were not documented or formalized within the residency programs.

Early in the project, it became apparent that a number of the physicians serving on the board shared differing opinions regarding who should be allowed to serve as a trainer, particular methods for central line placement, and the objectives of the training program. The instructional designer was responsible for neutralizing the heated discussions that took place among the committee, working with the team to design and develop instructional materials and developing non-instructional materials to support the various phases of the credentialing process.

Case Analysis

While the hospital administration did not impose a specific deadline for creating the credentialing program, the medical residency physicians and the director of the ICU wanted to develop appropriate training materials and protocols as soon as possible. During the first few meetings with the credentialing committee, it became quite apparent that there was no consensus among the physicians regarding an approach for teaching central line placement. While each discipline followed similar approaches, they varied enough to where it could pose challenges establishing guidelines and protocols to be followed throughout all units of the hospital. This led to several additional meetings over six months where the members of the committee began to debate which approach was better and which discipline should be the authority of central line placements in the hospital.

Several challenges were identified by the committee:

1. Each discipline (i.e., general surgery, emergency medicine, internal medicine, and anesthesiology) required different techniques for central line placement.
2. Different residency programs required different clinical rotations which posed challenges for sequencing when resident physicians would be trained on particular medical procedures.
3. The residency program directors were providing insufficient documentation to accrediting bodies for training procedures.

Problem Resolution

A critical systems thinking approach was employed to help mitigate the challenges associated with this complex training need within the healthcare organization. Critical systems reflect organizations that are nonlinear, complex, and hierarchical across a larger-scale system (Bammer, 2003). When designing solutions that involve multiple stakeholders within the system, it is important that time is spent obtaining buy-in and agreement to ensure there is a shared mental model for implementing change (Cabrera & Carbrera, 2019).

The intentional selection of committee members who represented the various disciplines and functions that would be involved in the program ensured that different perspectives would be represented during program development. It was also important that committee members were familiar with the routine and culture of the hospital to ensure that recommended changes to procedure would align with the existing system.

When it became apparent that each discipline had been training their medical residents differently, the committee had to spend time agreeing upon a suitable process for credentialing. In addition to establishing an agreed-upon process, the committee also had to agree to what content would be covered during initial training sessions. Once a shared mental model was developed for establishing agreed-upon procedures for central line placement training, the committee worked with medical experts to develop performance checklists and other evaluative assessments that would be used during the credentialing process.

Table 8.1 provides an overview of the interventions the committee developed to support central line placement training in the hospital. The committee developed a written policy that would explain the protocols and training required before a resident physician could perform a central line placement unsupervised. This policy was included in each of the handbooks and orientation materials for the

TABLE 8.1 Overview of Interventions Developed for Central Line Placement Training

Intervention	*Instructional*	*Non-instructional*
Develop written policy to be included in residency handbooks		x
Develop a Phased Training Program • Knowledge test • Demonstration of five central line placements in the simulation lab • Demonstration of ten observed central line placements in the intensive care unit	x	
Training for preceptors responsible for assessing resident physicians' performance	x	
Communication plan to physicians and nursing staff of new policies and protocols		x
Maintain a record of evaluative instruments (i.e., knowledge tests and performance checklists) for accreditation reports		x

ICU and the respective medical disciplines. The policy represented a consistent approach to central line placement to be practiced across all disciplines who did clinical rotations in the ICU.

A phased training program was developed to instruct resident physicians on central line techniques that were agreed upon by the senior physicians in the hospital. The training program consisted of knowledge acquisition tests, simulated activities, and precepted central line placements under the supervision of an approved physician. The purpose of the training program was to assist the resident physicians with demonstrating proficiency in central line placement and adhering to policies that supported the quality improvement initiatives within the hospital.

Each medical discipline identified several physicians who were qualified to serve as preceptors for the central line placement training. The physicians participated in a central line training program to review the training procedures and simulated activities that each resident would be expected to complete. The preceptors also participated in a simulated training session to calibrate themselves as reviewers.

The new policies and training program was communicated to physicians, nurses, and other allied health support staff in the ICUs and other medical areas where central line placements may occur. Staff was informed that if someone has not completed the mandatory training, they were prohibited from performing a central line placement unsupervised.

The instructional designer worked with the residency program directors to ensure that appropriate record-keeping was maintained to document each resident physician's progress in the central line training program. These records were used in the annual reports to the accrediting body that oversees residency education.

Lessons Learned

Due to the number of different medical disciplines involved in deliberating over an appropriate training and credentialing process at the hospital, it took a year to develop and implement the central line placement training program. The design and development stages associated with this project brought forth several successes and challenges to the team.

The most successful aspect of this project was the development and implementation of a credentialing process that would be completed by all resident physicians before performing any central line placements independent of a preceptor. This would ensure that there would be consistent training, a mechanism for reporting training activities for accreditation bodies, and protocols that clearly communicated the training process and performance expectations of residency physicians related to central line placement.

Several challenges emerged throughout the process which required the team to embrace a systems view of the situation. While it was important to have representation from each medical discipline, it became quite difficult for the committee to agree on what approach would be considered the most appropriate for training the resident physicians. Obtaining consensus from expert physicians who would serve as trainers for credentialing proved to be quite challenging as they each felt that their approach was the only correct approach.

Once the multidisciplinary committee was formed, it became quite apparent that attention needed to be given to the systemic implications that a credentialing process could impose on the various residency programs. It was important to consider when each discipline would require their residents to receive training on central line placement, the clinical rotations that required training, and the technique that would be followed by the supervising physicians. This required that additional information and training be provided to those individuals who would be responsible for precepting the junior residents.

Conclusion

This case provided an overview of how a number of instructional and non-instructional interventions were put in place to support the development of a central line placement training program. Upon the formation of a committee, the majority of the effort was focused on accounting for logistics required to implement and support the training and preceptorship of resident physicians. This case demonstrates the importance of ensuring appropriate infrastructure is in place to support instructional interventions introduced in a complex healthcare system comprising a variety of functions and disciplines.

Reflective Questions

- What are the overarching challenges presented in this case?
- Why is it necessary to develop instructional and non-instructional interventions to address the problems described in this case?
- Why do you think it was important to have representation from the various disciplines (i.e., general surgery, emergency medicine, internal medicine, and anesthesia) who require their residents to perform central line placements?
- What recommendations would you make to the team to ensure that all disciplines are aware of the changes to central line placement training?

Additional Resources

Hales, B. M., & Pronovost, P. J. (2006). The checklist: A tool for error management and performance improvement. *Journal of Critical Care, 21*(3), 231–235.

Michelson, J. D., & Manning, L. (2008). Competency assessment in simulation-based procedural education. *The American Journal of Surgery, 196*(4), 609–615.

Roberts, J. P., Fisher, T. R., Trowbridge, M. J., & Bent, C. (2016, March). A design thinking framework for healthcare management and innovation. *Healthcare, 4*(1), 11–14.

Ross, M., & Stefaniak, J. (2019). Promoting a holistic approach to delivering performance feedback: Introducing the behavioral analysis feedback model. *Performance Improvement, 58*(6), 17–27.

Segall, N., & Bennett-Guerrero, E. (2016). Should checklists for central venous catheter insertion be used in training, credentialing, or routine clinical care? *Critical Care Medicine, 44*(10), 1943–1944.

Stalter, A. M., & Mota, A. (2018). Using systems thinking to envision quality and safety in healthcare. *Nursing management, 49*(2), 32–39.

Steadman, R. H., & Huang, Y. M. (2012). Simulation for quality assurance in training, credentialing, and maintenance of certification. *Best Practice & Research Clinical Anaesthesiology, 26*(1), 3–15.

Wachter, R. M. (2013). Personal accountability in healthcare: searching for the right balance. *BMJ Quality & Safety, 22*(2), 176–180.

References

Bammer, G. (2003). Embedding critical systems thinking in the academy. In CMS conference. Retrieved from www.mngt.waikato.ac.nz/ejrot/cmsconference/2003/abstracts/orsystems/bammer.pdf

Beck, A. H. (2004). The Flexner report and the standardization of American medical education. *Jama, 291*(17), 2139–2140.

Cabrera, D., & Cabrera, L. (2019). What is systems thinking? In M. J. Spector & B. B. Lockee, & M. Childress (Eds.), *Learning, design, and technology: An international compendium of theory, research, practice, and policy* (pp. 1–28). Springer. https://doi.org/10.1007/978-3-319-63880-5_2

Reeves, S., Perrier, L., Goldman, J., Freeth, D., & Zwarenstein, M. (2013). Interprofessional education: Effects on professional practice and healthcare outcomes. *Cochrane Database of Systematic Reviews, 3*, 1–43.

West, C., Graham, L., Palmer, R. T., Miller, M. F., Thayer, E. K., Stuber, M. L., … & Joo, P. A. (2016). Implementation of interprofessional education (IPE) in 16 US medical schools: Common practices, barriers, and facilitators. *Journal of Interprofessional Education & Practice, 4*, 41–49.

PART III

Implementing Change

9

APPLYING SYSTEMS THINKING TO CONSIDER THE INTERDEPENDENCIES AMONG SUBSYSTEMS (HIGHER EDUCATION)

Todd Adrian and Kendall St. Hilaire

Introduction

Indian River State College is a mid-size community college serving approximately 28,000 students each year. The college experienced significant organizational changes over the past decade, due to rapid changes in technology and the services provided by the college. These changes have affected all stakeholders, including students, faculty, staff, and administration. Implementing systemic changes required collaboration among departments across the college. This collaborative approach allowed the college leaders to address the complexities of the issues related to awareness and adoption of a new Enterprise Resource Planning (ERP) system. This case will cover the departments involved with the project, an analysis of the scope of the work, lessons learned, and considerations and strategies for other institutions embarking on similar projects.

System and Key Players

The Institutional Technology division at the college contains the ERP system, student information system (SIS), learning management system (LMS), and information technology systems (IT) (see Figure 9.1). These subsystems are interdependent. Thus, implementing technology initiatives requires collaboration among the stakeholders across this division. A change management team (see Table 9.1) was created to plan and strategize how technology would be used for various business processes. The change management team consisted of 30 people who are members of Enterprise Systems, IT, and the Virtual Campus. The team met with stakeholders from academic departments, student affairs, and finance to plan and strategize how technology would be used for various business processes.

DOI: 10.4324/9781003028772-12

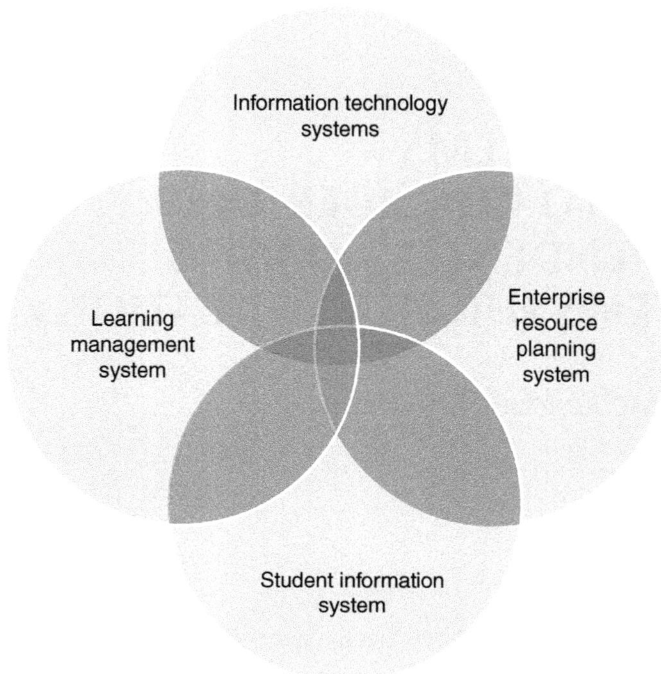

FIGURE 9.1 Institutional Technology Systems at Indian River State College

According to Reigeluth (2006), higher education institutions are connected inside a suprasystem, which at the college consists of interrelated components typically encompassing various academic and support departments that interact within the system and have a tremendous influence on systemic change. During the planning phase stakeholders designed a strategic plan for implementation. Systems thinking principles were applied to develop a comprehensive change management plan to meet the demands and challenges associated with implementing technology.

Case Analysis

Systems thinking, which enables teams to identify the complexities and interdependencies among subsystems or departments (Frank, 2016), benefited the institution during the ERP migration. There are many challenges associated with adopting and implementing a new ERP. The challenges for stakeholders (see Table 9.1) were broken into three phases: planning, implementation, and evaluation (see Figure 9.2).

TABLE 9.1 Key Systems Stakeholders

Stakeholder	*Role*
Information Technology	Network architecture and security systems integrations
Virtual Campus	Online course design, development, and deployment, systems integrations
Enterprise Systems	Enterprise resource planning functionality and business processes, systems integrations
Finance and Human Resources	Human capital and finance Tuition and financial aid
Academic Departments	Course offerings, faculty assignments Student experiences
Student Affairs	Student experiences Financial aid

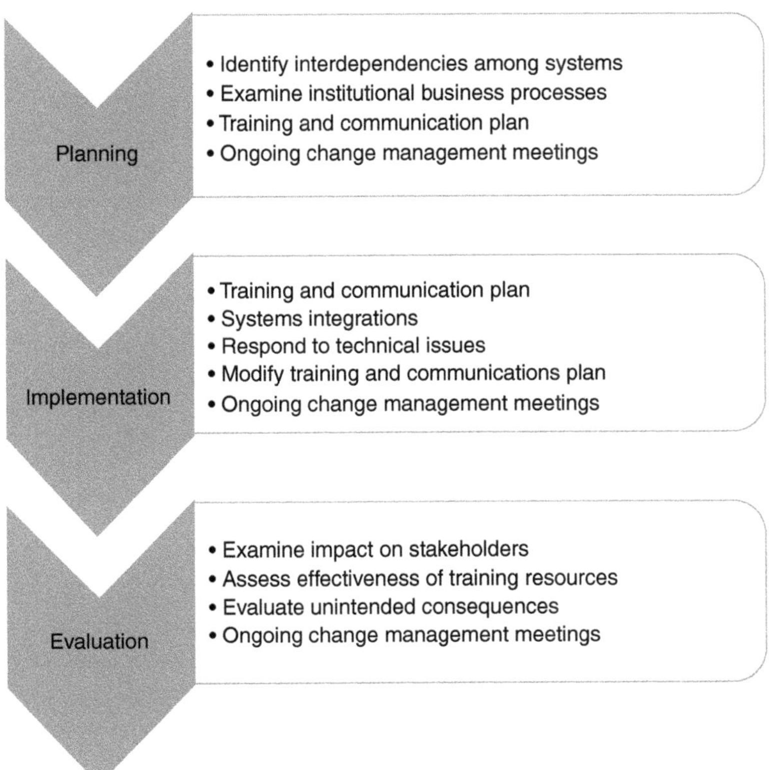

FIGURE 9.2 Technology Integration Phases

Planning Phase

During the planning phase, the focus was on the interdependencies among the subsystems. The change management team determined the impact the technology adoption would have on the interdependencies among the subsystems (see Figure 9.1) within the system at the college. The planning phase examined the institution's business processes and the users who conduct them. The timing and manner in which these changes occur is critical to the stability of the institution. Meetings were held to discuss the appropriate timeframe for implementing the new business processes. The team examined how each stakeholder would be impacted by the new ERP, which also functions as the SIS, by identifying academic deadlines for enrollment and tuition payment due dates according to semester start and end dates. Additionally, instructional designers were included on the change management team to provide guidance related to the creation of training materials and support resources. The team was charged with creating a communication plan that included appropriate and timely information for the institution's stakeholders.

Implementation Phase

The success of technical implementation hinges upon thorough planning. The change management team identified critical components for implementing the new ERP system, including instructional design, training, and communication. The change management team considered potential technical issues and used clear communication during the implementation phase through email and the college's website. Organizations use systems thinking during change management to examine how business process changes may impact various stakeholders in the organization (Stroh, 2015). Despite the best efforts of the change management team during the planning phase, stakeholders experienced unforeseen technical issues during the implementation phase, such as students being added and dropped from multiple course sections. To address the technical issues related to adding and dropping courses, LMS administrators modified the integrations between the systems during the implementation phase.

Evaluation Phase

The final phase of the project evaluated the effect of the system change on stakeholders. The change management team evaluated the business processes and procedures utilized during the ERP adoption. There were complexities, as the project consisted of various moving parts requiring attention to details, considerations related to the timeliness for implementation, and the appropriate use of communication strategies for the expected outcomes. Student Learning Coordinators used technology-supported systems and social media to monitor student feedback related to technical issues on the newly implemented systems. Frequent change management meetings led to timely responses to the unforeseen issues caused by the technology implementation.

When the institution migrated to the new ERP system, the learning curve associated with that change impacted stakeholders. The adoption of the new ERP and integration among the current systems created complexities and issues with existing business processes. It was critical to identify the business processes that existed with the previous ERP as it related to the impact of the migration. The ERP migration required new procedures and protocols. New business processes designed to address systems interdependencies can create roadblocks for stakeholders who expect the new system to function the same way the previous system operated. When the institution launched the new ERP that included SIS functions, faculty, staff, and students quickly realized business processes related to course IDs, semester durations, canceled courses and add/drops, and course records changed.

New Course IDs

When the institution migrated to the new ERP, course identification numbers were modified. As such, the creation of course shells and the categorization of the semester shells' course IDs were formatted differently. The traditional Course ID contained six numbers that did not convey any information about the course. When the new ERP launched, the Course IDs were modified to reflect the course name, term, campus location, modality, and section number. Initially, the new Course ID naming schema confused faculty, staff, and students. The change management team responded to feedback by providing a job aid inside the LMS. When users logged into the LMS they saw a message that explained the Course ID naming schema. After the first year, stakeholders became accustomed to the new format, which dramatically decreased the number of inquiries related to the Course ID naming schema.

New Semester Durations

As the institution transitioned to the new system, stakeholders were encouraged to evaluate business processes and determine whether to continue with the same practices under a new system. For example, the new system capabilities coupled with student scheduling needs led to changes in semester length options. The college continued to offer 16-week semesters and added accelerated semesters to the schedule to allow for students to progress through their courses more quickly. This change to the business process impacted the LMS, which led to some confusion from faculty and students and required additional communication to clarify the changes. The issue related to new semester durations was not created by migrating to the new ERP; however, it was an unintended consequence, which generated complaints about the new system on social media, email and phone support.

Canceled Courses and Add/Drops

Another disruption to business processes includes the way that records between the SIS and the LMS were exchanged and processed. The new ERP did not integrate with the LMS, creating discrepancies in rosters listed in the SIS but not in the LMS. These discrepancies created confusion about course rosters in the LMS. Students and faculty raised concerns through the technology support system that records were inaccurate. The technical teams investigated the issue and began troubleshooting.

Course Records

The institution policy on incompletes requires students to finish coursework by the end of the next semester in order to receive credit. Before the ERP migration, students could be added to a different course section to complete the course. The new business process requires that the LMS records match the ERP records. Faculty were provided information on the requirements for students to finish incomplete coursework in the original course section. An unintended consequence was that the new system did not allow students to be added to courses where payment was not collected, which avoids potential auditing issues.

Another change in the new system is the process for faculty requests to add other faculty members to courses. These requests were previously completed through the LMS, but now they are completed through the ERP. For the records to reflect accurately in the LMS, the LMS records must match what is in the ERP. This change caused confusion among stakeholders, but eventually stakeholders learned the new procedure. Problems addressed by the change management team during the evaluation phase eventually led to system improvements. These issues created a heightened awareness of the complexities and nuances of the various systems performing daily college business operations.

Problem Resolution

Systems thinking can assist with viewing connections, understanding parts, and predicting future behavior (Meadows, 2008). The change management team used systems thinking during the ERP implementation to determine how the problems and complexities of technology changes in subsystems are interconnected. The transition to the new ERP disrupted personnel and business processes. The underlying issues were related to the fact that existing ERP and other systems had been in place for many years, and personnel and business processes had grown around the systems' capabilities. Strategies addressed during the change include planning the implementation, delegating the responsibilities of each project phase, and managing the expectations of the key stakeholders. Decisions were made in the best interest of the stakeholders; however, as the system continued to evolve, the change management team meetings remained a priority for the continued success of the ERP migration. As the business processes associated with the new ERP became ubiquitous, the change management team provided stakeholders additional training options to maintain the positive gains.

Lessons Learned

Organizations contain subsystems, and one must consider all aspects of each subsystem when implementing a system change. The planning and implementation phases for the ERP migration revealed the interdependencies among the subsystems at the college. The planning and implementation phases of a systems or technology change require continuous feedback among stakeholders. Communication among the stakeholders enabled the change management team to examine what was working and what needed to be modified. A communication plan incorporating the changes required for all stakeholders is a vital component during and after a technology migration.

As with any system change, there are unexpected obstacles, but open communication with end users allowed the college to address these issues in an efficient manner. Communicating the expectations of how the new ERP was designed to improve stakeholders' work experience was critical. The team determined that additional proactive communication could have alleviated the issues associated with the new Course ID naming schema. Additionally, the change management team determined failure to evaluate and effectively communicate information related to the ERP technology change could lead to unintended consequences.

When institutions are challenged with implementing a systemic change that encompasses a technology change, the focus should be on a new system that is designed to meet the current and future institutional needs (Watson & Watson, 2013), rather than focusing on using the new technology to fit the needs of the system that already exists. The continuation of change management after the implementation was completed was critical for the ongoing steering of the initiative. Last, another consideration related to a technology adoption is a well-conceived plan does not always correlate with a successful implementation. Being prepared and willing to adapt to unintended consequences is imperative for successfully moving a technology adoption initiative forward.

Conclusion

Many considerations should be made when an organization adopts new technology. The factors associated with adopting new technology encompass layers of complexities, including new business processes, stakeholder learning curves for using the new technology, and unintended consequences created during the adoption process. Adopting new technology comes with challenges, requiring organizations to adopt a systems thinking approach to consider how the interconnected subsystems will be impacted when the technology is adopted. Implementing new technology is an exciting challenge that, when executed well, can have a positive impact on the organization and stakeholders. Thus, when an organization considers a technology adoption, utilizing systems thinking can be instrumental in a successful technology implementation.

Reflective Questions

Technology leaders charged with adopting technology should consider the following:

- How will adopting new technology impact all stakeholders in the organization?
- What new business processes will be created and how will existing business processes evolve?
- How will the organization respond to unforeseen technology issues and unintended consequences?
- What systems will be affected by a change and how should the stakeholders of those systems be brought to the table?

Additional Resources

Arnold, R., & Wade J. (2015). A definition of systems thinking: A systems approach. *Procedia Computer Science, 44*, 669–678. http://dx.doi.org/10.1016/j.procs.2015.03.050

Williams, A., Kennedy, S., Philipp, F., & Whiteman, G. (2017). Systems thinking: A review of sustainability management research. *Journal of Cleaner Production, 148*, 866–881. http://dx.doi.org/10.1016/j.jclepro.2017.02.002

References

Frank, M. (2016). *Systems thinking: Foundation, uses and challenges*. Nova Science Publishers, Inc.

Meadows, D. (2008). *Thinking in systems*. Chelsea Green Publishing.

Reigeluth, C. (2006). General influence of suprasystems on systemic change. *Tech Trends: Linking Research & Practice to Improve Learning, 50*(2), 26–27. http://dx.doi.org/10.1007/s11528-006-7585-y

Stroh, D. (2015). *Systems thinking for social change*. Chelsea Green Publishing.

Watson, W. & Watson, S. (2013). Exploding the ivory tower: Systemic change for higher education. *Tech Trends: Linking Research & Practice to Improve Learning, 57*(5), 42–46. http://dx.doi.org/10.1007/s11528-013-0690-9

10

IMPLEMENTING A PERSONALIZED LEARNING INITIATIVE IN A LARGE URBAN SCHOOL DISTRICT (K-12)

M. Elizabeth Azukas

Introduction

There are frequent calls for educational reform in the United States based on a myriad of concerns including graduates not being adequately prepared for college and career, stagnant performance on standardized testing, low graduation rates, and continued achievement gaps between affluent and economically disadvantaged students. Achieve (2005) found high school graduates ill-prepared for college and career. Thus, college and career readiness has become an urgent priority of the nation's education agenda. The global, knowledge-based economy of today requires a better-educated workforce than previous generations (Symonds et al., 2011).

The United States also has an alarming number of low-performing students, which can have severe consequences for both individuals and the national economy. The Program for International Student Assessment (PISA) defined low performance as scoring in the lowest achievement level on the mathematics, reading, and/or science assessments (National Center for Education Statistics, 2016). Students who were identified as low performers by the age of 15 were more likely to drop out of school and were less likely to maintain better-paying, more rewarding jobs (OECD, 2016). Additionally, low-performing students were not evenly distributed across the country; they were often highly concentrated in urban and impoverished areas (OECD, 2016).

The 2017 National Assessment of Educational Progress (NAEP) report documented a widened gap between high and low-achieving students on national math and science exams (USDOE, 2017). The 2019 NAEP scores revealed decreased proficiency for 4th grade math and 8th grade reading (USDOE, 2019). Moreover, the tests showed continued, large achievement gaps between the nation's

DOI: 10.4324/9781003028772-13

white and non-white students as well as between economically disadvantaged children and affluent children (USDOE, 2019).

Several recommendations have been made to address these education concerns. One popular recommendation has been "personalized learning" (PL). In 2012, the U.S. Department of Education (USDOE) offered a series of federal grants known as Race to the Top, to address deficits in college and career readiness and low-performing students (USDOE, 2012). The first priority of these grants was the development of personalized learning environments. Other requirements included:

- supports for teachers and students aligned with college and career-ready standards
- increase the effectiveness of educators
- expand access to the most effective educators to raise student achievement
- decrease the achievement gap across student groups
- increase the rates at which students graduate from high school prepared for college and careers.

USDOE, 2012, p. 1

This case focused on a large urban school district who received these grant funds to create personalized learning environments to address challenges with student achievement, equity, engagement, and a variety of system disconnects. Change in schools is notoriously difficult (Harris, 2011). Research suggests that focusing on the larger, systemic context of districts rather than individual schools is integral to understanding school-level improvement and in implementing and sustaining successful improvement and reform efforts (Coburn, Choi, & Mata, 2010; Daly & Finnigan, 2012; Fullan et al., 2009). This case analysis applied a systems lens to a personalized learning initiative in a large urban school district.

System & Key Players

The context for this study is a large urban school district that received federal grant money to construct personalized learning environments. The goal of the program was to develop a community of educators building schools around the needs, strengths, and motivations of individual students by implementing targeted online and blended learning initiatives. A system-wide approach was used in identifying key players for the team (Stroh, 2015). Table 10.1 summarizes the roles of the different members of the team.

Case Analysis

The goal of the system was to support schools to meet the needs, strengths, and motivations of individual students by implementing targeted online and blended learning initiatives. It was thought that providing students with personalized instruction would help every student to reach their full potential and increase

TABLE 10.1 Members and Responsibilities of the Personalized Learning Implementation Team

Members of the PL Implementation Team	*Role on the Team*
Personalized Learning Innovation Unit	Central Office Team Coordinating the Personalized Learning Initiative • Conducted the content RFP • Solicited applications from schools for participation and made selections • Developed training materials • Planned content marketplace
Principals	82 Principals Participated • Attended principal training • Collected data on needs of students • Developed school-based implementation plan • Sent teachers to professional development • Supported teacher implementation
Teachers	Approximately 2,000 teachers participated from 82 schools • Attend professional development sessions • Implement personalized learning plan with students • Collect data from students/monitor student achievement • Share successes and challenges
Implementation Coordinators	• Liaise between the PLIU and the schools • Supported teacher implementation
Technology Infrastructure	• Improve building infrastructure to support effective technology use
Technology Hardware	• Order required hardware
Technology LMS and Help Desk	• Coordinate the customization of an LMS • Implement single sign-on • Established a help desk for technical support
Project Management Office	• Developed the initial project plan and held regular project check-in meetings
Vendors	• Supplied online courses and content • Provided professional development on the use of their products • Exhibited products
Professional Development Unit	• Planned professional development on personalized learning, blended learning, and online learning • Coordinated vendor PD

not only student growth, but satisfaction. Checkland and Sholes (1999) suggested comparing the conceptual model to the real world when conducting a case analysis. Several challenges occurred in the system. Table 10.2 compares the conceptual model to the real world.

Problem Resolution

The problems of large organizations are too complex for simple quick fixes and require the involvement of a multitude of stakeholders. Jackson (1991) recommended Total Systems Intervention (TSI) for problem solving in large complex organizations. TSI principles were used in addressing the identified district systemic problems, including the use of system metaphors and systemic cycles of inquiry involving the PLIU central office and "clients" which included other administrative teams and school personnel. This approach allowed for several problem solutions to be developed because the problem-solving work was distributed throughout the system (Shaked & Schechter, 2019).

According to Jackson's (1991) TSI, this was a complex, pluralistic situation that would require multiple methodologies to achieve success, therefore, varied strategies were implemented to address the problems that arose with technology. First, a series of meetings were held to hear the different perspectives of everyone involved in the array of technical processes. A common purpose was emphasized to try to bring the different perspectives into closer alignment. The Chief Technology Officer (CTO) used the metaphor of a restaurant to facilitate the understanding of the different teams. In a restaurant, there are many roles including the chefs, waitstaff, dishwashers, bussing staff, hosts, managers, and so on, and there is quite a bit of activity going on behind the scenes in the kitchen, but the goal is to serve the customers a wonderful meal, without them knowing what is going on behind the scenes. The CTO argued that in this case we were delivering wonderful educational content to students and it should arrive flawlessly without their awareness of any of the work going on behind the scenes.

This common purpose and the recognition that multiple solutions may be needed to address the complex problems prompted a variety of actions. The technology infrastructure team developed a Bandwidth Utilization Tool that schools could use to better understand their needs. Additional funds were sought to conduct electrical upgrades in some schools. A sub-team was developed to consult with building owners and with the city on building codes. The technology equipment team sought out additional suppliers for laptops. They also ended up allowing some flexibility in the types of equipment schools were permitted to order which allowed schools to purchase the same equipment they already had in their buildings, that is, Apple products, but this did present additional challenges with support and maintenance of computers since they were all different. The Help Desk Team continued to market their services to schools and made magnets with the Helpline to send to every participating school, increasing the number of

TABLE 10.2 Conceptual Model vs Reality

Conceptual Model (what we thought would happen)	*Real World (what did happen)*
Technology Infrastructure Team to provide infrastructure support by upgrading Internet bandwidth	• Schools unable to provide accurate information about their bandwidth • Schools needed electrical upgrades • Not all buildings owned by the district
Technology Equipment Team orders and delivers laptops	• Suppliers could not meet demand • Schools wanted to select their own equipment
Technology Help Desk supports schools with LMS and vendor curriculum needs	• Schools continued to rely on their own tech support • Schools called the vendors directly and they did not understand our set up
PLIU provides schools with a budget to purchase online curriculum	• Schools wanted more money to purchase materials
Vendors provide online curriculum at a reduced cost	• Vendors were providing the same pricing to schools outside of the personalized learning initiative
Vendors deliver curriculum in content packages that can be imported into LMS	• Some vendor content was not compliant • Some vendors refused to separate their content from their proprietary learning management systems
Students and Teachers access their curriculum through a single sign-on	• Some schools had separate systems and services which required separate sign-ons
PLIU would provide professional development on the LMS and on online and blended learning pedagogy	• Schools would not send teachers to the PD because they required subs • Leaders needed PD on how to facilitate personalized learning environments
Vendors would provide PD on their products consistent with goals of personalized learning initiatives	• Vendors did not understand personalized learning • Vendors sent consultants to do PD; not familiar with our program
Implementation Coordinators would provide on-the-ground support to schools	• Implementation Coordinators had many of schools to support • Implementation managers would observe ineffective implementation practices
Project management team would develop and implement a project plan and liaise between all of the teams and departments	• Project managers did not understand school schedules and were inflexible with due dates • Project managers did not always understand the work involved • No direct contact between the project managers and the schools

calls to our help desk. Finally, the LMS and Help Desk Team were able to work with some vendors to create technical pass-throughs to enhance the single sign-on opportunities, but not all schools' vendors could be included.

Working with outside vendors over whom we had no control added to the complexity of these system challenges, therefore systemic cycles of inquiry were used (Jackson, 1991). Creativity sessions were employed to identify issues, problems, and dominant and dependent concerns. The virtual marketplace was used as a metaphor for both establishing a common purpose and for simplifying processes. The idea was that schools could visit a virtual marketplace, similar to going to the mall, and purchase content to meet the needs for their diverse students. It was similar to parents having children of different ages with different interests who would need different things from the mall. In the choice phase, interventions were identified and selected. Next, the team implemented specific positive change proposals. These cycles were revisited multiple times over the two years to continue to move toward the common goal.

Several approaches were used to tackle challenges with vendors. The budget was reconfigured to expand money for curricular allotments. Additional negotiations were conducted with vendors, resulting in lower pricing. The PLIU conducted marketing to "sell" their innovation program and emphasize the spectrum of services schools would receive as a part of the innovation unit that they would not receive from vendors directly. Additional technical personnel were assigned to the project to work with the vendors on compliance and to conduct some manual work to support proper content display. The PLIU set up vendor education sessions to teach them about the PLIU personalized learning model.

Cycles of inquiry (Jackson, 1991) were also used to approach the challenges with professional development and implementation, resulting in a variety of solutions being implemented at different times, based on the needs of the team members. The PLIU conducted training sessions for the project managers in school operation and focus groups were conducted with school leaders to communicate directly to the project management team what was and was not working for them. The PLIU and the professional development team began offering sessions after school and on weekends to avoid the need for subs. These teams also began offering "train-the-trainer" sessions so that schools could send fewer people initially, reducing the need for subs, and these trainers could conduct PD in the buildings at times that were convenient for them. Implementation coordinators were assigned schools by location to reduce travel time. The PLIU highlighted effective implementation strategies in the PD sessions and developed a website to promote and share best practices.

Lessons Learned

The overall purpose of applying a systemic approach for the design and development of personalized learning environments was to encourage debate and discussion among stakeholders to improve student achievement and engagement, promote equity, and to repair system disconnects. The pilot program was evaluated through teacher surveys, interviews, and focus groups. Resource support was highly effective. Perceived program impacts received mixed reviews. Teachers reported higher student motivation and self-regulation but raised concerns about higher-order thinking. Just over half of the teachers reported feeling as though they could better meet student needs.

The systems approach resulted in an improvement in the system disconnects but not a complete resolution. It was helpful to bring principals in to help articulate the problem, but teachers and students should also have been included. There were increased connections between the PLIU, professional development team, technology teams, and the schools but the accountability department was left out of the initial conceptual model. The accountability team analyzed effective instruction and rated both teachers and schools using a rubric that had not been aligned to the personalized learning program. Some schools received lower ratings on the accountability metrics which decreased the risk tolerance among some schools for the innovation. The accountability office must be included in future iterations of the process.

One cultural and political challenge that occurred in the creation of personalized learning environments was related to the centralization/de-centralization of autonomy and decision-making. The culture of the district was to empower principals and schools with the central office taking a support role. This culture permeated the personalized learning innovation and often resulted in the central office being reticent to provide direction so as not to stifle innovation and disempower the local school leaders. As a result, local schools were unaware of promising practices and implementation varied widely.

Systems thinking is not widely used in school organizations, largely because the school systems are often seen as too complex and the interconnectedness of the systems is often unclear (Kruse, 2021). Additionally, school systems are vulnerable to external environmental factors that can disrupt organizational workflows (Kruse, 2021). Research suggests, however, that distributed leadership that attends to the larger organizational system as an integral variable of leadership practice can both promote student achievement (Hallinger & Heck, 2010; Harion & Go, 2015; Louis et al., 2013) and organizational change (Leithwood, Mascall, & Strauss, 2009). This case demonstrated value in a systemic approach to planning and problem solving. More research is needed to examine leadership theory and change leadership in the context of systems thinking.

Reflective Questions

- How do systems approaches facilitate sense-making and contextual understanding in schools?
- How does systems thinking inform leadership practice?

- To what extent does organizational systems knowledge impact leaders' change efforts?
- What is the appropriate balance of centralized control and school autonomy to drive innovation while still ensuring equity and best practices?
- What are the best metrics to use to assess the effectiveness and impacts of large systemic educational change?

Additional Resources

Barnard, P.A. (2013). The systems thinking school: Redesigning schools from the inside-out (Leading systemic school improvement). R & L Education. *Journal of Educational Administration, 59*(1), 43–58.

Gurr, D., Longmuir, F., & Reed, C. (2021). Creating successful and unique schools: Leadership, context and systems thinking perspectives. *Journal of Educational Administration, 59*(1), 59–76.

Norqvist, L., & Ärlestig, H. (2021). Systems thinking in school organizations-perspectives from various leadership levels. *Journal of Educational Administration, 59*(1), 59–76.

Shaked, H., & Schecter, C. (2017). *Systems thinking for school leaders*. Springer International Publishing.

References

Achieve, Inc. (2005). *Rising to the challenge: Are high school graduate prepared for college and work? A study of high school graduates, college instructors and employers*. Achieve, Inc.

Checkland, P.B., & Sholes, J. (1999). *Soft systems methodology in action*. John Wiley & Sons.

Civic Enterprise & the Everyone Graduates Center. (2018). *2018 Building a grad nation: Progress and challenge in raising high school graduation rates*. Johns Hopkins University. http://gradnation.americaspromise.org/report/2017-building-grad-nation-report

Coburn, C.E., Choi, L., & Mata, W. (2010). I would go to her because her mind is math: Network formation in the context of district-based mathematics reform. In A. Daly (Ed.) *Social network theory and educational change*. (pp. 33–50). Harvard Education Press.

Daly, A.J. & Finnigan, K. (2012). Exploring the space between: Social networks, trust, and urban school leaders. *Journal of School Leadership, 22*(3), 493–530.

Fullan, M., Cuttress, C., & Kilcher, A. (2009). 8 forces for leaders of school change. In M. Fullan (Ed.) *The challenge of change: Start school improvement now!* (pp. 9–20). Corwin Press.

Hallinger, P., & Heck, R.H. (2010). Collaborative leadership and school improvement: Understanding the impact on school capacity and student learning. *School Leadership and Management, 30*(2), pp. 95–110.

Harion, S., & Goh, J.W.P. (2015). Pursuing the elusive construct of distributed leadership: Is the search over? *Educational Management Administration and Leadership, 43*(5), pp. 693–718.

Harris, A. (2011). System improvement through collective capacity building. *Journal of Educational Administration, 49*(6), 624–636.

Jackson M.C. (Ed.) (1991). Creative Problem Solving: Total Systems Intervention. *Systems methodology for the management sciences: Contemporary systems thinking*. Springer. https://doi.org/10.1007/978-1-4899-2632-6_11

Kruse, S. (2021). Hiding in plain sight: Systems thinking and school organization. *Journal of Educational Administration, 59*(1), 43–58.

Leithwood, K., Mascall, B., & Strauss, T. (2009). *Distributed leadership according to the evidence.* Routledge.

Louis, K.S., Mayrowetz, D., Murphy, J., & Smylie, M. (2013). Making sense of distributed leadership: How secondary school educators look at job redesign. *International Journal of Educational Leadership and Management, 1*(1), 33–68.

National Center for Education Statistics. (2016). Program for international student assessment, PISA. Retrieved from https://nces.ed.gov/surveys/pisa/

Organization for Economic Co-operation and Development (OECD). (2016). *Low performing students: Why they fall behind and how to help them succeed.* OECD. www.oecd.org/publications/low-performing-students-9789264250246-en.htm

Payne, C. (2008). *So much reform, so little change: The persistence of failure in urban schools.* Harvard Education Press.

Shaked, H., & Schechter, C. (2019). *Leading holistically, how schools, district, and states improve systemically.* Routledge.

Stroh, D.P. (2015). *Systems thinking for social change: A practical guide to solving complex problems, avoiding unintended consequences, and achieving lasting results.* Chelsea Green Publishing.

Symonds, W. C., Schwartz, R., & and Ferguson, R. (2011). Pathways to prosperity: Meeting the challenge of preparing young Americans for the 21st century. Cambridge, England: Pathways to Prosperity Project, Harvard Graduate School of Business.

U.S. Department of Education (USDOE). (2012.). Race to the top: District competition. Retrieved from www.ed.gov/race-top/district-competition/absolute-priorities.

U.S. Department of Education, Institute of Education Sciences, National Center for Education Statistics, National Assessment of Educational Progress (NAEP). (2017) *2017 NAEP Mathematics and Reading Assessments.* www.nationsreportcard.gov/reading_math_2017_highlights/

U.S. Department of Education, Institute of Education Sciences, National Center for Education Statistics, National Assessment of Educational Progress (NAEP). (2019) *2019 NAEP Mathematics and Reading Assessments.* https://nces.ed.gov/pubsearch/pubsinfo.asp?pubid=2020012

11

SYSTEMS THINKING IN UNDERGRADUATE HEALTHCARE EDUCATION AND SIMULATION-ENHANCED INTERPROFESSIONAL EDUCATION (HIGHER EDUCATION)

Dana Powell Baker

Introduction

Seldomly, the academic background and professional training of medical laboratory science professionals is discussed in systems thinking or systems-based practice. Given the vital role of laboratory professionals on the healthcare team, it is important to connect the transfer of practice from the academic setting to the clinical environment as it relates to patient safety concepts. Van Cott (1994) briefly mentioned the role of medical laboratories in describing the early perspectives of systems-based practice regarding healthcare delivery systems such as inpatient hospital units, ambulatory care services, and physician office practices. Collectively, these delivery systems interact with each other in the delivery and provision of quality care to patient populations (Van Cott, 1994). Plack et al. (2019) suggested that competence in systems-based practice requires healthcare professionals to understand the interrelationship between system practices and its impact on the optimization of patient safety and improved outcomes.

The American Society for Clinical Laboratory Science (ASCLS) recognized the need for integrating patient safety concepts into pre-certification curricula for clinical laboratory science (CLS) programs (ASCLS, 2015). This framework was guided by the 2001 Institute of Medicine's report, "Crossing the Quality Chasm," and provided six aims for improving patient care: safe, effective, patient-centered, timely, efficient, and equitable (IOM, 2001). Other healthcare professions, such as medicine and nursing, have integrated entry-level competencies and activities into their respective program curricula focused on the improvement of patient safety and the delivery of quality care.

Over the years, studies on teamwork in healthcare settings indicated that the lack of collaboration among healthcare teams contributed toward a marked

DOI: 10.4324/9781003028772-14

decrease in patient safety (Aebersold & Tschannen, 2013; Beard et al., 2015; Busari et al., 2017; Reinhold, Otieno, & Bacon-Baguley, 2017). Traditional undergraduate clinical (or medical) laboratory science program students tend to learn in silos, while other healthcare disciplines facilitate team learning experiences in both the academic setting and clinical environment. The expectations of today's healthcare environment consider work or clinical training in silos to be an antiquated process that no longer meets patient safety initiatives established by healthcare systems (Taylor et al., 2017).

System and Key Players

Attitudes and beliefs of the key players in the system influence the interrelationships that take place within a systemic structure (Senge, 2012). The mapping diagram below represents the system components portraying the structure of the undergraduate CLS program and its relationship to macro-level systems, including the academic medical center, the hospital system, and the simulation center. As demonstrated in Figure 11.1, the mapping diagram, there is a notable dynamic relationship that exists between the healthcare system and the academic medical center. Although both entities share the same brick and mortar location, each system possesses its own organizational structure. Within the academic medical center, there are three healthcare discipline-focused schools, including the School of Health Professions (SHP).

As a subsystem of the academic medical center, SHP houses several clinical specialties including the Department of Clinical Laboratory Science. This department was one of the SHP pre-certification programs seeking opportunities for integration of program students into simulation-based education (SBE) activities on campus. At the micro level of this subsystem, the program director for the undergraduate CLS program in the Department of Clinical Laboratory Sciences directly reports to the dean of the SHP. The CLS program faculty consists of full-time faculty members with a diverse representation of academic backgrounds

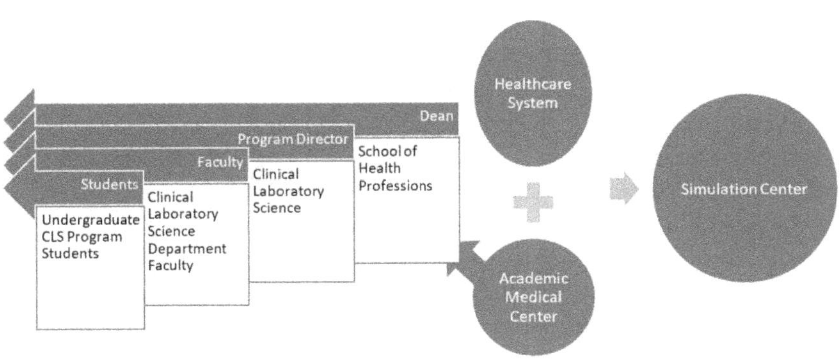

FIGURE 11.1 Mapping Diagram of Healthcare System and Academic Medical Center

and discipline-specific expertise. The undergraduate CLS program students were being considered for integration into a SBE activity with other pre-certification/ pre-licensure healthcare program students. Specifically, the undergraduate CLS program students being considered were those in their fourth and final year of the pre-certification curriculum. The students completed one full year of CLS profession-specific didactic and laboratory coursework.

The relationship of the academic medical center and the healthcare system is highlighted by their strategic partnership with the simulation center. The simulation center serves as a joint initiative between the academic medical center and the healthcare system providing advanced healthcare education through uniprofessional and interprofessional simulation activities to ensure optimal education related to the improvement of patient outcomes. The simulation education and operations delivery team collaborate with academic medical center leadership, faculty, and students to carry out healthcare simulation activities.

Case Analysis

The CLS department was presented with the opportunity to develop innovative learning approaches, such as the use of healthcare simulation, for integration into the programmatic curriculum. The integration of undergraduate CLS program students into simulation-enhanced interprofessional learning experiences was met with challenges. Some of these challenges can be directly attributed to the interrelationship between the academic medical center, the healthcare system, and the simulation center. The interrelation of these three entities is influential in shaping the system-based practices utilized in the organization. Peter Senge (2012) explained how systems continually send signals through circular loops similar to the structure of cause-and-effect relationships. These feedback mechanisms can be used to demonstrate how systems operate separately and together (Senge, 2012). Senge (1990) described mental models as "deeply ingrained assumptions, generalizations, or images that influence how we understand the world and how we take action" (p. 11). Oftentimes, individuals within a system are not consciously aware of their mental model and its influence on their behavior (Senge, 1990, p. 11). The lack of a shared mental model among system key players influenced the process for the initial integration of undergraduate CLS program students into the SBE activity.

Regarding learner engagement, undergraduate CLS program students had minimal involvement in simulation activities due to barriers such as limited opportunities for simulation-enhanced interprofessional education (Sim-IPE) development and scheduling constraints. Meanwhile, other healthcare program students were continuously exposed to TeamSTEPPS® effective communication and teamwork concepts within their program curricula. To further support the need for this implementation in educational practice, the 2015 Institute of Medicine report stated the increased complexity of patient cases in healthcare necessitates collaboration between healthcare professionals (National Academies of Sciences, Engineering and Medicine, 2015). Proposed educational interventions, such as Sim-IPE, have been proven to effectively create complex, reality-based patient cases which promote these aspects of teamwork, collaboration, knowledge sharing, and communication (INACSL, 2016).

Problem Resolution

There were two main challenges encountered in the integration of undergraduate CLS program students into Sim-IPE activities: (1) determining the overarching goal for the educational activity and (2) leveling the educational content to the level of the learner (e.g., 1st year medical student versus 4th year CLS student). During the planning stages, faculty representation from each program met with the simulation education delivery team to discuss the gaps in each respective programs' curriculum in addressing graduation requirements set forth by their program accrediting bodies. Regarding medicine students, one of the six core competencies mandated by the Accreditation Council for Graduate Medical Education (ACGME) includes systems-based practice which breaks down into subcompetencies including the ability to work in interprofessional teams to enhance patient safety and working effectively in various health care delivery settings and systems (Stanford Medicine, 2018).

Developing an Overarching Goal for Interprofessional Education

Based on other similar profession-specific competencies, it was suggested for the healthcare team to identify a commonly referenced tool for further developing effective communication and teamwork competencies. Program faculty members agreed that the TeamSTEPPS® communication toolkit was a reliable technique for practicing interprofessional communication and teamwork on healthcare teams. The integration of Interprofessional Education Collaborative (IPEC) Core Competencies and TeamSTEPPS® tools supported the pursuit of achieving competencies in interprofessional practice.

Leveling of Content Across Learner Participants

To address the challenge of leveling the content of the patient case to the curriculum level of the learner, it was proposed to develop a Sim-IPE activity within one of the undergraduate medical education blocks. By comparing graduate expectations and accreditation requirements from the academic programs, we were able to identify clinical content covered across all three healthcare program curricula. The educational activity was structured to represent clinical content leveled to the academic curriculum of each program including the opportunity to practice profession-specific skills (e.g., medical laboratory scientist reporting of abnormal laboratory results). The educational delivery approach of scaffolding IPEC Core Competencies using TeamSTEPPS® tools facilitated the reinforcement of best practices in fostering teamwork and collaboration in providing safe patient care (AHRQ, 2015).

Lessons Learned

Although the educational intervention seemed to address the teaching of systems-based practice to pre-certification students, there were unanticipated lessons learned in the process. The initial attempts to implement changes in the undergraduate CLS program curriculum lacked focus and clarity in the change process as it related to faculty involvement. More specifically, the steps toward integration of SBE into the CLS curriculum missed certain key components such as the anticipation for faculty reluctance or structuring a reform process. Evans (2001) cautioned that "major innovation is likely to fail and to damage the chances for future reform" (p. 143). Those involved in the implementation process did not fully consider the organizational capacity, the readiness (or lack thereof) of participants, and the preparation of the academic programs in adapting this change (Evans, 2001).

Assessment of Organizational Capacity

Evans (2001) described the following six content areas that can impact an organizations' capacity (or readiness) for adopting change: occupational framework, politics, history, stress, finances, and culture. The concept of occupational framework shapes the design, focus, and tone of the academic institution including the behavioral attitudes of its faculty (Senge, 2012). The unique pressures of the occupational setting include professional isolation (work carried out away from faculty peers) and multiplicity as many of us are charged with more than one responsibility within the department (Evans, 2001). The issues within this context, including social issues, provide a stark reality that education itself can be viewed as a negative experience for some key players involved (Evans, 2001).

The context of politics is commonly overlooked but it plays a significant role in the schools' ability to unite and maintain a stable core during the implementation process (Evans, 2001). Evans stated "reform can only be built on a platform of trust and consensus" (2001, p. 125). Striving for a consensus for change is necessary for effective, profound change to be successful. The history or background experience with innovation will influence the responses of key players toward current proposed changes in curriculum design (Evans, 2001). Historically, there have been disagreements between the key players within the institution in how to effectively integrate Sim-IPE into the curriculum.

Another area of consideration is the probable demand on educators and organizational resources which has been well noted in research literature regarding SBE integration into healthcare education programs. The current culture or *ethos* of the system is very supportive in the adoption of simulation education within the academic curricula of all healthcare programs. The support and shared mental model of impacted key players (e.g., administration, surrounding healthcare community) helps to reaffirm the need for academic reform to our healthcare programs, thus bolstering the meaningfulness of the work (Evans, 2001). The commitment to organizational reform is evident in the mission statement of the academic institution as well as the allocation of funding resources in support of SBE activities.

Future Implications

Moving forward, it will be imperative to explore methods of incorporating systems-based practice competency for all stakeholders including leadership, faculty, and students. This approach can prove to be effective in enhancing the systems thinking and systems-based practices integrated into the existing CLS curriculum. Future opportunities to engage in interprofessional practice in a longitudinal curriculum exist to promote collaboration and systems-based practices in healthcare teams. The implementation of best practices and theory-based concepts will help address institutional needs for increasing learner competency.

Conclusion

The integration of IPEC Core Competencies and TeamSTEPPS® tools further supported interprofessional practice of pertinent collaborative skills such as communication and teamwork for student participants. Due to the scope and complexity of integrating this new educational method, the path to transformation of systems thinking includes further exploration of faculty assumptions, beliefs, and attitudes beyond the surface. To sustain any type of longitudinal curricular change, the structure will require a supportive organizational culture that maintains feasibility and reaffirms the meaningfulness of the work itself (Evans, 2001, p. 140).

Reflective Questions

- What are some potential solutions for fostering collaborative work among faculty and system leadership to ensure the successful integration of systems-based practice in pre-certification/pre-licensure curriculum?
- How will consensus building among leadership and faculty contribute to the undergraduate healthcare education of students on the topic of systems-based practice?
- What methods exist for effective educational delivery of systems-based practice concepts in healthcare programs? Why should this be important for key players involved in the healthcare system and the academic medical center? For example, student transfer of knowledge into future professional practice.

Additional Resources

INACSL Standards of Best Practice website: www.inacsl.org/inacsl-standards-of-best-practice-simulation/history-of-the-inacsl-standards-of-best-practice-simulation/

Interprofessional Education Collaborative (IPEC). (2016). *Core competencies for interprofessional collaborative practice: 2016 update*. Interprofessional Education Collaborative.

IPEC Core Competencies website: www.ipecollaborative.org/ipec-core-competencies

Palaganas, J. C., Maxworthy, J. C., Epps, C. A., & Mancini, M. E. (2015). *Defining excellence in simulation programs* (1st ed.). Wolters Kluwer.

Pulcrano, M., Chahine, A. A., Saratsis, A., Divine-Cadavid, J., Narra, V., & Evans, S. R. T. (2015). Putting residents in the office: An effective method to teach the systems-based practice competency. *Journal of Surgical Education, 72*(2): 286–290. https://doi.org/10.1016/j.jsurg.2014.09.001

Team-Based Competencies, Building a Shared Foundation for Education and Clinical Practice website: https://ipec.memberclicks.net/assets/Team-Based.pdf

References

Aebersold, M., & Tschannen, D. (2013). Simulation in nursing practice: The impact on patient care. *The Online Journal of Issues in Nursing, 18*(2): 6.

Agency for Healthcare Research and Quality. (2015, January). University of Kansas Medical Center uses TeamSTEPPS® to educate future clinicians. www.ahrq.gov/policymakers/case-studies/201423.html

American Society for Clinical Laboratory Science. (2015, July). Patient safety and clinical laboratory science. www.ascls.org/position-papers/185-patient-safety-clinical-laboratory-science

Beard, T. S., Robertson, T. M., Semler, J. R., & Cude, C. J. (2015). A study of interprofessional collaboration in undergraduate medical laboratory science and nursing education. *Clinical Laboratory Science, 28*(2): 83–90.

Busari, J. O., Moll, F. M., & Duits, A. J. (2017). Understanding the impact of interprofessional collaboration on the quality of care: A case report from a small-scale resource limited health care environment. *Journal of Multidisciplinary Healthcare, 10*: 227–234. https://doi.org/10.2147/JMDH.S140042

Evans, R. (2001). *The human side of school change: Reform, resistance, and the real-life problems of innovation*. Jossey-Bass.

Institute of Medicine, Committee on Quality of Health Care in America. (2001). *Crossing the quality chasm: A new health system for the 21st century* [Press release]. National Academy Press: Author.

INACSL Standards of Best Practice: Simulation℠. (2016). Simulation-enhanced interprofessional education (Sim-IPE). *Clinical Simulation in Nursing, 12*: S34–S38. www.nursingsimulation.org/article/S1876-1399(16)30132-3/fulltext

National Academies of Sciences, Engineering, and Medicine. (2015). Improving *diagnosis* in *health care*. The National Academies Press. https://doi.org/10.17226/21794

Plack, M. M., Goldman, E. F., Scott, A. R., & Brundage, S. B. (2019). *Systems thinking in the healthcare professions: A guide for educators and clinicians*. George Washington University.

Reinhold, M. I., Otieno, S., & Bacon-Baguley, T. (2017). Integrating interprofessional experience throughout a first-year physician assistant curriculum improves perceptions of health care providers. *Journal of Interprofessional Education & Practice, 6*: 37–43. https://doi.org/10.1016/j.xjep.2016.12.001

Senge, P. (1990). *The fifth discipline: The art & practice of the learning organization*. Currency Doubleday.

Senge, P. (2012). *Schools that learn: A fifth discipline fieldbook for educators, parents, and everyone who cares about education* (1st ed.). Crown Business.

Stanford Medicine. (2018, January 23). *ACGME core competencies*. Graduate medical education. http://med.stanford.edu/gme/housestaff/all-topics/core_competencies.html

Taylor, J. R., Thompson, P. J., Genzen, J. R., Hickner, J., & Marques, M. B. (2017, February). Opportunities to enhance laboratory professionals' role on the diagnostic team. *Laboratory Medicine, 48*(1): 97–103. https://doi.org/10.1093/labmed/lmw048

Van Cott, H. (1994). Human errors: Their causes and reduction. In M. S. Bogner (Ed.), *Human error in medicine* (pp. 53–65). Lawrence Erlbaum Associates.

12

APPLYING INSTRUCTIONAL DESIGN PRINCIPLES TO A COMMON CHALLENGE IN HEALTH CARE RESEARCH (HEALTH CARE)

Janet K. Brishke, Christy Evans, Eileen M. Handberg, and Elizabeth A. Shenkman

Introduction

Despite a perception that health care professionals have all the answers, research is required to address health care's biggest questions: Which treatment works best? Why does one person get sick and another does not? To find answers effectively, researchers need an outside perspective that can help them stay grounded in reality. This outside perspective can vary by organization, but usually comes from a lay advisor (National Academies of Sciences, Engineering, and Medicine, 2018).

A group of lay advisors, called Citizen Scientists (CSs), work out of the University of Florida Clinical and Translational Science Institute (UF CTSI). While the term Citizen Scientist (CS) is more commonly used for individuals engaging in natural science fields through methods such as data collection (Wiggins & Wilbanks, 2019), the CSs play a role more similar to individuals at other health institutions who are often referred to as patient advisors, health care users, and stakeholders (Shippee et al., 2015). The CSs specifically chose their name to accentuate their involvement as integrated members of research teams and oversight councils. These individuals engage with researchers in a variety of ways throughout the research process. Activities may include recommending feedback on research ideas, reviewing proposals, advising on recruitment materials, improving research participant communication during the project, helping define the method and language for results dissemination to the lay public, and serving as study Co-Investigators.

DOI: 10.4324/9781003028772-15

System and Key Players

Working to complete this project were several stakeholders including CTSI leadership who helped guide the project; researchers within the CTSI who worked with the CSs on projects, committees, and studies; the curriculum project manager, who also managed the Citizen Scientist Program (CSP) and helped connect researchers with CSs as a study's needs necessitated; and instructional designers from the UF College of Education, who were hired by CTSI leadership to help ensure a worthwhile training product was created. The CSs themselves were a critical part of this process, as they were involved in the project from conception to implementation. The project stakeholders worked on five main focus areas of this project: project conceptualization, content identification, content creation, open educational resource (OER) creation, and implementation. As depicted in Table 12.1, some stakeholder roles within these focus areas overlapped, while some happened sequentially.

Case Analysis

As the CSs began working with researchers, a few problems arose. The most pervasive problems resulted from a lack of understanding of the research process. For example, a researcher would discuss a funding proposal with a CS and then, according to the CS perspective, the researcher would disappear. However, the reality was that the researcher was further refining the study protocol and/or waiting for funding or institutional approval, and the CS did not understand the timeline for health care research development and funding. The CSs became frustrated by the perceived lack of researcher follow through. Complicating this situation was the advent of the Patient-Centered Outcomes Research Institute, which mandated patient involvement in research projects (Frank et al., 2015). As such, consulting with lay advisors became a more common requirement from funders (Hahn et al., 2017). CS input was sought more frequently, increasing the CS perception that they were being used simply to meet a funding requirement. CSs were often left feeling frustrated and confused, as if their input was merely tokenistic (Hahn et al., 2017). CSs also struggled with unrealistic expectations stemming from their lack of understanding of the barriers, delays, and constraints that researchers face. For instance, a CS would offer an alternative project focus worth merit but struggled to understand that a researcher cannot change the central focus of a funded study. Likewise, CSs did not understand how federal and organizational regulations may impact the work of the researchers. Yet another problem was that CSs did not understand abbreviations and acronyms common to researchers. This made it difficult for the CSs to grasp the project information and provide meaningful feedback in a timely manner.

Additionally, onboarding new members to the UF CTSI Citizen Scientist Program (CSP) was a process lacking in consistency and rigor. New members

TABLE 12.1 Stakeholders and Roles on Project

Stakeholder	*Focus/Roles*
CTSI Leadership	• Project conceptualization: Project funding, reviewed framework and offered suggestions • Content identification: Identified content of importance • OER creation: Provided website to host OER course
Citizen Scientists	• Project conceptualization: Provided input on desired content format • Content identification: Identified content of importance • Content creation: Formative evaluation (viewed videos and completed learning assessments), provided feedback on content • Implementation: Completed final course in Canvas, obtained CS certification
CTSI Researchers	• Content creation: Served as video subject matter experts, provided slides for video lessons, reviewed/edited learning assessments created from video content
Instructional Designers	• Project conceptualization: Interviewed CSs about preferred format, identified instructional design model to guide project • Content creation: Formatted video slides, created learning assessments, adjusted slide/assessment content based on CS feedback • OER creation: Constructed website for OER course
Project Manager	• Content identification: Identified content of importance • Content creation: Recruited subject matter experts for videos, edited subject matter expert slides to ensure content was formatted correctly and in lay terms, coordinated with video studio for filming/editing • OER creation: Maintain website for OER course, disseminate course to other sites • Implementation: Ported course into Canvas for UF CTSI implementation, analysis of UF CTSI implementation course results

could begin work at any time throughout the year, and there was no formal approach to the onboarding process; in fact, new members were typically given journal articles to read and left on their own to make sense of group discussions and researcher interactions. This approach left new members feeling overwhelmed, unprepared, and less likely to contribute. Unless they started their tenure at the same time as another member, the onboarding trainings received by CSs differed between members, leaving each member with slightly different knowledge gaps.

All of these issues impeded the CSP from being able to provide the very thing researchers desired: a lay perspective on research studies. The CSs and researchers at the UF CTSI were simply not speaking the same language.

Problem Resolution

The UF CTSI created a formalized research training curriculum as a remedy to these challenges and prioritized this project through short-term funding, with an assumption that there would be a return on investment in the funding potential and quality of their research (Jagosh et al., 2012). The first charge for the curriculum team was to create an outline for content. The potential topics were endless; however, there is a fine line between providing a bit of background information and over-educating, causing the trainee to lose their lay perspective. To help strike this balance, the team sought input on content from UF CTSI leadership and CSs, and included only the topics deemed necessary as a primer to clinical research. This approach to establishing a shared vision ensured support for, and participation in, the final curriculum (Senge, 2006, p. 192). Next, the curriculum team interviewed the members of the CSP individually to determine the best method of information delivery. From these interviews, the curriculum team created a curriculum of seven modules composed of didactic lecture videos paired with online assessments and video examples of CSs at work. While primarily created to be informative, these videos challenge the mental model of CSs being passive participants in the research process (Senge, 2006, p. 163).

The team used the Analysis, Design, Development, Implementation, Evaluation (ADDIE) instructional design model (Morrison et al., 2010, p. 13) to develop the curriculum and made the course self-paced to ensure it could be usable for trainees from all backgrounds. Likewise, to accommodate a range of learning styles, a blended learning approach was adopted through the creation of an instructor's guide to aid in-person group discussions about the module contents (Hrastinski, 2019).

The final two steps of the ADDIE process were modified slightly to meet the specific needs of this project (Valle et al., 2018), as shown in Figure 12.1. Due to the short funding timeline, the evaluation occurred prior to the final implementation: once a didactic video and its assessment were finished, the CSs viewed the video and took the assessment as part of the formative evaluation (Harlen, 2007, p. 15). Changes were then made to the assessments and videos based on feedback collected during these sessions (Valle et al., 2018).

Completing the course were two new CSP members and six experienced members. The latter group participated in the formative evaluation of the videos and assessments and thus had reviewed the content previously. Due to the formative evaluation process and their tenure in the program, we expected the seasoned members to perform better on their first attempt than the new members. While this held true in most areas, their scores were not as high as expected and, in

FIGURE 12.1 Modified ADDIE Framework

some cases, their scores were lower than those of the new members (Table 12.2). Additionally, the patterns of retakes were similar for both groups. These results underscored the need for a standardized training curriculum for all CSs, regardless of their knowledge of research or health care upon entering the CSP.

UF CTSI leadership requested that the final materials be made publicly and freely available to assist others, as challenges with communication, trust, and training between community stakeholders and researchers are not limited to our organization (Sprague Martinez et al., 2018). As such, the curriculum content was intentionally designed to be broad and lack UF CTSI branding, and the final curriculum, including the instructor's guide with suggested implementation schedules, is available online as an OER (Fergusson et al., 2018). Our approach has been popular, and the content has been requested by, and shared with, other organizations. The interest in this curriculum indicates that these challenges are indeed not specific to the UF CTSI and that there is a growing desire to adjust the mental model of the researcher-CS paradigm. This diffusion of innovation (Dearing and Cox, 2018), coupled with the trend toward patient-centered research, suggests that this approach will be readily accepted by stakeholders.

Lessons Learned

Due to the abbreviated timeline of this project, follow-up after implementation was not possible. Additional analyses of the curriculum and its impact, such as user testing, a post-market analysis, user interviews, or interviews with researchers who worked with newly educated CSs, would have given a more thorough appreciation of the curriculum's impact as well as potential areas for improvement. As possible, these steps should be built into the timeline and budget of future projects of this nature.

TABLE 12.2 First Attempt Assessment Scores by Lesson: Seasoned Citizen Scientists vs New Citizen Scientists

Module	*Lesson Topic*	*Total Score – Seasoned Citizen Scientists Scores*	*Total Score – New Citizen Scientists*
Welcome and Orientation	Citizen Scientists: Who are they? What do they do?	94%	67%
	Intellectual Property and Confidentiality	92%	92%
Research Ethics	IRBs and Human Subjects Research	82%	55%
	Research Ethics	83%	67%
	Informed Consent	79%	59%
	Consent for Research vs Clinical Care	83%	70%
Sponsored Research	Research 101	83%	60%
	Federal Funding for Research	85%	80%
	How to Read a Research Article	80%	80%
Clinical and Translational Science	Translational Sciences 101	85%	80%
	Types of Research Studies	72%	55%
Stakeholder Engagement	What is Stakeholder Engagement?	98%	95%
Cultural Diversity in Research	Cultural Competence	77%	90%
Biomedical Informatics	Biomedical Informatics and Big Data	73%	80%
	Big Data in Health Care	88%	85%

Note: The total group scores per lesson are the number of correct response points from group members divided by the number of points possible for group members.

A valuable lesson learned through this process was to keep expertise on hand, even if funds are not available. Funds for the instructional design experts lapsed prior to the implementation phase, leaving the UF CTSI members of the curriculum team to add the content into the Canvas learning management system. The team struggled to create the course with a lock-step sequence that required that the learner complete one activity before proceeding to the next item. Compounding lack of expertise in Canvas with lack of educational expertise, the team also did not realize the importance of setting a minimum passing score for the assessments to more closely align with a mastery learning approach (Yudkowsky et al., 2015). Without a defined minimum passing score, CSs decided when they had mastered a lesson, which resulted in several retakes where satisfactory scores had already been achieved. If the UF CTSI team had reached out to the instructional design experts with one-off questions, these problems could have been resolved more quickly. Fortunately, neither of these issues caused insurmountable challenges that impacted the overall outcome.

One of the circumstances that appeared to initially threaten the project turned out to be a success in the end: A new staff member joined the curriculum team near the start of the project and was new to some of the areas of research to be included in the curriculum content. This aided content review, as the new team member also needed to learn the information. If that person did not understand the content, this indicated to the team that the materials needed modification to successfully work for a lay audience.

Despite a lack of formal follow-up, anecdotal feedback and lived experiences following implementation indicated that CSs are able to better follow research team discussions and give well-reasoned input. Members of the CSP have gone on to serve on national committees and as Co-Investigators on projects and have provided meaningful, substantial input to many large-scale, national clinical trials like ADAPTABLE and All of Us, as well as local investigator-initiated projects. In addition, the CSs have been engaged in a national clinical trial in response to the COVID-19 pandemic, providing valuable input to the National Institutes of Health as part of the federal government's efforts to identify medications to prevent clotting associated with the virus. Researchers have noted that this training has allowed for a strengthened relationship between researchers and CSs, and that they now view CSs as true collaborators.

Conclusion

The CS curriculum project aimed to alleviate communication problems between researchers and CSs. While the curriculum largely resolved this issue, there remains occasional friction between CSs and researchers that is often attributed to how some researchers perceive the concept of a lay stakeholder's perspective, not the lack of training of the CSs. Subsequent steps to adapting our systems to more efficiently foster relationships between CSs and researchers must also include an examination of how these stakeholders are approached, engaged, and appreciated, as well as a consideration to how elements of trust can influence these interactions (Allen et al., 2017). Trust is a multi-faceted concept in this case. Researchers need to trust that CSs know what they are talking about: they have lived experiences and valuable input. CSs need to trust that researchers will listen and value their input. However, a third and often overlooked aspect of trust is that CSs need to trust themselves. They have to be comfortable in their understanding of the topic or study, and must feel empowered to speak up, especially in group settings. The curriculum helps CSs gain this confidence by providing a basic knowledge of research and/or the topic at hand.

Because this curriculum was added into the operations of our existing CSP, we know that when we connect a researcher with a CS, we can be confident that the CS is prepared to provide meaningful feedback. The creation and implementation of this curriculum has helped us connect researchers to knowledgeable, professional lay stakeholders. When stakeholders better understand the research process, they can offer clear, actionable feedback and thereby help improve health care for all.

Reflective Questions

- What are some indicators that a lay stakeholder is becoming over-educated?
- How might your own lived experiences impact a clinical research study?
- What may be the benefits and disadvantages of different formulations of a lay advisor system (one person, a few people, a large group of people)?
- How might researchers ensure that their approach to interactions with stakeholders is more than merely tokenistic?

Additional Resources

The University of Florida Clinical and Translational Science Institute Citizen Scientist Curriculum is posted online at https://citizenscientist.ctsi.ufl.edu/.

References

Allen, M. L., Salsberg, J., Knot, M., LeMaster, J. W., Felzien, M., Westfall, J. M., Herbert, C. P., Vickery, K., Culhane-Pera, K. A., Ramsden, V. R., Zittleman, L., Martin, R. E., & Macaulay, A. C. (2017). Engaging with communities, engaging with patients: amendment to the NAPCRG 1998 Policy Statement on Responsible Research with Communities. *Family Practice, 34*(3), 313–321. https://doi.org/10.1093/fampra/cmw074

Dearing, J. W. & Cox, J. G. (2018). Diffusion of innovations theory, principles, and practice. *Health Affairs, 37*(2), 183–190.

Fergusson, D., Monfaredi, Z., Pussegoda, K., Garritty, C., Lyddiatt, A., Shea, B., Duffett, L., Ghannad, M., Montroy, J., Hassan Murad, M., Pratt, M., Rader, T., Shorr, R., & Yazdi, F. (2018). The prevalence of patient engagement in published trials: a systematic review. *Research Involvement and Engagement, 4*, 17. https://doi.org/10.1186/s40900-018-0099-x

Frank, L., Forsythe, L., Ellis, L., Schrandt, S., Sheridan, S., Gerson, J., Konopka, K., & Daugherty, S. (2015). Conceptual and practical foundations of patient engagement in research at the patient-centered outcomes research institute. *Quality of Life Research: An International Journal of Quality of Life Aspects of Treatment, Care and Rehabilitation, 24*(5), 1033–1041. https://doi.org/10.1007/s11136-014-0893-3

Hahn, D. L., Hoffmann, A. E., Felzien, M., LeMaster, J. W., Xu, J., & Fagnan, L. J. (2017). Tokenism in patient engagement. *Family Practice, 34*(3), 290–295. https://doi.org/10.1093/fampra/cmw097

Harlen, W. (2007). *Assessment of Learning*. Sage Publications.

Hrastinski, S. (2019). What do we mean by blended learning? *TechTrends, 63*(5), 564–569. https://doi.org/10.1007/s11528-019-00375-5

Jagosh, J., Macaulay, A. C., Pluye, P., Salsberg, J., Bush, P. L., Henderson, J., Sirett, E., Wong, G., Cargo, M., Herbert, C. P., Seifer, S. D., Green, L. W., & Greenhalgh, T. (2012). Uncovering the benefits of participatory research: implications of a realist review for health research and practice. *The Milbank Quarterly*, *90*(2), 311–346. https://doi.org/10.1111/j.1468-0009.2012.00665.x

Morrison, G. R., Ross, S. M., Kemp, J. E., & Kalman, H. (2010). *Designing Effective Instruction*. John Wiley & Sons.

National Academies of Sciences, Engineering, and Medicine. (2018). *Learning Through Citizen Science: Enhancing Opportunities by Design*. The National Academies Press. https://doi.org/10.17226/25183

Senge, P. M. (2006). *The Fifth Discipline: The Art & Practice of The Learning Organization*. (2nd ed.). Doubleday/Currency.

Shippee, N. D., Domecq Garces, J. P., Prutsky Lopez, G. J., Wang, Z., Elraiyah, T. A., Nabhan, M., Brito, J. P., Boehmer, K., Hasan, R., Firwana, B., Erwin, P. J., Montori, V. M., & Murad, M. H. (2015). Patient and service user engagement in research: a systematic review and synthesized framework. *Health Expectations: An International Journal of Public Participation in Health Care and Health Policy*, *18*(5), 1151–1166. https://doi.org/10.1111/hex.12090

Sprague Martinez, L., Carolan, K., O'Donnell, A., Diaz, Y., & Freeman, E. (2018). Community engagement in patient-centered outcomes research: Benefits, barriers, and measurement. *Journal of Clinical and Translational Science*, *2*(6), 371–376. http://doi.org/10.1017/cts.2018.341

Wiggins, A., & Wilbanks, J. (2019). The Rise of Citizen Science in Health and Biomedical Research. *The American Journal of Bioethics*, *19*(8), 3–14. https://doi.org/10.1080/15265161.2019.1619859

Valle, N., Brishke, J., Ritzhaupt, A., Evans, C., Nelson, D., & Shenkman, E. (2018). Using instructional design to support community engagement in clinical and translational research: A design and development case. *Journal of Formative Designs in Learning*, *2*(1), 20–35. https://doi.org/10.1007/s41686-018-0018-4

Yudkowsky, R., Park, Y. S., Lineberry, M., Knox, A., & Ritter, E. M. (2015). Setting mastery learning standards. *Academic medicine: Journal of the Association of American Medical Colleges*, *90*(11), 1495–1500. https://doi.org/10.1097/ACM.0000000000000887

13

INCLUSIVE HISTORIES

Using Systems Thinking and a Team-based Approach to Develop and Implement a U.S. History Curriculum Rooted in Social Justice (K-12)

Khary Fletcher

Introduction

The National Council for the Social Studies (NCSS) (2016) asserts that a rigorous social studies curriculum provides strategies and activities to engage students while encouraging them to critically think about what they are learning and connect the new learning to their prior knowledge. The NCSS position statement, in essence, calls for students to learn social studies content in a manner which allows them to apply the learning to their lives. The call for critical and creative thinking aligns with that of a social justice-based curriculum.

Social justice education aims to help teachers and students develop the necessary knowledge and tools "to examine issues of justice/injustice in their personal lives, communities, institutions, and the broader society" (Bell, 2016, p. 4). The ability to engage students in an examination of social identities, power, privilege, and structural inequalities in society and their own lives requires educators/leaders to examine both the design of the curriculum and who they are (their role) as the instructor (Bell, Goodman, & Ouellett, 2016). In September 2018, a collaboration of teachers, coaches, district administrators, and university professors engaged in the process of designing an African American and Latinx perspective, high school United States (U.S.) History curriculum.

Our goal is the collaboration of all stakeholders to ensure successful implementation of the social studies curricula, resulting in frequent communication about assessments, resources, and instructional methods. Stakeholders wanted a curriculum that represented the community. Latinx and African American students represent a majority of the student population; it is important to implement curricula that provide windows into others' lived experiences, and mirrors that reflect

DOI: 10.4324/9781003028772-16

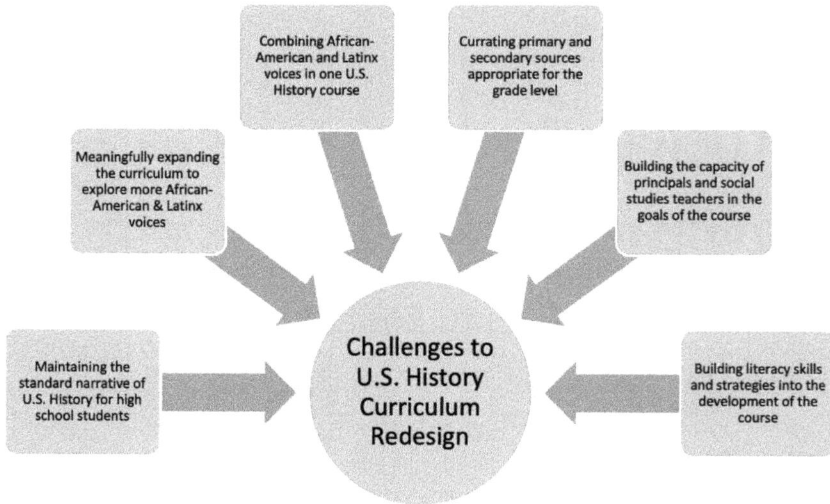

FIGURE 13.1 Challenges of Curriculum Innovation

their lived experiences to foster positive social identity development (Teaching Tolerance, 2020).

Students' exploration of U.S. History was a "window" into the lived experiences of Americans; this did not represent their identity groups. In other words, students were not exploring the challenges and successes of African Americans and Latinx peoples in U.S. History. The challenges of redesigning a U.S. History curriculum for high school 11th grade students were many (see Figure 13.1). Nevertheless, this innovation was necessary to provide students with "voices and experiences of people from the African and Latinx Diasporas in the Americas to offer [an often neglected] interpretation of United States history" (Ortiz, 2018, p. 1).

A team of teachers were assembled to work with professors from several universities to develop a Black and Latinx U.S. History curriculum. Strong consideration of the desired goal resulted in a curriculum enriched with the narratives of Black and Latinx peoples. Utilizing systems thinking from the onset of this initiative, the team intentionally structured time during professional learning to inform teachers of the upcoming changes. In doing so, the goal was to "focus on building collaborative relationships and structures for change" and create an interest in joining the Curriculum Redesign Team (Senge et al., 2012, p. 404).

System and Key Players

The development of this initiative was dependent upon the actions of several key participants. This included central office administrators, building principals, district instructional coaches, social studies teachers and out of district content experts.

The common structures of the K-12 educational system have a clear delineation between the district office and each school building. However, it was necessary for communication to be on-going during this time. This, too, was true of the coordinated efforts between in and out of district support networks. The establishment of important check points were developed to keep key stakeholders apprised to the development of the course. An added benefit of this was the opportunity to sell members of the school community on the ideas needed to properly implement the redesigned curriculum (Senge et al., 2012).

The components represented below sequence the order in which this innovation was discussed, developed, and implemented throughout the system:

Planning of the redesign and the shift to implementation of the curriculum in several high schools throughout the district. The innovation transition from the planning to implementation was clearly stated at the onset of the project. The basis of a Black & Latinx curriculum is to provide students in the district the opportunity to analyze their world from an historical perspective through thematic units of study while providing teachers the resources to engage in such teaching and learning. However, the plan of curriculum creation could have easily become the sole focus for the key participants. Evans (1996) describes this as "reification" or the tendency for the plan to become the end product rather than the means to a goal (p. 13). In order to avoid this after the initial discussions and planning at the central office level of the system, the Curriculum Redesign Team engaged in work with two endpoints in mind: the development of a U.S. History curriculum with resources centered on the perspectives of Black and Latinx peoples while maintaining the chronology of the United States standard

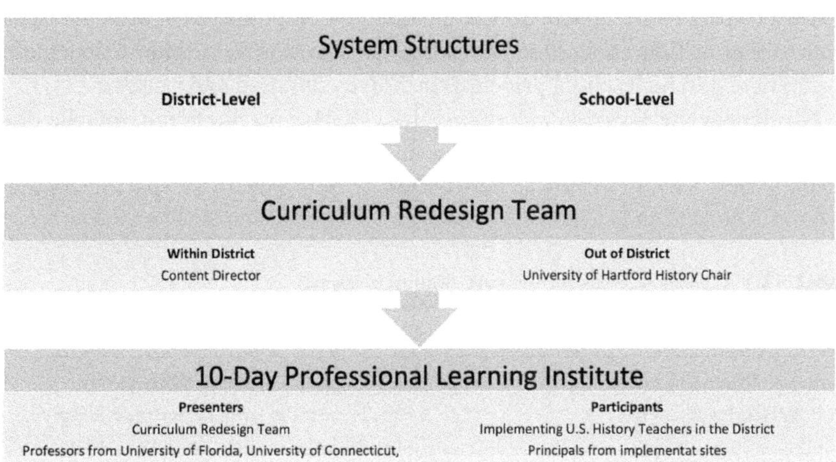

FIGURE 13.2 System and Key Participants for Implementation of a Black and Latinx Curricula

narrative of historical events, and preparation to launch professional learning at the end of the 2019–2020.

Case Analysis

In order to provide students with an opportunity to put historical thinking into context and make meaning from it, the Curriculum Redesign Team had to overcome several barriers: conceptual design of the curriculum; identification of U.S. History teachers to implement the new curriculum; listing the curriculum as a new course; and facilitation of professional learning needed to implement the curriculum during COVID-19 social distancing.

The conceptual design of this course was unfamiliar to the district team, including professors, that engaged in the early curriculum design (e.g., thinking of how the African American, Black, and Latinx history can cohesively exist as one curriculum while attending to the standard narrative). The team had no known template to address the design aspect of the curriculum. To remedy this, the design team identified a foundational text (Ortiz, 2018) which combined African American and Latinx U.S. History. The text served as a conceptual model for the content design of the curriculum. With the inability to find a secondary source with a readability measure appropriate to 11th grade students, the team approached the several sources (see Table 13.1) and the professors on the design team to curate primary source materials to teach content that challenged the standard narrative of U.S. History (Singer, 2012).

Additionally, the team faced the challenge of having the developed course listed in the high school's course offerings. However, another U.S. History course would be seen as an elective; especially since all high schools in the district offered U.S. History as part of the graduation requirement. Communication with the State Department of Education, District leaders, the Board of Education Curriculum Committee, and high school principals provided education and clarity.

Challenges also rested in identifying the U.S. History teachers across the district that have the background in African American and Latinx. This included teachers that have intersecting knowledge of not only these specific groups,

TABLE 13.1 Consulted Texts for Primary Source Materials

Author/Editor	*Title*
Games & Rothman	*Major Problems in Atlantic History*
Holt & Barkley Brown	*Major Problems in African-American History Vol. I & II*
Valerio-Jimenez & Whalen	*Major Problems in Latina/o History*

but of social justice educational practices and culturally relevant pedagogy. Communication of curriculum implementation intentions during the 2019–2020 district-wide professional learning piqued the interest of several U.S. History teachers. By selling the importance of the curriculum, we were able to identify four high schools and six teachers to implement the curriculum for the following year.

Selected teachers did not have specialized content knowledge in African American or Latinx U.S. history. They were not experts in Social Justice Education or applying culturally relevant pedagogy as a perspective of the work we do in education. However, these were dedicated history teachers willing to deepen their practices outside of teaching the standard narrative of U.S. History. Recognizing these factors, members of the design team developed a ten-day professional learning institute. The impact of Covid-19 and social distancing compelled the team to utilize technology to invite presenters that otherwise would not be able to attend the professional learning institute.

The ten-day professional learning institute was specifically designed to address several key factors: unpack the curriculum, deepen content knowledge, and create a working implementation guide. Ultimately, what began as ten days of professional learning quickly morphed into a professional learning community (Stroll et al., 2006). The group was able to address gaps within their learning with members of the Curriculum Redesign Team as well as the content experts invited to expand the level of knowledge needed to implement the innovation. Moreover, participants had the opportunity to directly apply this knowledge to the curriculum.

Problem Resolution

Senge et al. (2012) suggest that working collaboratively toward a set goal is beneficial to a system in terms of building a shared vision and offers five developmental stages (telling selling, testing, consulting, and co-creating). However, "co-creating" is not a natural task for teachers who have not been asked to collaborate in this manner as evidenced in the early days of the ten-day institute (p. 94). To combat the tension of allowing a newly formed team to co-create the learning plan for each unit of study, the facilitators of the institute used a combination of telling and selling strategies. First, the facilitators named the tension that arose during the co-creation time. Next, the facilitators re-engaged the group on the idea that they were having direct input on the curriculum that they were expecting to implement in the fall. The flexibility in the design of the professional learning allowed the facilitators and participants "to talk openly about the assumptions and interpretations that have led to any irreconcilable views" (p. 95). Thus, resulting in greater small group collaboration in creation of each unit's learning plan.

Lessons Learned

Evans (1996) suggests that change is a multidimensional process involving all aspects of an organization. In this change effort, social studies teachers were asked to look beyond the ways in which they have traditionally taught a course and share in a vision in which they could not yet see. The organization itself had to adapt to the introduction of a curriculum that did not change listing of a course, per se, but a major shift in the conceptualization of content of a U.S. History curriculum. Not to mention the undertaking of such efforts during the onset of a global pandemic. Throughout it all, flexibility and communication were key strategies relied upon in order to accomplish the tasks. Addressing misconceptions and unintended drifts from the goal happened often. In reflection, participants in both the Curriculum Redesign Team and the learning institute expressed gratitude for the norms which established such an environment.

Although success was measured by the work that took place during the ten-day learning institute, the reality that participating social studies teachers still needed support during the school year. Implementing teachers were surveyed at the start of the year to determine when the best time would be to continue the professional learning community (PLC). The survey resulted in bi-weekly meetings in which four teachers, two instructional coaches, and the content director met to discuss pacing and literacy strategies (two goals selected by the implementing teachers during the initial PLC). On-going support in a PLC became necessary in order to halt what Senge et al. (2012) define as the balancing process or a system's return to the way it used to operate. For U.S. History teachers, the process would be a lack of support leading to a return to the standard narrative of history in which African American and Latinx contributions are marginalized to a select few events and peoples. In this, the system continues to find ways to collaborate while attempting to practice new behaviors and adopt new beliefs (Evans, 1996). This will enable the growth in implementation of a diverse U.S. History curriculum in every high school in the district.

Conclusion

Conceptualizing the design of a Black and Latinx United States History curriculum was a challenging feat for the members of the Curriculum Redesign Team. On-going support through the PLC proved to be valuable to the implementing teachers as well as the content director supervising the implementation of the new curriculum. Through continued collaboration with teachers, steps have been taken to further modify each unit's implementation guide to ensure connections students' identities are visible. Using systems thinking as a lens, the focus continues to be on building collaborative relationships and structures for change that will best serve the societal interest of students in the district.

Reflective Questions

- How are students' lived experiences and histories represented in the curricula they encounter?
- Sometimes change initiatives require collaboration between individuals with various levels of content expertise, residing inside and outside of the organization adopting the change. In this form of collaboration, what is the best way to structure the team to reach the desired goal?
- How do collaborative teams work together in setting multiple goals for the development, professional learning, and implementation of a curriculum project?

Additional Resources

Baldwin, J. (1962). *The fire next time.* Vintage.

Coates, T. (2015). *Between the world and me.* Spiegel & Grau.

Gee, J.P. (1989). What is literacy? *Journal of Education, 171*(1), 18–25.

Gonzalez, J. (2000). *Harvest of empire: A history of Latinos in America.* Penguin.

Ladson-Billings, G. (1994). But that's just good teaching! The case for culturally relevant pedagogy. *Theory into Practice, 34*(3), 159–165.

Tatum, A.W. (2009). *Reading for their life: (Re)building the textual lineages of African American adolescent males.* Heinemann.

References

Bell, L.A. (2016). Theoretical foundations for social justice education. In Adams, M., & Bell, L.A. (Eds.), *Teaching for diversity and social justice* (3rd ed., pp. 3–26). Routledge.

Bell, L.A., Goodman, D.J., & Ouellett, M.L. (2016). Design and facilitation. In Adams, M., & Bell, L.A. (Eds.), *Teaching for diversity and social justice* (3rd ed., pp. 55–93). Routledge.

Evans, R. (1996). *The human side of school change: Reform, resistance, and the real-life problems of innovation.* Jossey-Bass.

National Council for the Social Studies. (2016). A vision of powerful teaching and learning in the social studies: A position statement of the National Council for the Social Studies. *Social Education, 80*(3), 180–182.

Ortiz, P. (2018). *An African American and Latinx history of the United States.* Beacon.

Senge, P., Cambron-Mcabe, N., Lucas, T., Smith, B., Janis, D., & Kleiner, A. (2012). *Schools that learn: Update & revised: A fifth discipline field book for educators, parents, and everyone who cares about education.* Crown Business.

Singer, A.J. (2012). Teaching challenging topics with primary sources. *Social Education, 76*(6), 324–328. www.socialstudies.org/social-education/76/6/teaching-challenging-topics-primary-sources

Stoll, L., Bolam, R., McMahon, A., Wallace, M., & Thomas, S. (2006). Professional learning communities: A review of the literature. *Journal of Educational Change,* 7(4), 221–258.

Teaching Tolerance. (2020, July 26). *Window or mirror?* Teaching Tolerance. www.tolerance.org/classroom-resources/teaching-strategies/close-and-critical-reading/window-or-mirror

14

A JOURNEY TO QUANTIFIED BLOOD LOSS IN A TERTIARY PERINATAL SETTING (HEALTHCARE)

Riad Homsi, Gina Horne, and Suha Rahif Tamim

Introduction

Severe maternal morbidity and mortality rates are on the rise in the United States with obstetric hemorrhage being the leading cause of pregnancy-related mortality and the most frequent cause of preventable maternal harm (The American College of Obstetricians and Gynecologists, ACOG, 2019). The rate of obstetric hemorrhage associated morbidities exceeds the morbidity rates of all other obstetric and medical conditions. Delay in diagnosis and treatment, ineffective management, and lack of proper preventive measures for hemorrhage lead to pregnancy-related death and extreme morbidity that could be prevented (ACOG, 2019).

The Alliance for Innovation on Maternal Health (AIM) is a data-driven program endorsed by ACOG that aims to improve maternal outcomes, one of which is obstetric hemorrhage (ACOG, 2020). The program is based on the 4Rs: Readiness for Every Unit, Recognition and Prevention for Every Patient, Response for Every Hemorrhage, and Reporting Outcome Metrics (Council on Patient Safety in Women's Health Care, 2020). This program includes multiple components at each level. One of the components in the Recognition and Prevention for Every Patient level is the accurate quantification of blood loss during delivery that allows for early identification of obstetric hemorrhage, timely intervention, and more seamless management of blood products replacement (California Department of Public Health, CDPH, 2015).

The World Health Organization (2012) recommends the use of protocols by health care facilities to standardize the prevention and treatment of obstetric hemorrhage. Therefore, in 2016, and in adherence to the recommendations of ACOG, the Council on Patient Safety in Women's Health Care, and the World Health Organization, Baptist Memorial Hospital for Women in Memphis,

DOI: 10.4324/9781003028772-17

Tennessee established a process for early recognition of obstetric hemorrhage with a standardized approach to the quantification of blood loss (QBL). The goal was for blood loss to be quantified for over 90 percent of deliveries. Before the AIM obstetric hemorrhage initiative, blood loss was estimated visually, often underestimated by as much as 50 percent (California Department of Public Health, 2015). Underestimation resulted in the delay of critically needed interventions, while overestimation resulted in unnecessary and costly treatments with a greater risk for the patient (Association of Women's Health, Obstetric, and Neonatal Nurses, 2015). Visual estimations of blood loss have been historically completed by the delivering provider and/or the anesthesia provider. Subsequent to a literature review highlighting work completed by the California Maternal Quality Care Collaborative (CMQCC) in 2015 and the AIM, an obstetrician and a labor and delivery nurse (champion physician and champion nurse) began working on a protocol for the standardization of blood loss measurement following delivery. Additional literature was analyzed in order to establish methods for best practice, although this initiative was still in its infancy on a national level. They used the PDSA model to address the complexity of refining a method of measurement to provide the greatest accuracy. PDSA refers to a process for Plan-Do-Study-Act. It represents a quality improvement model widely used in healthcare settings, where small tests of change are completed before a final process is determined (Taylor et al., 2014). It is flexible and adaptable enough to determine "whether an intervention works in a particular setting … to [make] adjustments accordingly to increase the chances of delivering and sustaining the desired improvement" (Reed & Card, 2016, p. 147). The first stage, Plan, consists of identifying the change needed, selecting a team, and developing a plan for improvement. The second stage, Do, involves the implementation and testing of the planned process for change. The third stage, Study, comprises an analysis of the results and the success of the plan. The fourth stage, Act, includes a reflection on results, deciding whether to adopt, revise, or abandon the plan (Taylor et al., 2014; The Agency for Healthcare Research and Quality, 2020).

System and Key Players

The Plan stage of the PDSA cycle was set in motion when the physician and nurse champions identified the problem through the AIM initiative. The identification of the problem helped to establish the aim of raising awareness regarding the amount of blood loss incurred on each delivery (Donnelly & Kirk, 2015). Next, a team was selected in order to develop a plan for the quantification process. The selection process followed a systems thinking approach in order to encourage motivation, allow collaboration, focus on the work, and promote continuous learning by involving key players essential to the implementation of standardized quantitative blood loss calculation in the process (Stroh, 2015). Therefore, the champion physician and nurse created and facilitated the work of an ad hoc committee to move the change forward collaboratively. The ad hoc committee consisted of an obstetric nurse representative, the blood bank director, the blood bank technician, an anesthesia representative, in addition to the physician and nurse champions. The new initiative aided in the creation of a standardized and accurate method for quantifying blood loss following all deliveries. Table 14.1 summarizes the duties of each committee member in the hospital and their role in the ad hoc committee.

TABLE 14.1 Duties and Roles of ad hoc Committee Members

Ad hoc Committee Member	*Duties in the Hospital*	*Role on Committee*
Physician Champion	OB/GYN Provider	Conducts literature review. Provides feedback related to PDSA cycle changes. Acts as role model for physician staff support on process. Volunteers patients for small tests of changes.
Nursing Champion	Labor and Delivery (L&D) Educator	Conducts literature review. Implements process change through PDSA cycles in Delivery Room. Monitors Outcome Metrics. Educates nursing and physician staff. Acts as role model for nursing and physician staff support on process.
Obstetric Nurse Representative	Frontline L&D staff Member of C-section Team	Implements process change through PDSA cycles in Operating Room. Act as role model for nursing and physician staff support on process.
Blood Bank Director	Blood bank supervision	Assists with blood bank process for massive transfusion protocol (MTP). Creates policy for MTP.
Blood Bank Technician	Monitor outcome metrics related to blood utilization	Continues with blood utilization metrics and adds number of MTP each month.
Anesthesia Representative	Assist nursing staff with most efficient quantification process identified in the operating room Role model for anesthesia staff support	Collaborates and gives feedback about the patient's status during delivery.

The committee members reviewed the protocol and refined it, bringing individual perspectives from each of their areas of expertise. By April of 2016, the QBL protocol was refined enough to begin small tests of changes with the patients of the champion physician and other physician volunteers, as part of the Do-Study-Act phases of the PDSA cycle. Members of the ad hoc committee collaborated on different facets of the implementation and the management of the complex problem (Senge et al., 2012). For example, in the operating room, the obstetrician had to identify the amniotic fluid and separate it from blood loss; the obstetric nurse had to complete blood loss measurement by weighing all the bloody pads; the pharmacist supplied medication, the anesthesiologist had to support the patient status and administer the medications; while the blood bank technician provided any blood product needed.

As a subsystem of the hospital system at large, the ad hoc committee that laid the foundation for the protocol's implementation had to reach out to the next subsystem in which it resides, the Perinatal Quality Committee. This is a multidisciplinary committee in which all areas of hospital involved in obstetric services are represented. Any change in clinical practice requires approval by this group. Each month, the ad hoc committee for the QBL process reported process changes and subsequent progress to the Perinatal Quality Committee. Once the Perinatal Quality Committee reviewed and approved the protocol, the ad hoc committee presented it to the Department of OB/GYN, composed of obstetric medical staff, nursing leaders, and hospital administrators, for another round of review and approval. The protocol was later sent to the OB-GYN Advisory Committee, represented by physician, nursing, and business executives at the highest levels for review and recommendations for dissemination across the nine-hospital system. Baptist Memorial Hospital for Women in Memphis represents a referral perinatal center for the eight remaining hospitals in the region, delivering about 80 percent of pregnancies and representing about 90 percent of all physician providers. This overarching system includes nine acute care hospitals that provide perinatal services to the region. Figure 14.1 represents the system at large involved in the AIM initiative and the process of development and adoption of the protocol within it.

The systematic approach in the development of the protocol followed a bottom-up approach to leadership that led to effective implementation of change. In this case, the hospital managers and administrators valued the strengths and autonomy of the medical professionals, realized their influence on decision making, and fostered a climate of positive communication, productivity, and engagement (Ham, 2003; Northouse, 2021).

Case Analysis

Sustainment for the QBL initiative was accomplished over a period of two years, tackling a number of obstacles in the interim. Challenges to this change process centered around the reversal of responsibility from a prior subjective blood loss

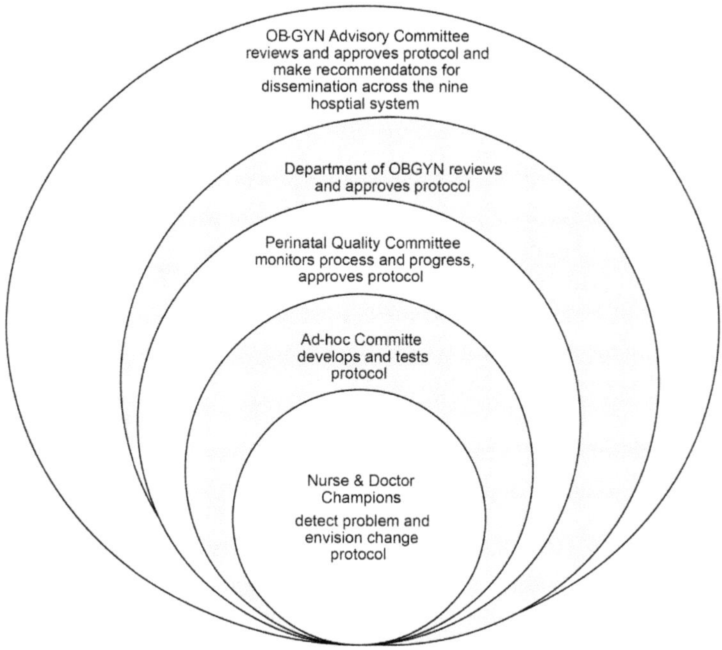

FIGURE 14.1 AIM Initiative System at Large

estimation from providers to a measured quantification completed by nursing and technician staff. First, the reversal of responsibility resulted in lack of engagement that was crucial for the project's success, especially from obstetric and anesthesia providers, who had traditionally been the "estimators of loss." A difficult transition for all, the responsibility for blood loss assessment was now reversed. While obstetric and anesthesia providers were losing a bit of autonomy, other staff members were taking on more responsibility. Second, the need for refining the method for measurement that provided the greatest accuracy developed reluctance by the nursing and technician staff with what they viewed as a complicated process and a skepticism that this method of measurement would prove to be more accurate than visual estimation.

However, through a series of PDSA cycles with changes in methods for measurement, measuring instruments and supplies, and personnel responsible for blood loss measurement, a largely smooth procedure for blood loss measurement was created.

By 2018, the QBL initiative was disseminated to the remaining facilities in the Baptist Memorial Healthcare system that provide obstetric services. Undertaking the standardization of blood loss calculation at this referral center was a good starting point to disseminate the information to the rest of the hospitals in the system.

Problem Resolution

The first test of change regarding the quantification process included the use of a graduated drape on vaginal deliveries for measurement of amniotic fluid and subsequent quantification of blood loss. Tabletop scales were initially used for weighing bloody materials manually. Laminated guides were placed in each room for the subtraction of dry weights. Later, a QBL calculator was designed for the electronic medical record, with all dry weights included for accurate computation on all deliveries. The tabletop scale was quickly replaced with the use of the infant scale in the room, which was ideal for measuring blood loss at the recommended 1 gm = 1 ml conversion. On Cesarean sections, the use of two suction canisters (one for the amniotic fluid, switched to another for blood loss) was later refined to the use of one canister to identify blood loss, to be marked after suctioning all amniotic fluid to accurately calculate subsequent blood loss. The Panda infant warmers in the operating rooms with embedded scales were used for weighing bloody materials on C-sections. These small tests of change resulted in a collaborative refinement of the QBL protocol through dialogue and team learning (Senge et al., 2012) Additionally, it helped team members align their mental models on the process by challenging their knowledge and beliefs and testing them against evidence emerging from the PDSA cycles (Cabrera & Cabrera, 2019).

Moreover, medical personnel responsibilities needed to shift. Initially, nursing staff were designated for the measurement of all bloody materials. It soon became apparent that for vaginal deliveries, the surgical technician was the more appropriate staff member for weighing laps and providing a number for quantified loss via the graduated drape, as the nurse was otherwise occupied with the mother and the infant. Over time, the quantification of blood loss was deferred by the physician and the anesthesia provider to the nurse or the technician in the room, who was diligently calculating and providing a cumulative measurement by which the physician could make educated decisions regarding the need for uterotonics (medication used to stop bleeding after delivery), additional interventions, or the replacement of blood products. This process facilitated the creation of a massive transfusion protocol to be used with significant hemorrhages, and based in part on quantified blood loss measurement.

On the other hand, a vital element for the success of QBL was providing the systems' team members with the education and the instruments necessary to accurately measure loss and to gain their confidence and acceptance regarding the new practice (Ladouceur & Goldbort, 2019). Beginning with the tertiary perinatal center, system-wide education was provided regarding the need for quantitative measurement and the evidence supporting it. Blood measurement labs were offered to all staff with simulated blood loss, incorporating visual estimations compared with the same loss in a quantified amount. This raised awareness regarding the inaccuracy of estimation.

The initial challenge of medical personnel reluctance was addressed through evidence of feasibility and accuracy of blood loss quantification. The smoothness of the procedure confirmed its feasibility and the accuracy of blood loss quantification proved how the initiative can alleviate a major problem faced in obstetrics care. Notably, the support of the physician champion was paramount for the engagement of all of the providers of care by presenting the change as growth not as loss, which in turn eased the resistance to change (Evans, 1996/2001).

Lessons Learned

The PDSA model for improvement reminded us that many times going back to the drawing board is necessary. The QBL process resulted in the timely identification of excessive blood loss, encouraging early intervention and the prevention of severe maternal morbidity and mortality subsequent to postpartum hemorrhage. Additionally, the process confirmed the importance of clear communication and addressing reluctance to clarify the feasibility of change for key players.

Conclusion

Change does not come quickly or easily. Hospital and medical staff engagement is critical for any large-scale change to occur. This process was initiated at the Baptist Memorial Healthcare system's tertiary care hospital and was spread to the remaining eight facilities which provide obstetric services. These nine facilities worked together to refine methods, protocols, and order sets in order to make the quantification process seamless and habitual for all staff.

Reflective Questions

- How would the dynamics in the system be changed if the hospital leadership followed a top-down approach?
- How would the key players measure the impact of change in blood loss quantification?
- How would the ad hoc committee measure the impact of change on the culture and perception of quality of care within L&D system?

Additional Resources

American College of Physicians. (n.d.). ACP Quality Connect: PDSA Planning Worksheet, 2018. https://30qkon2g8eif8wrj03zeh041-wpengine.netdna-ssl.com/wp-content/uploads/2017/05/ACP_PDSA-Planning-Worksheet.pdf.

California Department of Public Health (CDPH, 2015). Definition, early recognition, and rapid response using triggers. *California Maternal Quality Care Collaborative Obstetric Hemorrhage Toolkit, version 2.0*, 70–77.

Coury, J., Schneider, J. L., Rivelli, J. S., Petrik, A. F., Seibel, E., D'Agostini, B., … Coronado, G. D. (2017). Applying the Plan-Do-Study-Act (PDSA) approach to a large pragmatic study involving safety net clinics. *BMC Health Services Research, 17*(1), 1–10. https://doi.org/10.1186/s12913-017-2364-3

Gorenflo, G., & Moran, J. W. (2010). *The ABCS of PDCA. Public Health Foundation.* www.phf.org/resourcestools/Pages/The_ABCs_of_PDCA.aspx

Hall, L. L. (2019). *Plan-Do-Study-Act (PDSA): Accelerate quality improvement within your practice.* American Medical Association. https://edhub.ama-assn.org/steps-forward/module/2702507?resultClick=1&bypassSolrId=J_2702507

Leis, J. A., & Shojania, K. G. (2017). A primer on PDSA: Executing Plan-Do-Study-Act cycles in practice, not just in name. *BMJ Quality and Safety, 26*(7), 572–577. https://doi.org/10.1136/bmjqs-2016-006245

References

American College of Obstetricians and Gynecologists (ACOG, 2020). Alliance for innovation on maternal health (AIM). www.acog.org/practice-management/patient-safety-and-quality/partnerships/alliance-for-innovation-on-maternal-health-aim

American College of Obstetricians and Gynecologists (ACOG, 2019). Quantitative blood loss in obstetric hemorrhage: Committee opinion No. 794. *Obstetrics & Gynecology, 134*(6), e150–e162.

Association for Women's Health, Obstetric, and Neonatal Nurses (AWHONN, 2015). Quantification of blood loss: AWHONN practice brief number 1. *Journal of Obstetric, Gynecologic, and Neonatal Nurses, 44*, 96–98. doi:10.1111/1552-6909.12519

Cabrera, D., & Cabrera, L. (2019). What is systems thinking? In M. D. C. Michael J Spector, Barbara B Lockee (Ed.), *Learning, design, and technology: An international compendium of theory, research, practice, and policy* (pp. 1–28). Springer. https://doi.org/10.1007/978-3-319-63880-5_2

California Department of Public Health (CDPH, 2015). Cumulative quantitated assessment of blood loss. *California Maternal Quality Care Collaborative Obstetric Hemorrhage Toolkit, version 2.0*, 80–89.

Council on Patient Safety in Women's Health Care (2020). *Obstetric hemorrhage (+AIM).* https://safehealthcareforeverywoman.org/patient-safety-bundles/obstetric-hemorrhage/#link_acc-1-3-de

Donnelly, P., & Kirk, P. (2015). How to … use the PDSA model for effective change management. *Education for Primary Care, 26*, 279–281.

Evans, R. (1996/2001). *The human side of school change: Reform, resistance, and the real-life problems of innovations*. Jossey-Bass.

Ham, C. (2003). Improving the performance of health services: The role of clinical leadership. *Lancet, 361*(9373), 1978–1980. https://doi.org/10.1016/S0140-6736(03)13593-3

Ladouceur, M. K., & Goldbort, J. (2019). A proactive approach to quantification of blood loss in the perinatal setting. *Nursing for Women's Health, 23*(6), 471–477. doi:10.1016/j.nwh.2019.09.007

Northouse, P.G. (2021). *Introduction to leadership: Concepts and practice* (5th ed.). Sage.

Plan-Do-Study-Act (PDSA) Directions and examples. Content last reviewed September 2020. Agency for Healthcare Research and Quality. www.ahrq.gov/health-literacy/improve/precautions/tool2b.html

Reed J.E., & Card, A.J. (2016). The problem with Plan-Do-Study-Act cycles *BMJ Quality & Safety, 25*, 147–152.

Senge, P., Cambron-McCabe, N., Lucas, T. Smith B., & Duttoon, J. (2012). Schools that learn (Updated and Revised): A fifth discipline fieldbook for educators, parents, and everyone who cares about education. Currency.

Stroh, D. P. (2015). *Systems thinking for social change*. Chelsea Green Publishing.

Taylor, M.J., McNicholas, C., Nicolay, C., et al. (2014). Systematic review of the application of the plan-do-study-act method to improve quality in healthcare *BMJ Quality & Safety, 23*, 290–298.

World Health Organization (2012). *WHO recommendations for the prevention and treatment of postpartum haemorrhage.* https://apps.who.int/iris/bitstream/handle/10665/75411/9789241548502_eng.pdf;jsessionid=EB519BB951334A10246E7722E1527C05?sequence=1

15

STRUCTURING AND SUPPORTING AN ONLINE DOCTORAL PROGRAM

Administrative and Academic Challenges (Higher Education)

Rhonda Jeffries, Suha Rahif Tamim, Yasha Jones Becton, and Christopher Bogiages

Introduction

The Education Doctorate (EdD) in Educational Practice and Innovation with a concentration in Curriculum Studies (CS) is a doctoral program in the College of Education at the University of South Carolina focused on providing educators with an in-depth knowledge of social justice in diverse communities. The program equips education professionals with the ability to resolve problems of practice through collaboration with critical key players. Its unique design helps students to acquire the disposition of a scholarly practitioner needed for leadership positions at the school (instructional), district (administrative), and other institutional (e.g., higher education, non-profit) levels.

The EdD-CS concentration emphasizes concerns for equity and social justice, self-knowledge, cultural issues, and human growth and development through a balanced approach to diversity education consisting of theory and practice. This concentration provides an in-depth understanding of the theory, history, concepts, current techniques, strategies, and issues of diversity in schools, as well as other social institutions and community settings; and facilitates self-reflection for engaging in social justice education. Graduates of the EdD-CS program return to the field of education well equipped to strategically address opportunity gaps within K-12 and higher educational systems, as well as ameliorating unjust learning conditions for traditionally marginalized student populations.

Since its inception, the EdD-CS program has embraced a responsibility to improve educational outcomes for the students and teachers of South Carolina. In order to respond to immense changes in teaching and learning in the 21st century, South Carolina teachers needed access to quality professional development, especially those living in remote, rural, and sometimes impoverished communities.

DOI: 10.4324/9781003028772-18

Expanding access to professional learning became one motivating factor for the development of our 100 percent online EdD-CS program. Moving from offering distance courses through live video meetings that were relegated to satellite sites throughout the state of South Carolina, the shift to web-based online offerings removed limitations of access to courses and created the beginning of a global program as early as 1999. In 2000, the program dedicated significant effort toward focusing the degree on equity issues through a series of curriculum and course changes. Previously operating as a curriculum generalist degree, the revised focus on diversity, equity, and inclusivity was coupled with a major program format change from a traditional campus-based doctoral program to a hybrid model including approximately 50 percent of the program of study being offered online and the remaining 50 percent of the program of study being offered on campus. In 2014, the program of study shifted to a 100 percent online degree continuing to offer 60 credit hours of graduate level coursework. This shift responded immediately to geographical access issues existing not only throughout the state of South Carolina, but nationally and internationally. Other variables that were impacted through this reform effort include asynchronous scheduling solutions, financial access through management of cost to obtain the degree, and time to degree completion.

System and Key Players

Changing the EdD-CS program from brick and mortar to 100 percent online demanded a collaborative effort with several key players at different levels in the university. University administrators responded over time to doctoral student requests and marketplace competition which were primary drivers for the program change over time to a 100 percent online platform. Change decisions ultimately rested with university administrators. Doctoral students gradually shifted from consumers of knowledge to consumers of goods in the systems change decision trail. Department and program faculty provided expertise to inform university administrators' reform initiatives, but ultimate decisions may not have fully acknowledged faculty voice. This chapter will describe the systems dynamics among key players including university administrators, department and program faculty, and doctoral students.

Case Analysis

Moving the program online entailed three major changes: the adoption of an accelerated program of 36 months, which included completion of a dissertation, the shift from the conventional semester-long courses to compressed eight-week courses, and the selection of a cohort model where students take one course at a time. Several advantages drove these design decisions. First, accelerated programs attract adult learners who perceive this model as manageable with a clear strategy for completion (Serdyukov, 2008). Second, cohort models help students balance academic, professional, and personal responsibilities (Fenning, 2004); cohorts enhance the sense of community among students and help them bond as scholarly practitioners (Swayze & Jakeman, 2014); and cohorts facilitate program delivery and management (Browne-Ferrigno & Muth, 2003). Third, compressed courses keep students focused and are perceived by them as more time efficient than semester-long courses, even though they embed the same learning outcomes and credit hours (Serdyukov, 2008). These advantages that benefit students and support program management posed administrative and academic challenges.

Administrative and academic challenges revolved around creating balance among the goals and objectives of established and emerging systems and the philosophies and expectations of key players. Administratively, university leadership decided to partner the program with an online program management (OPM) provider that directed recruitment and motivated enrollment decisions. The choice to create an OPM partnership was primarily based on the university's desire to increase enrollment but did not fully consider faculty resistance to the consumer of goods model implemented by the OPM system. Communication among the OPM partnership, university administration, and program faculty was rarely synchronized and resulted in a myriad of misunderstandings between prospective doctoral students and program faculty regarding admissions requirements and matriculation expectations. The OPM staff were incentivized by student enrollment, and they often advised prospective students that they could perfunctorily complete application forms and register for classes to begin the program. This advisement pattern diametrically opposed the program's admission criteria that heavily considered students' writing skills and dispositions as critical to their success in the program and ultimately determined their admission decision. OPM providers operating for profit are chosen by university administrators to structure and support online programs to provide some of the start-up web-based course development skills and specialized marketing techniques that may not exist within the existing university structure (Springer, 2018). In this case, the program's 15-year history with web-based courses that were offered during its hybrid phase positioned the faculty to understand and implement this aspect successfully without the OPM's assistance. Furthermore, the marketing efforts provided by the OPM were generic and disregarded the faculty's academic expertise. While this partnership was intended to support program recruitment and development, these efforts significantly conflicted with the academic goals and standards set by the program faculty and needed to be reconsidered.

Academically, the expanded 100 percent online program required balance between the quality of teaching and learning and the faculty's ability to manage increased numbers of students. Faculty and students navigated the compressed core courses relatively well; however, the faculty's ability to handle a sizable number of dissertations simultaneously emerged as a pressing challenge, which is common in cohort online programs (Kumar & Johnson, 2019). Consequently, the alignment of the dissertation process across courses and among faculty prompted program changes. These changes entailed embedding dissertation elements into research and theory courses to maintain the accelerated design, which resulted in students receiving dissertation guidance from multiple professors. In this new model, students write drafts of the first three chapters in three courses designed independently by each professor who is not necessarily their advisor. As the initial cohorts rotated through coursework and collaborated with their advisors to finalize the dissertation, inconsistencies in quality and process surfaced. These inconsistencies were expected due to the dynamic interplay between the components of the program's complex system (Bryk et al., 2015), namely student, faculty, and the cohort accelerated online model. On one hand, mentoring dissertations online is not easy for faculty. They need to provide detailed asynchronous feedback to a significant number of students, negotiate variation in students' research and writing skills, and manage divergent research topics. On the other hand, students in online doctoral program need structure, clear expectations, and support (Kumar & Johnson, 2019) in order to overcome transactional distance (Moore, 2013). The problem of producing quality student outcomes created the need to find solution strategies (Pretz, Naples, & Sterberg, 2003).

Problem Resolution

The inability to synchronize systems goals and objectives among the key players including OPM, university administrators, and program faculty ultimately resulted in the dissolution of the partnership. Variables including the terms of contract, the inability of the OPM staff to accurately represent the program, and the financial albatross of the partnership produced high levels of faculty, staff, and student dissatisfaction. With student recruitment being the OPM priority and insignificant levels of support being provided to address student retention, this variable became elemental in addressing program quality and institutional accountability (Shaw, Ferguson, & Burrus, 2016). Therefore, program faculty and college administration collectively designed internal systems of marketing and web site management in addition to hiring a college recruitment officer and an online faculty student manager to address retention. These efforts responded to the ineffective and inefficient partnership which was dissolved at the end of the five-year contract. The administrative challenges of OPM systems are well documented (Combe, 2005; Hughes, 2012; Russell, 2010), and it is clear that decision making, expectation alignment, collaboration, and accountability are the variables that drive universities to terminate these partnerships after recognizing that the externally provided services can be better offered internally (Springer, 2018). This transformation mirrored Kotter's (2018) eight-step process for leading change. It began with establishing a sense of urgency triggered by the dissatisfaction and the financial burden of the partnership. The optics of a doctoral program that enrolls students, collects tuition dollars, and graduates low numbers of students was simply unacceptable. Then, it aimed at creating a guiding coalition of members with diverse roles, developing a vision and a strategy, communicating it, and empowering action through the coordinated work between program faculty and college administration, resulting in dissolving the partnership and designing internal systems of marketing. Finally, it is focused on sustaining change, achieved through hiring a college recruitment officer and an online faculty student manager.

Once this first phase of change was accomplished, efforts shifted toward addressing inconsistencies in the quality of student outcomes to sustain student retention further (Kotter, 2018). The faculty expressed the need to collaborate (Browne-Ferrigno & Muth, 2003) and develop a guidance document of criteria for quality of the dissertation process and product. A program sub-committee reviewed dissertation-embedded course expectations to determine appropriate alignment. Varied experiences and assumptions among faculty ranged from epistemological beliefs about research methodologies and views about advising students virtually. These inconsistencies were explored in a series of meetings designed to think, learn, and act together (Senge, 2012). The sub-committee created a virtual space to collaborate on reviewing the guidelines and the rubrics that guide the writing process. This virtual space provided a visual representation of the inconsistencies (Bryk et al., 2015) and allowed for mental organization of the problem and solutions (Pretz, Naples, & Sterberg, 2003). Moreover, through inquiry and reflection, continuously questioning the causes behind inconsistencies and conversing about their views and assumptions, the committee members resolved disagreements, determined the desired criteria, and created a shared vision on the components of each chapter (Bryk, 2015; Senge, 2012), which resulted in common guidance criteria and documents. These guidance documents were shared with the full program faculty and with doctoral students for feedback and improvement to ensure buy-in and to disseminate the shared vision across the program's system. The work of the committee at the micro level (expectations and product of dissertation chapters in specific courses) revealed the disequilibrium the program changes caused to the dissertation process. On the other hand, it set the stage for a collective transformation (Reigeluth, 2019) on guidance of the dissertation at the program level and led to a review of the course sequence. Moreover, it established the foundation of a professional learning community (Hilliard, 2012) tasked with strengthening the advisement on the dissertation process to continuously reflect and adjust (Senge, 2012) and to benefit both students and faculty. This systems thinking approach enabled buy-in from every faculty member and the adoption of the agreed upon dissertation guidance documents (Senge, 2012).

Reigeluth (2019) explained: "for a system to be healthy, it must coevolve with its environment: It changes in response to changes in its environment, and its environment changes in response to its changes" (p. 2). He continued, "systems can be in a state of disequilibrium, in which case, they approach 'the edge of chaos'" (pp. 4–5). This is when the system transforms, "modifying the structure of a system, usually in response to new needs" (p. 5). Administratively, the system responded to data from faculty, students, and the relevant literature indicating needed changes in OPM. Academically, faculty responded to outcome indicators that drove the need to sustain and improve quality.

Lessons Learned

Transitioning to a 100 percent online graduate program presented several successes and challenges. Successes included key players understanding and accepting the need for change, which created a sense of ownership and established a shared vision. In addition, key players took a collaborative approach for change, allowing the input of multiple perspectives and contributions (Peck, 2019). On the other hand, the shift to 100 percent asynchronous online instruction that introduced an immediate expansion of the program created the challenge of meeting the needs of students. The creation of an online faculty student manager provided an initial advisor for every student which ensured smooth advancement in this accelerated program. Also, the addition of new faculty members into the program enabled increased mentoring opportunities for the increased number of student cohorts. From the students' perspective, the program expansion provided a much more diverse pool of doctoral candidates and a great deal of dialogue and rich virtual communication. While the communication provided a rich environment for the sharing of ideas, it was a particular challenge when dealing with sometimes controversial content such as ableism, gender, heteronormativity, race/ethnicity, religion/spirituality, and social class and how these issues influence instructional methods and educational environments.

Conclusion

The strategies used to address the challenges and opportunities generated from the decision to shift the program to 100 percent online at the administrative and academic levels were collaborative and evolutionary. Critical to these adjustments are the program's commitment to maintain its focus on social justice and advance its mission toward activism while mitigating the administrative policies that govern the university setting. These opportunities for reform will likely expand as universities presently adjust to pre- and post-COVID-19 economic and social challenges which are invariably driving more university faculty to accommodate students' online learning needs.

With increased marketplace competition and technological advancements, budget model reforms must account for the qualitative factors that support engaged faculty governance and produce strong student outcomes. Kastens and Manduca (2017) suggested this be done by identifying mutually beneficial methods of problem solving, establishing criteria that produce replicable outcomes, designing streams of feedback to guide behaviors and future choices, and evaluating critical information that impacts the larger system of higher education. Systems change decisions will need to draw from the talented faculty and students who are invested in the organization to attract new key players and keep the system vibrant and thriving.

Reflective Questions

- How might university administrators and program faculty best negotiate the competing agendas of increased student enrollment, institutional budget challenges, and faculty welfare?
- This doctoral program transitioned from a hybrid program to a 100 percent online program. How might the shift from a synchronous hybrid model to an asynchronous online program impact the type of student recruited by the program?
- How could faculty mitigate the challenges faced in the dissertation process to set clear expectations for students while maintaining a level of autonomy and differentiation on dissertation guidance?

Additional Resources

Cabrera, D., & Cabrera, L. (2019). Complexity and systems thinking models in education: Applications for leaders. In M. J. Spector, B. B. Lockee, & M. D. Childress (Eds.), *Learning, design, and technology: An international compendium of theory, research, practice, and policy* (pp. 1–29). Springer. https://doi.org/10.1007/978-3-319-17727-4_101-1

Fullan, M. (2006). The future of educational change: System thinkers in action. *Journal of Educational Change*, 7, 113–122. https://doi.org/10.1007/s10833-006-9003-9

Grady, M. L. (2018). Online doctoral education: Strategies and resources for faculty advisors. *Journal of Learning in Higher Education, 14*(1), 17–20. Retrieved from http://files/504/Grady – 2018 – Online Doctoral Education Strategies and Resource.pdf

Lowenthal, P. R., Nyland, R., Jung, E., Dunlap, J. C., & Kepka, J. (2019). Does class size matter? An exploration into faculty perceptions of teaching high-enrollment online courses. *American Journal of Distance Education, 33*(3), 152–168. https://doi.org/10.1080/08923647.2019.1610262

Singh, V., & Thurman, A. (2019). How many ways can we define online learning? A systematic literature review of definitions of online learning (1988–2018). *American Journal of Distance Education, 33*(4), 289–306. https://doi.org/10.1080/08923647.2019.1663082

References

Browne-Ferrigno, T., & Muth, R. (2003). Effects of cohorts on learners. *Journal of School Leadership, 13*(6), 621–643. https://doi.org/10.1177/105268460301300602

Bryk, A. S., Gomez, L. M., Grunow, A., LeMahieu, P. G. (2015). *Learning to improve: How America's schools can get better at getting better.* Harvard Education Press.

Combe, C. (2005). Developing and implementing an online doctoral programme. *International Journal of Educational Management, 19*(2), 118–127.

Costa, A. de, & Kallick, B. (2004). *Assessment strategies for self-directed learning*. Corwin Press.

Fenning, K. (2004). Cohort based learning: Application to learning organizations and student academic success. *College Quarterly*, *07*(1), 1–11. http://eric.ed.gov/?id=EJ852017

Harasim, L. M. (2012). *Learning theory and online technology*. Routledge.

Hilliard, A. T. (2012). Practices and value of a professional learning community in higher education. *Contemporary Issues in Education Research (CIER)*, *5*(2), 71. https://doi.org/10.19030/cier.v5i2.6922

Hughes, R., Jr., Bowers, J. R., Mitchell, E. T., Curtiss, S., & Ebata, A. T. (2012). Developing online family life prevention and education programs. *Family Relations*, *61*(5), 711–727.

Kastens, K. A., & Manduca, C. A. (2017) Using systems thinking in the design, implementation, and evaluation of complex educational innovations, with examples from the InTeGrate Project. *Journal of Geoscience Education*, *65*(3), 219–230. DOI: 10.5408/16-225.1

Kotter, J. P. (2018). *The eight-step process for leading change*. www.kotterinc.com/8-steps-process-for-leading-change/

Kumar, S., & Johnson, M. (2019). Online mentoring of dissertations: the role of structure and support. *Studies in Higher Education*, *44*(1), 59–71. https://doi.org/10.1080/03075079.2017.1337736

Moore, M. G. (2013). The theory of transactional distance. In M. G. Moore (Ed.), *Handbook of distance education* (3rd ed., pp. 66–85). Routledge.

Moore, M. G., & Kearsley, G. (2005). *Distance education: A systems view*. Thomson Wadsworth.

Peck, K. L. (2019). A change model mashup to guide educational system change participants. In M. J. Spector, B. B. Lockee, & M. D. Childress (Eds.), *Learning, design, and technology: An international compendium of theory, research, practice, and policy* (pp. 1–24). Springer. https://doi.org/10.1007/978-3-319-17727-4_89-1

Pretz, J. E., Naples, A. J., & Sterberg, R. J. (2003). Recognizing, defining, and representing problems. In J. E. Davidson & R. J. Sternberg (Eds.), *The psychology of problem solving* (pp. 1–394). Cambridge University Press. https://doi.org/10.1017/CBO9780511615771

Reigeluth, C. M. (2019). Chaos theory and the sciences of complexity: Foundations for transforming educational systems. In M. J. Spector, B. B. Lockee, & M. D. Childress (Eds.) *Learning, design, and technology* (pp. 1–12). Cham: Springer International Publishing. doi: https://doi.org/10.1007/978-3-319-17727-4

Russell, A. (2010). *Outsourcing instruction: Issues for public colleges and universities. A higher education policy brief.* American Association of State Colleges and Universities. Retrieved from www.aascu.org/policy/publications/policy-matters/2010/outsourcing.pdf

Senge, P. M. (2012). *Schools that learn: A fifth discipline fieldbook for educators, parents, and everyone who cares about education*. Crown Business.

Serdyukov, P. (2008). Accelerated learning: What is it? *Journal of Research in Innovative Teaching*, *1*(1), 35–59.

Shaw, M., Ferguson, K., & Burrus, S. (2016). Factors that influence student attrition in online courses. *Proceedings of the Distance Learning Administration Conference*. University of West Georgia Distance & Distributed Education Center.

Springer, S. (2018). One university's experience partnering with an online program management (OPM) provider: A case study. *Online Journal of Distance Learning Administration*, *21*(1), 1–15. www.learntechlib.org/p/188465/.

Swayze, S., & Jakeman, R. C. (2014). Student perceptions of communication, connectedness, and learning in a merged cohort course. *Journal of Continuing Higher Education*, *62*(2), 102–111. https://doi.org/10.1080/07377363.2014.915446

16

LET'S IDEA RELAY

Strategy for Harnessing Collective Intelligence (Higher Education)

Meng-Fen Grace Lin, Ariana Eichelberger, and Peter Leong

Introduction

Higher education faces unprecedented pressure to continuously innovate and stay relevant. In addition to the challenges of bureaucracy and divergent goals among stakeholders, academic units often have limited resources to develop new and meaningful ideas for change. When universities respond to change, it often happens at the department level through faculty collaboration and decision-making. However, departments tend to be composed of faculty with diverse perspectives and cultural backgrounds. Cultural differences have been found to account for varying expectations of communication and behavioral meeting norms (Köhler, Cramton, & Hinds, 2012) and for impacting team and meeting processes (Brannen & Salk, 2000). Meetings can be emotionally laden due to their goal-related activities, social interactions, and status dynamics (Rogelberg, Scott, & Kello, 2007). Yet, the ultimate goal of a successful faculty meeting is one in which transformational conversations can take place where members deeply listen to each other and collectively seek solutions (Bowman, 2015). The question then becomes, how can university departments harness the uniqueness and diversity of its individual members into a collective intelligence that leads to innovative solutions for departmental problems? From a systems thinking perspective, units in higher education should move from focusing on individual expertise to collective intelligence. This case study describes one academic department's experience implementing an idea relay strategy to harness the diverse expertise of participants to develop innovative ideas for programmatic change.

DOI: 10.4324/9781003028772-19

System and Key Players

The department is situated in a college of education (COE) comprised of ten departments, 225 faculty and 1,947 undergraduate and graduate students. This COE is the primary preparer of teachers going into the state's public school system and is a distance education leader at its campus, with the highest number of distance programs of any college at its campus. The department was made up of ten faculty members, all but one had earned tenure. The number of years faculty had spent with the department ranged from less than three years to over 30. In addition to cultural differences, faculty members varied in age, cultural background, experience, tenure status, and administrative experience. In the department's traditional face-to-face meetings, some members tended to assert more control over decision-making than others. Not all participants felt comfortable expressing their opinions and few clear decision-making processes were in place.

Case Analysis

The department had experienced a significant drop in enrollment and was exploring innovative programmatic changes that would better address student needs. Faculty and administrators in American institutions of higher education typically participate in policy and decision-making through shared governance (Leach, 2008) which commonly requires participation on committees and in meetings (Olson, 2009). Meetings are critical to smooth operations of organizations (Angouri & Marra, 2011) and have important functions for information sharing, decision-making, and social interaction (Mroz et al., 2018). Meetings in which participants can interact on issues related to their group norms and personal values increase trust and cooperation, which are related to an institution's effectiveness (Birnbaum, 2004). An institution's effectiveness is partly the result of its ability to generate innovative solutions, yet all too often individuals within complicated systems resist change as it would disrupt the benefits they receive in the short term. Truly innovative solutions often require stakeholders to forfeit some short-term gains in service of longer-term benefits (Stroh, 2015). Clearly, the challenges higher education institutions now face need innovative solutions. However, it is not enough to focus solely on solutions, the decision-making processes themselves also need to be considered (Eckel, 2006). Collaboration can be a powerful strategy in decision-making toward innovative solutions (Eddy, 2010) and supports formation of a group's collective or shared vision, a critical component of long-term change (Senge, 2006).

Within department meetings, a whole-group discussion was the primary method of communication and decision-making. However, this method posed issues in that not all members felt willing or able to contribute. Those most willing to speak up were most often heard from, guided the discussion, and strongly influenced the subsequent decisions made. Cultural values and tenure status may have played a role in these interpersonal dynamics.

In addition, while productive ideas and details often arose in meeting conversations, they may not have been written down, or if recorded, they were recorded by one individual. Therefore, the level of detail would depend on the note-taker's knowledge of the subject.

Furthermore, if a proposal for change was agreed upon, traditionally the person who proposed the idea would be charged with leading, developing, and implementing it. The fact that members of the department already had full workloads often discouraged the sharing of new ideas.

Cultural differences have been found to account for varying expectations of communication and behavioral meeting norms (Köhler, Cramton, & Hinds, 2012) and for impacting team and meeting processes (Brannen & Salk, 2000). The department's diversity in faculty members, which included a mix of junior and senior faculty at various career stages from different cultural backgrounds brought a multitude of perspectives and lenses through which to view problems. Yet, the traditional large group discussions did not capture its diversity of knowledge and experience.

Problem Resolution

The department usually held an annual all-day retreat to discuss issues beyond the scope of a monthly departmental meeting. In previous retreats, the department had used various techniques to harness collective intelligence of the diverse members of the department to seek innovative solutions for departmental problems. Examples of techniques used in previous retreats include online, anonymous, modified Delphi processes, small group verbal consensus building using affinity diagrams, generating "How Might We" questions, and large group voting (Lin & Eichelberger, 2020, 2019).

A goal of a recent retreat was to develop programmatic change and experiment with new communication and decision-making techniques. A pre-retreat online survey helped identify and rank programmatic solutions that the department could implement. Solutions included creating an undergraduate minor, developing a micro-credentialing program, and creating an undergraduate-to-masters pathway (4+1). To facilitate a process that would foster equal voice and emphasize the "collective intelligence" of the department, an idea relay technique was used at the retreat to develop each solution proposal.

Participants were randomly divided into three small groups, with each group assigned to work on a proposal. A set of prompts was developed by the retreat's faculty facilitators to assist participants to expand on each proposal. Sample prompts included "What do we know about this proposed solution?" "How would this benefit the department?" "How would success be evaluated?" and "What are the expected outcomes?" Three Google docs with the same prompts were created, one for each of the top-ranked solutions. In the first round, groups were given 20 minutes to collaborate and respond to the prompts in their shared document. The

Google docs were then rotated between groups and 20 more minutes were spent to further develop each proposal. In round two, participants were encouraged to expand, add to, or modify existing ideas. The Google docs were then rotated a final time, and a final 20 minutes spent integrating the ideas provided by the previous two groups. In this way, each group worked on each individual proposal.

Several salient yet important design strategies are worth noting. First, three shared Google docs where all participants had editing privileges were used. The use of a shared document afforded the group to openly build additional ideas on top of ideas suggested by others. Using a shared document not only created the environment and expectation of a transparent process, but the document also functioned as documentation of all opinions. In this fashion, no one voice was lost but was instead expanded upon. Second, each small group was instructed to use a different color text in each round of editing. This small step created a transparent record of the process. Through this process, participants were able to trust that their contributions were recorded and would stay on record. Last, the time-limit focused discussions, created an agile and fun process, and encouraged participants to think on their feet. This process facilitated more spontaneous idea formation, a contrast to traditional meetings in which ideas can be overanalyzed, judged prematurely, and it takes a long time to make decisions. The artificial time constraint helped foster creativity. These strategies were designed based on Kowch's (2019) notion that systems thinking involves the dynamic interplay of an individual's culture and ideas. Furthermore, these strategies enabled team members to test and align their shared understanding of the proposed solution against their own mental model and prior knowledge (Schaveling & Bryan, 2017).

Lessons Learned

As evidenced through post-retreat interviews, participants overwhelmingly appreciated the idea relay activity. They drew on each other's expertise and learned along the way. Participants reported that they felt they had an equal opportunity to voice their opinions in a non-threatening way and that all voices had been considered without censorship. The technique successfully harnessed collective intelligence and facilitated collaboration. Some specific lessons gleaned from the activity include:

1. Equalize Voice and Perspectives

Feedback indicated that the idea relay captured the department's collective intelligence. One participant explained,

> One of the things I appreciated about the process is I feel like the process is sort of set up to both distill a group direction and provide individuals their

> opportunity to give their own perspective, but also eliminate their ability to dissent with the group direction later.

Another participant said,

> You're kind of building your ideas on top of their ideas. And so it felt like that was kind of the true kind of group collaboration … building each other's ideas on top of each other's ideas. A good strategy to do the group work using a small group setting [dividing] bigger group work into small groups. So I thought that strategy was really good.

Yet another participant shared that the process facilitated both individual ideas and group discussion, saying, "this series of activities gave adequate time for people to reflect individually, adequate opportunity to share ideas and priorities, and also narrowed the field in a rational manner."

2. *Maintain the Momentum or Call for Action*

A day-long retreat took a tremendous amount of time for the facilitators to plan and facilitate. It was also costly as it demanded a full day of everyone's time. At the conclusion of the retreat, there were three documents containing a list of ideas as to how we might implement each of the solutions addressing the enrollment shortages. However, nothing happened after the retreat itself. The enthusiasm created at the retreat was lost and momentum dropped. In retrospect, a day of meaningful engagement resulted in no specific action plan. Follow-up and follow-through on action items is critical for moving an organizational forward (Francisco, 2007).

A more productive retreat ending would have included a brief planning session in which a list of action items was created, volunteers assigned to accomplish each item and a follow-up meeting scheduled.

3. *Cultivate a Designer's Mindset*

Post-retreat interviews also revealed that many felt they were not ready to commit to any of the top-ranked ideas at the conclusion of the retreat. There are several reasons why this might be the case. Selecting any programmatic change and shepherding it to fruition is a monumental task requiring time and resources. This may have seemed too big a decision to make after one day. Some felt they were not educated enough on the details of the ideas. While these concerns are real, they contrast with a designer's mindset. A designer experiments and builds their way forward, fails early, and learns along the way. Such a mindset calls for small and agile steps to problem solving (Brown, 2008).

4. Tackle Traditional Challenges

Within the traditional systems of higher education such as tenure and promotion, many faculty are already overburdened by the expectations of service, teaching, and research. Committing to additional tasks might overwhelm already tight schedules. Hence, it is not surprising that no action was taken after the retreat.

Conclusion

This first experiment with an idea relay strategy yielded positive results for the department. Within the system of one academic unit, the strategy tapped into the interconnectedness of its members to create a shared consensus. Drawing on this experiment, and following the systems thinking perspective, the next logical step would be to invite other stakeholders such as alumni and administrators to participate in a similar activity.

Reflective Questions

- What other strategies could an academic department utilize to encourage equal voice in order to capture its collective intelligence?
- How might an academic department cultivate a designer's mindset culture?
- How might an academic department cultivate a culture of innovation and motivate faculty to take on additional tasks?
- How might an academic department use a single event such as a retreat as a starting point for new possibilities?

References

Angouri, J., & Marra, M. (2011). Corporate meetings as genre: A study of the role of the chair in corporate meeting talk. *Text & Talk – An Interdisciplinary Journal of Language, Discourse & Communication Studies, 30*(6), 615–636. https://doi.org/10.1515/text.2010.030

Birnbaum, R. (2004). The end of shared governance: Looking ahead or looking back. *New Directions for Higher Education, 2004*(127), 5–22. https://doi.org/10.1002/he.152

Bowman, R. F. (2015). Faculty meetings: Hidden conversational dynamics, *The Clearing House: A Journal of Educational Strategies, Issues and Ideas, 88*(5), 141–145, https://doi.org/10.1080/00098655.2015.1051499

Brannen, M. Y., & Salk, J. E. (2000). Partnering across borders: Negotiating organizational culture in a German-Japanese joint venture. *Human Relations, 53*(4), 451–487. https://doi.org/10.1177/0018726700534001

Brown, T. (2008). Design thinking. *Harvard Business Review, June 2008*, 1–9.

Eckel, P. D. (2006). *The shifting frontiers of academic decision making: Responding to new priorities, following new pathways*. Greenwood Publishing Group.

Eddy, P. L. (2010). *Partnerships and Collaboration in Higher Education: AEHE*. Wiley.

Francisco, J. M. (2007). How to create and facilitate meetings that matter. *The Information Management Journal, 41*(6), 54–58.

Köhler, T., Cramton, C. D., & Hinds, P. J. (2012). The meeting genre across cultures: Insights from three German–American collaborations. *Small Group Research*, *43*(2), 159–185. https://doi.org/10.1177/1046496411429600

Kowch, E. G. (2019). Introduction to systems thinking and change. In M. J. Spector, B. B. Lockee, & M. D. Childress (Eds.), *Learning, design, and technology* (pp. 1–14). Springer International Publishing. https://doi.org/10.1007/978-3-319-17727-4_133-1

Leach, W. D. (2008). *Shared governance in higher education: Structural and cultural responses to a changing national climate*. Available at SSRN 1520702 (SSRN Scholarly Paper No. ID 1520702). Social Science Research Network. https://papers.ssrn.com/abstract=1520702

Leach, D., Rogelberg, S. G., Warr, P. B., & Burnfield, J. L. (2009). Perceived meeting effectiveness: The role of design characteristics. *Journal of Business and Psychology*, *24*(1), 65–76. https://doi.org/10.1007/s10869-009-9092-6

Lin, M. F. G., & Eichelberger, A. (2019). Flip that meeting: Online consensus building in an academic department. *International Journal for Educational Media and Technology*, *13*(2), 44–52.

Lin, M. F. G., & Eichelberger, A. (2020). Design thinking as a catalyst for change: Faculty reaction to a redesigned meeting. *Journal of Formative Design in Learning*, *4*(1), 34–42. https://doi.org/10.1007/s41686-020-00046-2

Mroz, J. E., Allen, J. A., Verhoeven, D. C., & Shuffler, M. L. (2018). Do we really need another meeting? The science of workplace meetings. *Current Directions in Psychological Science*, *27*(6), 484–491. https://doi.org/10.1177/0963721418776307

Olson, G. A. (2009, July 23). Exactly what is "shared governance"? *The Chronicle of Higher Education*. www.chronicle.com/article/Exactly-What-Is-Shared/47065

Rogelberg, S., Scott, C., & Kello, J. (2007). The science and fiction of meetings. *MIT Sloan Management Review*, *48*(2), 18–21.

Schaveling, J., & Bryan, B. (2017). *Making better decisions using systems thinking: How to stop firefighting, deal with root causes and deliver permanent solutions*. Springer International Publishing AG.

Senge, P. M. (2006). *The fifth discipline: The art and practice of the learning organization*. Currency.

Stroh, D. P. (2015). *Systems thinking for social change: A practical guide to solving complex problems, avoiding unintended consequences, and achieving lasting results*. Chelsea Green Publishing.

17

THE CASE OF SITUATED LEARNING EXPERIENCES FOR SECONDARY SCHOOL ADULT CERTIFICATION (EDUCATION/INTERNATIONAL)

Mónica Sulecio de Alvarez

Introduction

In this chapter, the systemic approach to the design and development of six modules with their corresponding lessons is analyzed. Such modules were created for a secondary school program in Guatemala which is attended by young adults and adults who were not able to complete their school degree at the regular age.

Guatemala is a Latin American country located at the start of the Central American isthmus with a population of nearly 16.5 million people (*Estimaciones y proyecciones nacionales de población: Metodología y principales resultados*, 2020, p. 12). Spanish is the official language, but there are 22 other Mayan languages spoken, plus the language of Xinkas (Richards, 2003). Enrollment rates are higher for elementary school than for secondary school, but attrition is higher in secondary school (see Table 17.1). This situation leaves many adults without the diploma needed to enter college or access higher-income jobs.

Low enrollment in secondary school may be explained by different causes. One reason is the limited offering available, and since it is mainly from the private sector, it is hard to afford by low-income parents who need their children to start working early in order to contribute to their household. Reasons for not attending secondary school also include being over the official age group, racism (private secondary school in some places is mainly attended by non-indigenous students), sexual harassment, and bullying. Lack of enrollment is also affected by poor quality of education, violence in school and weak psychological and social well-being of teenagers (Molina & Peñate, 2014). When young men make it to the secondary level, they may stop attending in order to prioritize work to provide for their own family; young women may leave school due to pregnancy or the need to help with household chores and/or to take care of siblings or children of their

DOI: 10.4324/9781003028772-20

TABLE 17.1 Enrollment and Attrition Rates in Guatemala

Level		*Net Enrollment Rates*		*Attrition Rates*	
		Female (2015)	*Male (2015)*	*Female (2015)*	*Male (2015)*
Elementary (equivalent to grades 2nd–7th)		80.0%	80.8	3.2%	3.6%
Secondary School	Basic cycle (equivalent to grades 8th–10th)	44.8%	46.9%	5.6%	7.4%
	High school (equivalent to grades 11th–12th)	24.5%	23.5%	4.5%	6.6%

Source: República de Guatemala: Compendio Estadístico de Educación 2015, 2016.

own. In general, the country suffers from very low investment in teenagers and from absence of strategies that consider teenagers as a group to prioritize investment (Molina & Peñate, 2014).

For those individuals who were not able to finish secondary school, public programs are in place. Such programs offer varied and flexible schedules to allow participants to meet work and family responsibilities during the week, attending face-to-face classes in their spare time (at night or during the weekend). The problem observed with the current solution is that it can still be more effective and attractive for the target population by replacing school-like patterns that disconnect them from authentic life-long learning. Such patterns follow the traditional school dynamics, which was tailored for the industrial-age society (Aslan & Reigeluth, 2013) and which limits agency in learning and doing (Chavajay & Rogoff, 2002). The following are common components of the current solution:

- Content as an end, isolated in school subjects (math, language, science, etc.);
- School-type schedules with 40-minute classes to "teach" every subject;
- Teachers working in silos;
- Classroom arrangement with boards at the front and desks in rows for big groups of students to "receive" class;
- Homework targeted to practice subject content.

The education system has already failed these individuals once, and by following the traditional content-based/teacher-centered paradigm in adult programs, the system is at risk of failing them twice. The use of reductionist, analytic, and mechanistic approaches alone to solve educational problems has failed to provide long-term permanent solutions to the need for life-long learning (Haines, 1998); a systemic learning experience design is in demand to create better solutions for learners and facilitators combined.

System and Key Players

The Flexible Modalities Program (FMP), which is part of the out-of-school educational system, connects teenagers, young adults, and adults with educators and good will professionals to advance in the secondary school curriculum. The microcosm of the immediate learning experience includes the space, the textbook as mediating tool, the facilitators, and the learners (see Figure 17.1).

The flexibility of the FMP allows facilitators and learners to meet at convenient times and in out-of-the ordinary places such as the forest to reach forest rangers, lake shores to work with fishermen, public markets in the case of produce vendors, or even on the street, to meet shoe-shiners and informal vendors. This flexible focus of the FMP is a critical asset to serve their population in a meaningful way. The FMP also uses schools, community multi-purpose rooms and religious facilities to teach classes. However, it is in these more formal settings where instruction adopts the traditional school-like type of teaching described in the introduction to this chapter. In this sense, the space is a key component of the system as it seems to be shaping the learning experience (Oblinger, 2006).

Due to the community nature of the Program, facilitators may be graduated teachers or other community members with different professions and the good will to help.

Learners are characterized as follows:

- Between 15 and 70 years old;
- Living in rural and urban marginal areas across the country;
- Low income from a paid job or small businesses of their own (public transportation helpers, construction workers, fresh produce growers, market and informal vendors, trash collection helpers, small dining place waiters/waitresses/owners, etc.);
- Six years of schooling; extensive reading and writing not part of their lifestyle;
- Tired in the evening after long hard workdays;
- Indigenous origin in many cases, with systemic perspective about life and Spanish as second language.

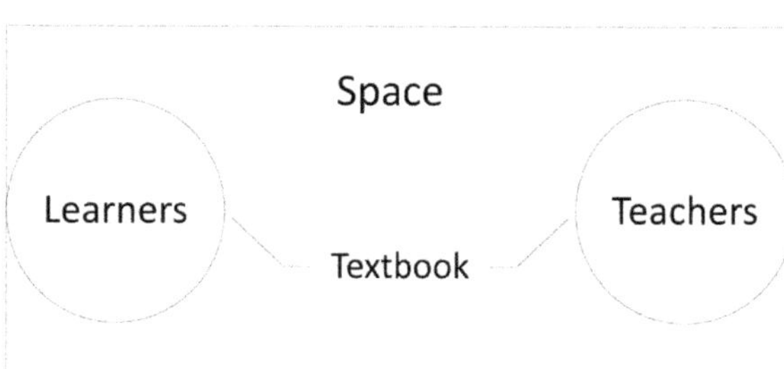

FIGURE 17.1 Microcosms of the Immediate Learning Experience

The textbooks are an important component of the system, as the mediating tools that guide the focus of instruction and the attention of the learners.

Case Analysis

A paradigm shift in the microcosm of the learning experience is needed to move the FMP from teacher-centered and content-centered education to learner-centered (Lee Watson, Reigeluth, & Watson, 2008) and context-centered authentic learning (Collins & Greeno, 2011) to make the experience meaningful for young adults and adults when going back to finish secondary education.

Despite the "interdisciplinary nature of the real world" (Prensky, 2014; Reigeluth & Karnopp, 2013) and the characteristics of the target population, the FMP had been using traditional textbooks which focused on specific topics in disconnected school subjects. In 2016, the FMP published two learning modules for 10th grade which used projects to apply school subjects. In 2018, these modules were used as a reference to create new modules for the remaining grades (8th, 9th, 11th, and 12th). The task was assigned to a group of 24 education consultants contracted as subject-matter experts to write 20 lessons each with integrated content from at least two school subjects. A holistic learning experience designer, who is the author of this chapter, completed the team to edit all the lessons and coordinate the entire production process. Lesson writers were distributed in six teams to produce the same number of modules which became the Program's textbooks.

Before starting, consultants were introduced to the holistic perspective of the project and the impact sought in the microcosm of the immediate learning experience. During the orientation session, they participated in specially designed activities to explore complexity and recognize the traditional "damaging discontinuities" between the different phases and settings for learning (Goodyear, 2002, p. 3) that were causing the school-like patterns observed. To change this situation, awareness was raised on the type of instructional design needed to create environments for activities that followed a holistic perspective to support real-world learning (Goodyear, 2002, p. 2). Orientation brought together their perspectives on the purpose of education (see Figure 17.2) and helped them to connect in one shared vision (Senge et al., 1994). Shared documents, an inspirational project website, and team chat groups kept them connected and generally focused on such vision.

The traditional focus on content as an end was redirected via the modules which used learner-centered instruction and assessment to prepare learners to "successfully operate in society" (Aslan & Reigeluth, 2013, p. 19) considering that they are already playing active roles in their communities and society. Projects and lessons were the two main instructional elements in the design of the modules. One project with its 20 lessons integrated a unit, and four units formed a module.

FIGURE 17.2 Integrated Perspectives (Text in Spanish)

Projects were oriented toward the real world, addressing topics such as: heritage, healthy habits, well-being, family economy, art, ecology, innovation, entrepreneurship, human rights, cooking/growing food, and knowing oneself, the community and the country. Open-ended projects gave room to creativity and exploration. Final creations were expected to be shared in an open event with community members and leaders.

Subjects were not explicit. Lessons only provided explanations using applied content in real-life examples that learners could relate to and transfer to their actual jobs, families, or initiatives. Despite being part of a unit under a leading project, lessons were "project independent." This meant that the explanations and the examples were "neutral," not related to any project. The link to the project was through the assignment which asked for a product that directly contributed to the project's success while serving to demonstrate the skills learned in the lessons. This design followed the learning object theory (Wiley, 2002) to make lessons and their sections "granular" enough to be used or combined in other settings. Assignments from all weekly lessons were interrelated and all five lessons of the same subject were interconnected to lead to complex performance (see Figure 17.3). Lessons integrated subjects as much as possible and guided remote self-paced learning between weekly face-to-face meetings. Suggestions for the weekly face-to-face encounters were also included following the sociocultural perspective for learning (Vygotsky, 1978).

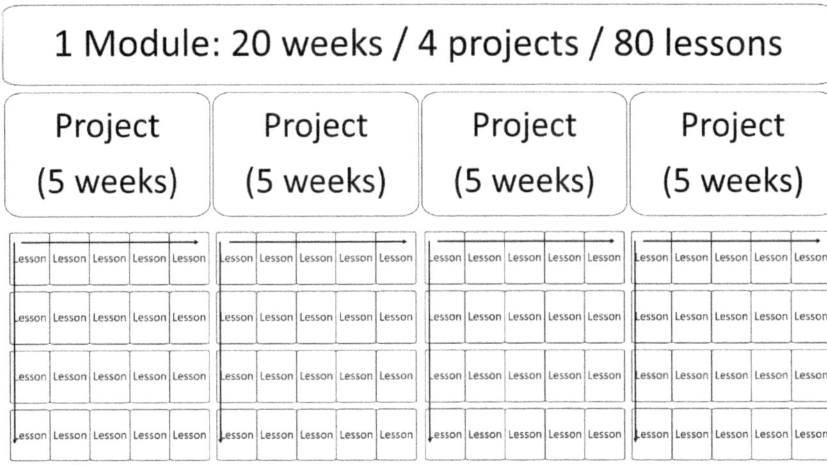

FIGURE 17.3 Module Structure

Problem Resolution

Following the systemic "leverage" principle by which "small, well-focused actions can sometimes produce significant, enduring improvements, if they're in the right place" (Senge, 2006, p. 64), the textbooks, as the mediating component of the system, were conceived as the doorway to begin influencing the microcosm of the immediate learning experiences in FMP. Their design would require further changes in the face-to-face meetings and the role of facilitators.

The modules were designed adapting inquiry-based methodologies (project/problem-based) and procuring integration of content from at least two subjects per lesson, following the new paradigm for learning in situated environments (Collins & Greeno, 2011; Reigeluth, 2012). There are multiple ways to integrate subjects in a curriculum (Kysilka, 1998). However, since almost all the consultants were doing it for the first time, no specific method was rigidly followed. Consultants were encouraged to use one subject as primary to connect the other one, integrating topics and skills whenever they found them interrelated.

The design process required consultants to go through a synthesis-analysis-synthesis process (see Figure 17.4). They were advised to start by reviewing the project that they had designed with their teams in order to identify the particular steps or minor products that learners could complete during a five-week period. Such steps or minor products guided the content for the lessons and needed to be aligned to the most relevant learning outcomes for each subject area. To evaluate the learning outcomes at the end of every five-week period, one single assessment criterion was created per subject. These criteria were included in the textbooks

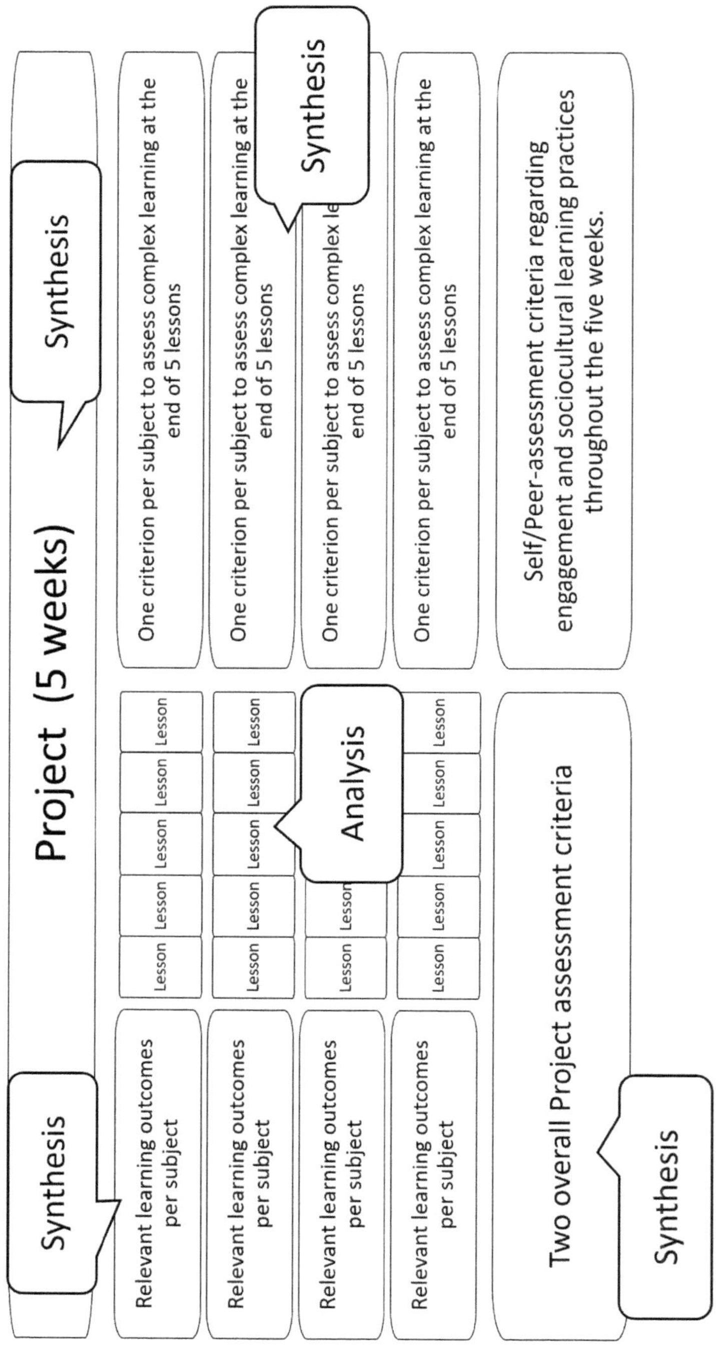

FIGURE 17.4 Synthesis-Analysis-Synthesis Process for Design

for self-assessment as well as formative and summative assessment from facilitators. Also included in the textbooks were two criteria to evaluate the overall outcome of each project and a fixed set of ten criteria to self- and peer-assess engagement and sociocultural learning practices in every unit.

Like a fractal (Reigeluth, 2019) of the unit, every lesson followed the same synthesis-analysis-synthesis trajectory (see Figure 17.5).

This construction and deconstruction of a part-whole configuration is one of the principles of systems thinking (Cabrera & Cabrera, 2015) and was the cornerstone in the design to help with integration and authentic learning, and to demonstrate textbook users that skills and content pieces are always part of a broader performance. In a reductionist pedagogical paradigm, subjects are broken down into multiple skills and pieces of knowledge. However, when knowledge is taught in this fragmented way, and no connections are made to help learners understand the purpose of the pieces, deep learning for real-world problem solving becomes limited. Productive engagement with complexity in authentic experiences is what warrants deep, complex learning for real life (Foster, 2013).

Consultants were encouraged to expose learners to major issues, key ideas, themes and principles within and across subjects; this helps them see and interiorize underlying schemas for deep understanding and transfer of learning to real-world settings (VanTassel-Baska & Wood, 2010). Such a way of organizing learning experiences around major issues in an integrated curriculum is a practice of accelerated learning which follows a systemic approach (VanTassel-Baska & Wood, 2010) and was recommended for this project (Charlick, n.d.).

Lessons Learned

The renewal of the educational system starts from the understanding that education means partnering with learners to help them transform and be able to consciously participate in the future that is emerging for everyone (Scharmer, 2013). Motivation of paradigm shifts through design implies continuous monitoring, feedback gathering, and iteration for improvement. Results are richer when system participants are aware of this constant improvement cycle and remain open to learn from it. This was particularly important in this case since the product expected from consultants differed strongly from what they traditionally did to guide learning. In this type of situation, diverse and abundant scaffolds are useful to help professionals perform better and feel confident with their tasks. Small-team and one-to-one coaching sessions also help to make sense of the new ideas and find creative ways to move forward.

All 24 consultants were asked to write lessons and were grouped in teams based on the module that they were producing. After three to four weeks of working together, the strongest skills of each consultant were evident: some were very good at the macro level (integrating content in projects, creating stories to demonstrate application in real life, describing complex performance), and others were better

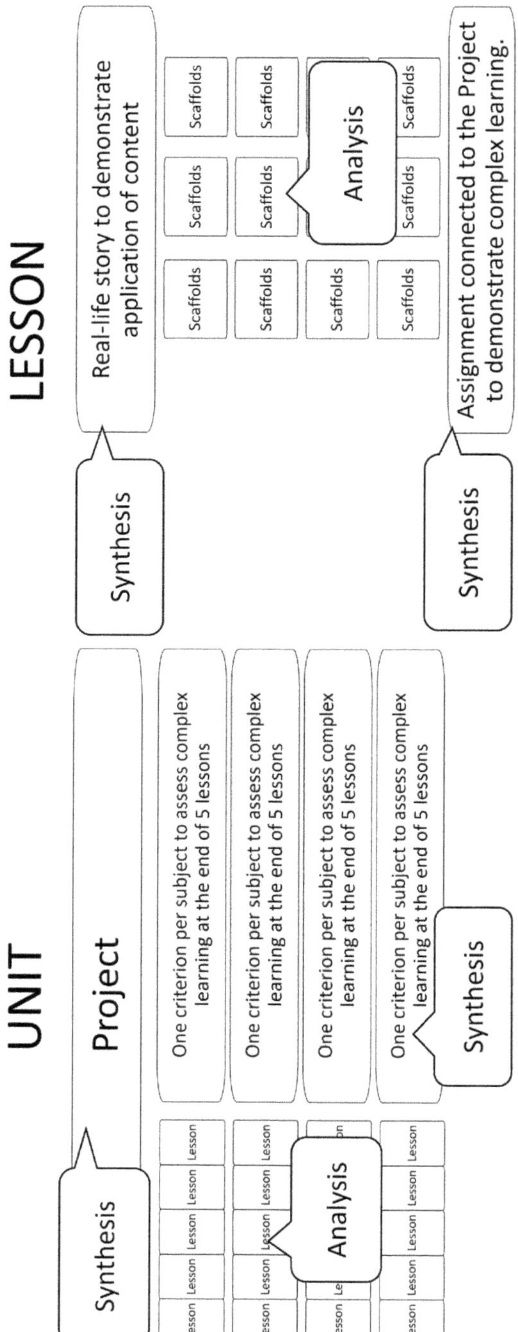

FIGURE 17.5 Lessons as Fractals of the Unit

at the micro level (choosing essential content from subjects, explaining concepts or step by step processes, providing examples); writing skills were also uneven. In future similar projects, a different team organization could be explored. Synergy is better achieved when each team player contributes with his or her own personal mastery to complement one another's efforts (Senge, 2006).

Conclusion

The evolution of education toward deep, authentic learning demands collaboration among all system participants: administrators, designers, facilitators, learners, and community members. They need to remain open to learn with a systemic "both/and" mindset throughout mindful iterations of designs in a virtuous cycle of improvement. Strategic implementation of key practices in such iterations as levers for change will make that evolution steadfast and fruitful.

Reflective Questions

- How can curriculum be an ally of deep, authentic learning?
- How can reductionism and holism be balanced to achieve deep, meaningful, life-long learning?
- What competencies do instructional designers need to be able to design learning experiences geared toward authentic learning?
- Which are the best leverage points to shift the direction of education toward its transformation to holistically improve life in our Planet?

Additional Resources

Collective Leadership Institute. (2018, December 19). *Dr. Petra Kuenkel and Dr. Humberto Maturana talk about "The Systems view of Life"* [Video]. YouTube. https://youtu.be/EJDWEJYSjyI

Maturana H. R. & Poerksen B. (2006) The paradox of education: A conversation. *Journal of Aesthetic Education* 40(1): 25–33. https://cepa.info/710

Maturana, H. R., & Varela, F. J. (1998). *The Tree of Knowledge: The Biological Roots of Human Understanding*. Shambhala Publications.

Rugut, E. J., & Osman, A. A. (2013). *Reflection on Paulo Freire and Classroom Relevance* 2(2): 23–28. www.aijssnet.com/journals/Vol_2_No_2_March_2013/3.pdf

References

Aslan, S., & Reigeluth, C. M. (2013). Educational Technologists: Leading Change for a New Paradigm of Education. *TechTrends* 57(5): 18–24.

Cabrera, D., & Cabrera, L. (2015). *Systems Thinking Made Simple: New Hope for Solving Wicked Problems*. Odyssean.

Charlick, J. A. (n.d.). *Accelerating Learning for Children in Developing Countries: Joining Research and Practice*. Creative Associates Internationale.

Chavajay, P., & Rogoff, B. (2002). Schooling and Traditional Collaborative Social Organization of Problem Solving by Mayan Mothers and Children. *Developmental Psychology* 38(1): 55–66.

Collins, A., & Greeno, J. (2011). Situative View of Learning. In V. G. Aukrust (ed.), *Learning and Cognition in Education*. Elsevier Ltd.

Compendio Estadístico de Educación. (2016). Instituto Nacional de Estadística de Guatemala. www.ine.gob.gt/sistema/uploads/2017/01/16/13EpHY9jEEyYORgJJAUwB758EoJL36aV.pdf.

Estimaciones y proyecciones nacionales de población: Metodología y principales resultados. (2020). Instituto Nacional de Estadística de Guatemala. www.ine.gob.gt/ine/wp-content/uploads/2020/08/01-Presentacion-de-Resultados-Nacionales.pdf

Foster, C. (2013). Resisting reductionism in mathematics pedagogy. *The Curriculum Journal* 24(4): 563–585.

Goodyear, P. (2002). Environments for lifelong learning: Ergonomics, architecture and educational design. In J. M. Spector, & T. M. Anderson (Eds.), *Integrated and Holistic Perspectives on Learning, Instruction and Technology: Understanding Complexity* (pp. 1–18). Kluwer Academic Publishers.

Haines, S. G. (1998). *The Manager's Pocket Guide to Systems Thinking & Learning*. HRD Press.

Kysilka, M. L. (1998). Understanding integrated curriculum. *The Curriculum Journal* 9(3): 197–209.

Lee Watson, S., Reigeluth, C. M., & Watson, W. R. (2008). Systems design for change in education and training. In Spector, M., Merrill, M. D., Elene, J. and Bishop, M. J. (eds.), *Handbook of research on educational communications and technology* (pp. 691–701). www.academia.edu/download/36455188/systems_handbook_chapter.pdf

Molina, G., & Peñate, M. (2014). *Adolescencia: Un presente y un futuro en claroscuro. Análisis de los Presupuestos Generales de Ingresos y Egresos del Estado de Guatemala, 2007–2013*. Instituto Centroamericano de Estudios Fiscales.

Oblinger, D. G. (2006). Space as Change Agent. In Oblinger, D. G. (ed.), *Learning Spaces*. Educause. www.educause.edu/learningspaces

Prensky, M. (2014). The World Needs a New Curriculum. *Educational Technology* 54(4), 3–15.

Reigeluth, C. M. (2012). Instructional Theory and Technology for the New Paradigm of Education. *RED. Revista de Educación a Distancia* 32(September 30, 2012). www.um.es/ead/red/32/reigeluth.pdf

Reigeluth, C. M. (2019). Chaos Theory and the Sciences of Complexity: Foundations for Transforming Educational Systems. In Spector, M. J. (ed.), *Learning, Design and Technology* (p. 12). Springer Nature. https://doi.org/10.1007/978-3-319-17727-4_95-1

Reigeluth, C. M., & Karnopp, J. R. (2013). *Reinventing Schools: It's Time to Break the Mold*. Rowman & Littlefield Publishers Inc.

Richards, M. (2003). *Atlas Lingüístico de Guatemala*. https://issuu.com/michaelrichards40/docs/atlas_ling____stico

Scharmer, O. (2013). *Leading from the Emerging Future: From Ego-system to Eco-system Economies* (Kindle). Berrett-Koehler Publishers.

Senge, P. M., Kleiner, A., Roberts, C., Ross, R. B., & Smith, B. J. (1994). *The Fifth Discipline Fieldbook: Strategies and Tools for Building a Learning Organization*. Doubleday, Random House, Inc.

Senge, P. M. (2006). *The Fifth Discipline: The Art & Practice of The Learning Organization* (Revised Edition, Kindle). The Crown Publishing Group.

VanTassel-Baska, J., & Wood, S. (2010). The Integrated Curriculum Model (ICM). *Learning and Individual Differences* 20: 345–357. https://doi.org/10.1016/j.lindif.2009.12.006

Vygotsky, L. S. (1978). *Mind in Society: The Development of Higher Psychological Processes*. Harvard University Press.

Wiley, D. A. (2002). Connecting Learning Objects to Instructional Design Theory: A Definition, a Metaphor, and a Taxonomy. In Wiley, D. S. (ed.), *The Instructional Use of Learning Objects* (pp. 3–24). Agency for Instructional Technology.

PART IV

Managing Change

18

A CASE STUDY OF SOCIAL-TECHNICAL SYSTEMS APPROACHES AND EDUCATION VIDEO ANIMATIONS (HEALTH CARE/INTERNATIONAL)

Julia Bello-Bravo, John Medendorp, Anne Namatsi Lutomia, N. Peter Reeves, Jeremy W. Bohonos, Rick Gardner, and Barry Pittendrigh

Introduction

Socio-technical systems are the foundation on which future societies will be built (Fuenfshilling & Binz, 2018; Saddiqi & Collins, 2017; Salmon & Read, 2018). Balancing human and technological factors has the potential to provide sustainability and well-being in a developing world. There is a considerable body of literature on the widening digital divide in international development (Fang et al., 2019; Hidalgo et al., 2020; Van Dijk, 2020). Although the benefits of access to information and communication technology (ICT) are evident, leveraging ICT to the benefit of marginalized and underserved populations remains elusive (Kondowe & Chigona, 2019) especially for the so-called "last mile" communities (Mittal, Mehar, & Hariharan, 2019; Tinsley & Agapitova, 2018). The "last mile" refers to rural, often isolated communities. The advent of COVID-19 has simply highlighted this deficit. This chapter's case study focuses on SAWBO's collaboration with CURE Ethiopia Children's Hospital in Addis Ababa, which provides surgical care for children with orthopedic conditions.

The application of socio-technical systems to this gap calls for fostering an understanding of connectedness in organizations and societal levels that leads to making changes that are stable and robust (Campbell, Coldicott, & Kinsella, 2018). The delivery of critical information is key to the success of socio-technical systems. This is especially true when the critical information is time-bound. Entities that need to deploy time-sensitive knowledge for time-sensitive outcomes can ill afford to have delays in the timely delivery of vital information. This especially includes

DOI: 10.4324/9781003028772-22

healthcare interventions at the personal/familial but also at the public level, especially in times of crisis (as COVID-19 makes abundantly clear).

Problem Statement

In this chapter we present a case study that explores a specific socio-technical system that addresses the key socio-technical challenge of interconnecting expert content-providers to target audiences that speak diverse languages and are of diverse literacy levels, thus forming a link between experts and diverse users. Specifically, we will explore the Ethiopian case of Ethiopia Children's Hospital in Addis Ababa. We do so by exploring through this case study (1) how informal social-technical networks acting as interlinking sub-systems expand the effective distributional range of web-based educational content with a multiplier effect and (2) how locally situated scientific experts and medical practitioners can operate as key linkage points between local social networks and the global scientific community.

Innovation

In 2011, Scientific Animations Without Borders (SAWBO) was created and launched. SAWBO is an academic research program inaugurated at the University of Illinois Urbana-Champaign and currently housed at Purdue University. SAWBO is an education innovation around developing efficient/low-transaction cost, social-technical systems for translating scientifically accurate and scalable educational solutions for low-literate learners who speak divergent languages.

Broadly speaking, SAWBO addresses the key challenge of the digital divide by linking experts with educational end users. The scientific-technical expert community is often well-networked with others in the scientific-technical expert community—often in a major global language such as English. However, these experts often have few, limited, or no linkages with the educational end users who may benefit from their knowledge. Even those experts with considerable links in a given scientific-technical expert community may have limited access to last mile communities. Conversely, there are significant global community developers (e.g., NGOs, government agencies, inter-government agencies) who are engaging low-literate audiences that would benefit from the use of highly accurate educational content usable directly with target audiences. SAWBO addresses this gap by creating linkages between information-producing and information-adopting communities—not only in a theoretical (systems thinking) sense but also as applied toward achieving direct tangible content, output, experimental testing, and case analysis.

The SAWBO "socio-technical system" involves the creation of educational content in virtual networks with global experts using scripts and storyboards toward animated video end-product development. Initially released in English, subsequent sets of local language experts are engaged to place the animated video's contents into regionally or locally usable translations. Local language versions are thus added over time as new underserved populations are identified. Content is then available for use and scaling by others on online and offline SAWBO platforms. In this way, SAWBO provides a critical link between information and people who find such information helpful, thus affecting information dissemination not only in a scalable fashion but also such that critical masses of users can address problems and crises in their communities or that span traditional borders of communities.

No system, however, is isolated (Meadows, 2008): they exist within other systems with varying forms of hierarchies, norms, regulations, and interconnectedness. Additionally, systems are nested within each other and are interwoven and required for collaboration (Meadows, 2008). Systems can be open or closed, but when new linkages are formed between systems or sub-systems, the functionality of the newly formed system can be expanded, thus improving its capacity in meaningful ways.

While some of the systems that SAWBO strategically engages include topics around food security, health, and women's empowerment (Bello-Bravo, Seufferheld, & Adebimpe, 2011) in Ghana, Nigeria and Niger, technical systems germane to the organization's work include digital ICT distribution channels, especially the Internet, mobile phones, and community-based charging hubs. Social systems include formal scientific, civil, religious, and political networks, as well as informal social systems that facilitate phone-to-phone sharing of e-learning content in areas where Internet access is marginal.

SAWBO aims to maximize the affordances of dynamic interchange between these several types of systems that position socio-technical systems approaches as valuable (Davis et al., 2014). Smartphones are now increasingly widespread in the global South, while as recently as five years ago the technology required was not available in many countries most in need of the type of information SAWBO distributes. More exactly, only mobile phones able to play downloaded or Bluetooth-shared animated video content are needed to access SAWBO videos. The Bluetooth capability of phone-phone transfer is particularly attractive, as it does not require the use of often locally very or prohibitively expensive data allowance plans.

System and Key Players

Since 2011, the lean SAWBO team has grown from the two co-founders to a team of eight employees—one program manager, one project manager and researcher, four researchers, one animator and one system engineer. Others are SAWBO consultants and partners with a global network of production units and technical experts to create animated videos on 90+ topics. These have since been translated into 145 language variants. A goal of SAWBO involves developing a socio-technical systems approach to bridge the divide between the Research for Development (R4D) community and global low-literate learners in reading, writing, mathematics, health, agriculture, and technology, who live on less than $3 a day, in diverse languages, particularly in countries with limited resources to deliver such content.

SAWBO explores how to effect this link between information-producing and information-adopting communities—not only in a theoretical (socio-technical system) sense but also as applied toward achieving direct tangible content, output, experimental testing, and case analysis. Briefly, then, the SAWBO "socio-technical system" involves the creation of educational content in virtual networks with global experts using scripts and storyboards as steps toward animated video end-product development that are then made accessible to "last mile" populations.

SAWBO first releases animated master videos in English. Subsequently SAWBO engages sets of local language experts to place the animated video's contents into regionally or locally usable translations in order to make the information accessible to "last mile" populations. Local language experts are volunteers who speak a local language and languages and English and they are interested in translating the content into specific local languages. Sometimes these local volunteers are educators or community leaders who want to share a solution for one specific problem with their community. Global or content experts are academics, researchers, extension personnel who are interested in sharing a solution for the social good. Different languages and dialect versions are thus added when there is a need and demand for it over time. Content is then available for use and scaling by others on online and offline SAWBO platforms through the SAWBO web-page (see Figure 18.1).

In contrast to reductionist approaches to systems, where systems are viewed in isolation or apart from one another, a systems thinking approach considers all parts of a system and how systems are connected (Meadows, 2008). The interaction between parts of the system is often critical for the system to achieve its intended function, which, in this case, represents the system's ability to tackle the orthopedic problems of club foot and hip dysplasia in underserved regions of the world. The knowledge to address the problem exists, but requires a technical component, represented in this case by the SAWBO linkage. SAWBO creates connections from experts to local users by providing educational content in local languages, thus creating the necessary link between expert knowledge and those in need of that knowledge.

Case Analysis

Our case analysis explains the process of SAWBO's collaboration with CURE Ethiopia Children's Hospital in Addis Ababa. The goals of the collaboration included developing and deploying two educational animations: one on recognizing club foot (which is readily recognizable even by non-healthcare

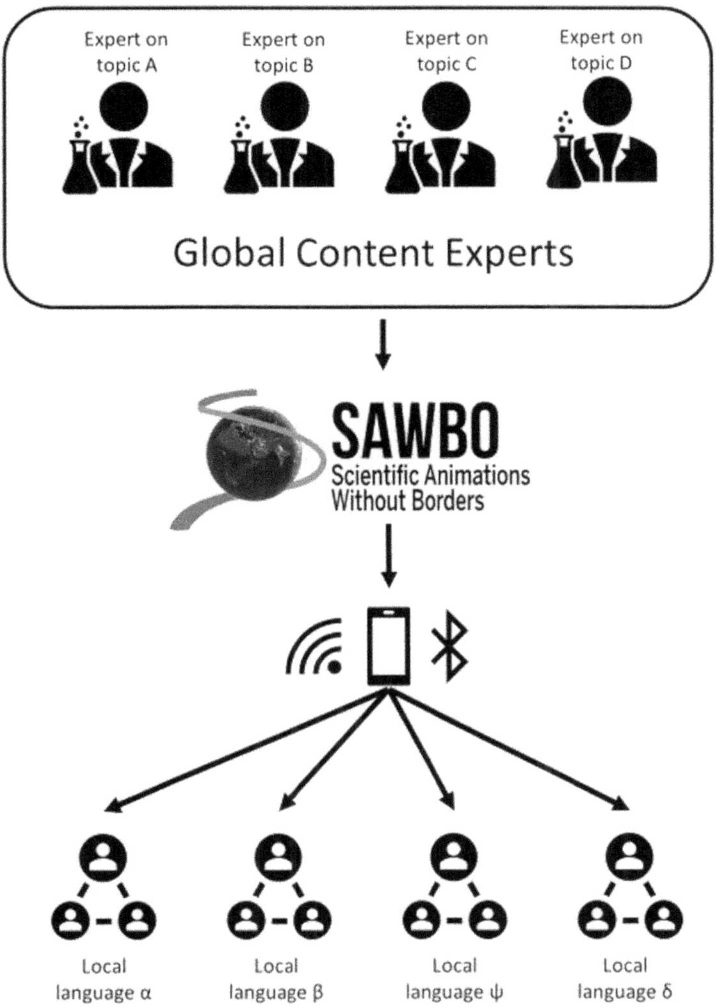

FIGURE 18.1 Model of SAWBO Social Technical Networks

professionals) and another to help parents, healthcare professionals, and midwives in Ethiopia detect the early signs of hip dysplasia, and the availability of treatment for both conditions.

Using a socio-technical systems approach, the animation was created by global health experts in club foot from different countries and deployed by integrating the educational animation in community health workers training programs in Ethiopia. This approach was driven by two key factors: (1) the "raw" scientific content developed by global and local experts and its growing library of educational materials in local languages, and (2) a strategic deployment of information through different channels, including mobile phones or any other electronic

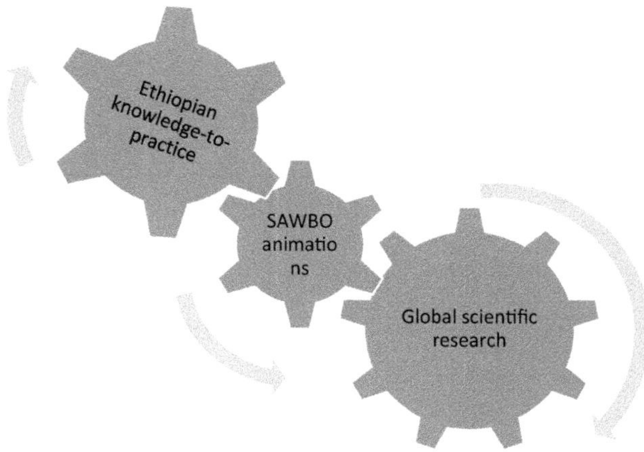

FIGURE 18.2 Leveraging Linkages Through Sociotechnical Systems Approaches

devices that could reach networks of people interested in sharing the information with target audiences with those needs (see Figure 18.2).

Complexity—Reaching Target Audiences. A recurrent challenge for healthcare policy setters and providers is how to reach target audiences with different health needs, especially when they live in rural or isolated areas with limited access to information, speak many different languages (but not the mainstream language), and have limited access to healthcare systems generally. The above linking of socio-technical systems shows how multiplier effects can be leveraged for increased impact. SAWBO's mission and vision is a holistic one to tackle each of the identified factors to improve livelihoods through informal education, finding the best communication strategies to reach the target audience.

SAWBO's approach brought a positive development for the field of health, reaching audiences with different needs in their own local languages by connecting world-class scientific-technical systems with local social systems. Specifically, CURE Ethiopia Children's Hospital understood the population needs in Ethiopia. Some 4,000 children in Ethiopia are born with clubfoot each year. Many are also born with a dislocated hip (also known as Developmental Dysplasia of the Hip, or DDH). Early detection is vital to correcting these developmental conditions without surgery. SAWBO working with CURE understood the context, the needs, the attitudes, social networks, and the opportunity for families to recognize these health conditions and seeking early treatment through educational video advocacy. Through the efforts of one physician, who worked collaboratively with SAWBO, a linkage was created between advanced technical systems and local social systems, which allowed otherwise unaddressed (or under-resourced) problems to receive a vital resource for helping to address them. According to the orthopedic surgeon and Medical Director at CURE

Ethiopia Children's Hospital, "The videos have been a hugely valuable way of communicating about each health condition and the management of them in a way that is hard to portray in pictures and text alone" (personal communication Rick Gardner).

Problem Resolution

The animations produced connected global expertise with a specific local need in treating hip dysplasia and clubfoot. For hip dysplasia, CURE (the partner) had the capacity to identify and treat the problem while SAWBO had the capacity to make the knowledge accessible and helpful for increasing public awareness and treatment compliance. In the case of clubfoot where the condition is visible to people not trained in medicine, community members were empowered to identify cases and seek assistance. The videos also opened educational pathways for the partners to help reduce cases of late-presenting hip dysplasia by alerting both birthing personnel and the public of the risk-potential, thereby increasing the likelihood of having the condition checked for.

Lessons Learned

The strategies of SAWBO in this case study show how linking scientific-technical systems with local social systems allows for a multiplication of impact in both systems. On the one hand, global experts collaborated with the local medical experts in Ethiopia toward developing comprehensive, comprehensible, and actionable content that was culturally sensitive (above all by translation into local dialects).

On other hand, after SAWBO delivered its work-project, the local partner's autonomy ensured best-practices decision-making for how to deliver the content to people most in need of it. Local partners deployed clubfoot animation throughout the country while the hip dysplasia animation found its most relevant use in the medical sector. Both contributed to the knowledge base and practices within the medical sector generally. The strategies of SAWBO in this case study show how linking scientific socio-technical systems with local socio-technical systems allows for a multiplication of impact in both systems. On the one hand, global experts collaborated with the local medical experts in Ethiopia toward developing comprehensive, comprehensible, and actionable content that was culturally sensitive (above all by translation into local dialects).

On other hand, after SAWBO delivered its work-project, the local partner's autonomy ensured best-practices decision-making for how to deliver the content to people most in need of it. Local partners deployed club foot animation throughout the country while the hip dysplasia animation found its most relevant use in the medical sector. Both contributed to the knowledge base and practices within the medical sector generally.

Analysis

A key to multiplying system impact is through inter-system linkages.

> Systems integration—holistic approaches to integrating various components of coupled human and natural systems (for example, social-ecological systems and human-environment systems) across all dimensions—is necessary to address complex interconnections and identify effective solutions to sustainability challenges.
>
> *Liu et al., 2015, p. 1*

Connecting systems through intermediaries allows for an expansion of the "reach" and "power" of the systems and in that sense act like gears that transfer force across a system (Ince & Güler, 2019). Gearing provides a helpful analogy of how the turning force of one socio-technical system might be applied to socio-technical systems that are remote and perhaps at different levels in terms of their resources, skills, and knowledge. Using an intermediary linkage to cause these two systems to engage each other across locations allows systems to have impact beyond their initial scope (see Figure 18.2).

The key to this case study is understanding how interlocking systems leverage each other for increased reach in the knowledge-to-practice output of the individual systems thanks to interconnecting linkages that make the power of one socio-technical system bring its force to bear on another.

In this case study, two systems, although initially separate from each other, were interlinked through leveraged linkages to produce a higher knowledge-to-practice scope and impact than the systems could have produced individually. The power of the large socio-technical system of global scientific research was brought to bear on a second smaller, and less dynamic socio-technical system through the use of a linking intermediary that allowed the force of the first system to influence outcomes in the second system through local knowledge supporting the diagnosis and treatment of club foot and hip dysplasia.

Prior to this intervention, the smaller socio-technical system was connected to the larger, more powerful system of scientific research, but only remotely, through a long concatenation of intermediaries applied in irregular interventions that in the end had only irregular and ineffective impact. By reducing the number of linkages between the scientific community and the local communities, the use of animated videos was able to eliminate many of the inefficiencies of the existing indirect linkages and was able to bring the force of the scientific research socio-technical community directly to bear on the system by adapting the nature of the linkage to bring the two systems directly in contact with one another. Because the interconnecting mechanisms between the global scientific base and the local knowledge base were too diffuse, the powerful force of the research system was lost through the complexity of the system, and the local knowledge base was less dynamically affected. In this case study, however, the force of the socio-technical research system was connected directly to the local knowledge-to-practice system through the use of SAWBO's scientific animations. This was possible by reproducing global scientific research in a medium accessible to non-global, non-scientific learners. The use of this direct integration of the power of the global scientific research into the local knowledge-to-practice system thus produced an increase in the influence of the research of the local knowledge-to-practice system, with resultant great benefits for the local systems in a very cost-effective way.

Conclusion

In general, the socio-technical systems approach depicts how to navigate the sometimes-confusing degree of analysis needed in local and global projects that include input, process, output, and feedback (Campbell, Coldicott, & Kinsella (2018). It accomplishes this by simplifying the complexity through scientifically narrowing project goals toward the strongest points of leverage into local systems.

The clearest signal of realities on the ground such as access to the Internet, phones, and airtime/local actualities is implementing the intervention in local people's most comfortably spoken dialect. Nonetheless, this theme of"translation" is as much cultural as it is linguistic. Engineering an effective gear *must* take both entities to be linked in their actual characteristics. To focus only on one side, or to try to force a fit, leads at best to jammed gears, if not blown engines. While this requires more up-front design costs, those costs are recouped on the back-end, both by successful solution uptake of the intervention, on the one hand, and fewer "repairs" to fix any breakdowns due to a poor gear fit in the first place. In this way, SAWBO affords a link between scientifically critical information and people who find such information helpful or critical, thus affecting information dissemination not only in a scalable way but also such that critical masses of users can address critical problems and crises in their communities or beyond the traditional borders of communities.

Reflective Questions

The following questions could inform future research and practice:

- How can designers more effectively connect technical and social systems through scientific animations such that complex technical issues are addressed in formal and non-formal social systems?
- How can designers optimize knowledge pathways in the field toward understanding outcomes in the field?
- How can designers standardize a system for linked partners to collect for problem solving?

Additional Resources

Chai, S., & Kim, M. (2012). A socio-technical approach to knowledge contribution behavior: An empirical investigation of social networking sites users. *International journal of information management, 32*(2), 118–126. https://doi.org/10.1016/j.ijinfomgt.2011.07.004

İpek, Ö. F., & Karaman, A. C. (2020). Systemic change in a higher education institution: Inquiring into organizational and instructional transformation. *Systemic Practice and Action Research*, 1–17. https://doi.org/10.1007/s11213-019-09516-6

References

Bello-Bravo, J., Seufferheld, F., & Adebimpe, A. (2011). Gender and farmer field schools in food and agricultural production systems in select crops and regions of West Africa. *The International Journal of Science in Society, 2*(4), 13–24. https://doi.org/10.18848/1836-6236/CGP/v02i04

Campbell, D., Coldicott, T., & Kinsella, K. (2018). *Systemic work with organizations: A new model for managers and change agents*. Routledge.

Davis, M. C., Challenger, R., Jayewardene, D. N., & Clegg, C. W. (2014). Advancing socio-technical systems thinking: A call for bravery. *Applied Ergonomics, 45*(2), 171–180. https://doi.org/10.1016/j.apergo.2013.02.009

Fang, M. L., Canham, S. L., Battersby, L., Sixsmith, J., Wada, M., & Sixsmith, A. (2019). Exploring privilege in the digital divide: implications for theory, policy, and practice. *The Gerontologist, 59*(1), e1–e15.

Fuenfschilling, L., & Binz, C. (2018). Global socio-technical regimes. *Research policy, 47*(4), 735–749.

Hidalgo, A., Gabaly, S., Morales-Alonso, G., & Urueña, A. (2020). The digital divide in light of sustainable development: An approach through advanced machine learning techniques. *Technological Forecasting and Social Change, 150*, 119754.

Ince, E., & Güler, M. A. (2019). Design and analysis of a novel power-split infinitely variable power transmission system. *Journal of Mechanical Design, 141*(5). https://doi.org/10.1115/1.4041783

Kondowe, C., & Chigona, W. (2019, May). Rethinking theory and practice of ICT4D. An analysis of the discourse embedded in the 2016 World Bank Report. In *International Conference on Social Implications of Computers in Developing Countries* (pp. 135–148). Springer.

Liu, J., Mooney, H., Hull, V., Davis, S. J., Gaskell, J., Hertel, T., Lubchenco, J., Seto, K. C., Gleick, P., & Kremen, C. (2015). Systems integration for global sustainability. *Science, 347*(6225), 1258832. https://doi.org/10.1126/science.1258832

Meadows, D. H. (2008). *Thinking in systems: A primer*. Chelsea Green Publishing.

Mittal, S., Mehar, M., & Hariharan, V. K. (2019). Information and communication technologies for strengthening extension services to reach the last mile in India. In *Agricultural Extension Reforms in South Asia* (pp. 255–274). Academic Press.

Pasmore, W. A. (1988). *Designing effective organizations: The sociotechnical systems perspective*. Wiley.

Salmon, P. M., & Read, G. J. (2018). Using principles from the past to solve the problems of the future: Human factors and sociotechnical systems thinking in the design of future work. *Human Factors Management, 28*, 277–280.

Siddiqi, A., & Collins, R. D. (2017). Sociotechnical systems and sustainability: current and future perspectives for inclusive development. *Current Opinion in Environmental Sustainability*, *24*, 7–13.

Tinsley, E., & Agapitova, N. (2018). *Reaching the last mile*. World Bank.

Van Dijk, J. (2020). *The digital divide*. John Wiley & Sons.

19

SYSTEMS IN K-12 EDUCATION AND THEIR IMPACT ON PROVIDING "EXCELLENCE" IN SUPERVISION (K-12)

Michele Connors

Introduction

"Excellence in education" is the phrase that begins the motto of Four Townships School District (FTSD) (pseudonym). A commendable goal to strive toward for sure, but what does excellence mean for the faculty and staff at the high school? How do supervision and evaluation impact their ability to provide an excellent education for students? And what systems affect the supervision and evaluation process at the high school and determine whether or not the employees are "excellent"?

Despite the wording in its motto, FTSD does not rate its employees under categories that include the word excellent. Instead, Charlotte Danielson's *The Framework for Teaching: Evaluation Instrument* (2013) is the preferred text widely used by teachers and administrators throughout the district to appraise an educator's performance as unsatisfactory, basic, proficient, or distinguished in four domains: planning and preparation, the classroom environment, instruction, and professional responsibilities. First published in 1996, Danielson's Framework has been revised to now include components that align to the demands of the Common Core State Standards (Danielson, 2013, p. 2). This Framework was used to develop an online Pennsylvania Electronic Teacher Evaluation Portal (PA-ETEP) in which district employees evaluate themselves and their subordinates after uploading evidence used as the basis for their evaluative score (Edulink, Inc., 2020). FTSD has been using this supervision and evaluation process for the past several years, and professional staff members have the option to complete either the direct observation, the differentiated observation, or the peer-review observation models. In direct observation, supervisors observe staff members on a mutually accepted date and time and provide detailed feedback in the portal to

DOI: 10.4324/9781003028772-23

be reviewed by both parties at a post-observation conference. The differentiated observation model requires staff members to create their own goal to work toward throughout the school year and upload evidence and descriptive narratives to support their own evaluation of themselves. In the peer-review model, a pair of colleagues works together to coach one another throughout the year by setting and sharing goals, participating in observations of one another, and collaborating on areas of success and ones that need improvement.

In the 2019–2020 school year, staff members faced significant challenges they had to overcome to provide a quality education for their students and work toward a distinguished ranking for themselves. FTSD transitioned between district-level administrators and reacted to the demands of a virtual continuity of education plan in response to the Covid-19 pandemic. Both obstacles provided challenges to overcome to provide an appropriate, rigorous, and engaging learning experience for the students and do so in a way that allows for a most desirable ranking on staff member evaluations.

Taking into consideration the various professional and support staff positions in the high school, the recent changes the school district has undergone, and the school district's motto, are the staff at the high school being supervised in a way that promotes "excellence in education" even throughout the unforeseen challenges of the 2019–2020 school year?

System and Key Players

Systems theory helps to explain the extent of the effect of the supervision and evaluation process at Four Townships High School (FTHS).

The supra-level systems include the United States Department of Education which enacts mandates states are required to follow and enforce on all public school districts who receive federal and state funding. Following the federal mandates, the Pennsylvania Department of Education (PDE) creates and regulates policies that FTHS must abide by. These policies include an appropriate system for evaluating teaching staff and developing plans for growth and professional development of educators. PDE through the PA-ETEP evaluation tool utilizes the Danielson Framework to satisfy the needs of these policies. A final system that should not be neglected at the supra level is society in general whose world students will enter after high school with the understanding that they are capable of being independent, successful adults.

In regards to macro level systems, FTHS is part of the FTSD and is the district's only high school. The communities FTSD serves elect nine representatives to the school board which is responsible for developing policies for the district faculty, staff, and students to abide by. In some regards, these elected officials determine the acceptable guidelines the district employees must strive for to meet their mission of providing excellence in education to all students. Additionally, the school board members have the ability to retain and dismiss staff based on regular evaluations of job performance.

There are 13 curricular departments at FTHS from which students can choose to take classes when making their course schedule each spring. (Students may also opt to take classes at the county's vocational-technical school for half of the day.) A variety of sports, clubs, and activities are available for students to participate in as well. When considering the mezzo level systems in effect at the high school, the groups of teachers in each department and extracurricular area, for the most part, work toward departmental guidelines in place to help staff members achieve a distinguished rating on their yearly evaluations.

Micro-level systems that affect the quality of supervision staff members receive at FTHS include the students—all who are in grades 9–12. The most recent Future Ready PA Index data (2019) indicates that FTHS has an overall school enrollment of 1,569. The school's demographics show that nearly 75% of its students are White, 13% are Hispanic, and 8% are Black. Additionally, nearly 35% of the students are classified as economically disadvantaged, and nearly 17% of students receive special education services.

Individual teachers, administrators, and other employees working in the building should also be considered as part of the micro level. In the 2019–2020 school year, there were 103 teachers who served as the high school's faculty, and seven administrators were housed in the high school as well. Additionally, nine secretaries, three curriculum coaches, a school psychologist, a social worker, a librarian, a nurse, an English as a Second Language (ESL) program specialist, an athletic trainer, two speech therapists, a probation officer, and five school counselors also worked from the high school. Staff members also included four technology room technicians, four full-time security officers, and numerous full- and part-time monitors, paraprofessionals, custodians, and lunch room staff members. Throughout any given school day, people among and within these various systems could play a role in the success of others.

With all of these system levels in place, do the procedures for supervision at FTHS support the district's mission and help to nurture an environment conducive to providing excellence in education for all students?

Case Analysis

Nine employees (all given pseudo names) at FTHS during the 2019–2020 school year volunteered to participate in a qualitative research study. Most of the interviews were informal phone conversations; however, the first one was conducted at lunch during a professional development workshop.

While enjoying lunch from a local delicatessen, Amy, a veteran special education teacher, explained that all of the teachers at the high school are evaluated by either the principal or one of the assistant principals; however, faculty members in her department receive their rating from the Supervisor of Special Education.

Amy immediately expressed her displeasure with the way she is evaluated because she spends most of her time in a co-teaching classroom environment, and special education paperwork and Individualized Education Program (IEP) meetings are only a small fraction of her school day. She prefers to receive her observations and feedback from one of the building principals as well as the Supervisor of Special Education so that she can learn how to improve in the content area classes she supports. Amy wants the most useful feedback possible so that she can use it to improve in all of her many job requirements.

Todd is the Director of Athletics and Activities for FTSD, and his office is housed in FTHS since that's the building where the majority of the district's extracurricular opportunities occur. On a busy Tuesday morning in June, his interview was conducted over the phone where other phone lines in his office and people coming and going could be heard throughout the course of the conversation; however, Todd, it seemed, had become very accustomed to multitasking and prioritizing. Todd's perspective on how he is evaluated was not unlike Amy's in that he too didn't have a clear understanding of which superior to report to—partly due to the fact that Todd's was a new position in the district, and due to the change in administration, the levels of hierarchy were still being developed. Because the school board of FTSD has an athletics and activities committee, Todd often finds himself answering to their questions, praise, and scrutiny in addition to that of his superiors. He commented that he desired more clarity in his job performance and a supervisor who could work with him to determine what he could do to grow in his position.

A busy doctoral student herself, Vanessa, one of the high school's instructional coaches, was willing to participate in an interview between assignments. Similar to the conversation with Todd and Amy, Vanessa also desired more clarity in the supervision and evaluation process in regards to her position in the district. She hoped for more meaningful feedback from an administrator which would allow her to grow.

On a positive note, Pam, Dave, and Susan are all teachers in the special education, mathematics, and science departments at FTHS respectively. All spoke highly of their supervision and evaluation process. Their administrators all shared a common theme—the administrators' own content area matched that of the people they provided feedback to. All commented that the shared content knowledge was beneficial to their growth as educators.

The difference in opinion between Amy, Todd, and Vanessa's supervision and evaluation process and Pam, Dave, and Susan's indicates a problem. All six of the employees are part of the same system within the district; however, their experiences with the supervision and evaluation process are conflicting. Pam, Dave, and Susan are classroom teachers who are evaluated by supervisors who once held their same position. These educators perceived their evaluation and supervision process as one that was positive due to the evaluators' level of knowledge and experience in each particular position. However, Amy, Todd, and Vanessa who are not in typical classroom teacher positions found their supervision and evaluation experience not as positive and lacking in evidence to help them grow as professionals. They were not clear as to whether or not they were providing excellence in education, and if not, what they could do to improve and work toward that district goal.

Amy, Todd, and Vanessa's problem may stem from a system higher than the micro system they and their administrators belong to. The educator evaluation and supervision process is mandated by PDE and the U.S. Department of Education, and these supra-level systems require educators to be supervised and evaluated by superiors who hold administrative certifications. Based on the work of systems thinking theorist Peter Senge, unless the system for evaluation is changed, educators such as Amy, Todd, and Vanessa will not glean the benefits of an evaluation from a supervisor in their same content area (Isaacson & Bamburg, 1992, p. 42). The supra level appears to lack knowledge of this problem that the micro-level system faces at FTHS and perhaps other schools as well.

Another tenet of systems thinking is that organizations can only learn and grow if their individual members are learning (Isaacson & Bamburg, 1992, p. 42). All educators at FTHS need to experience feedback that enhances and encourages their growth in order for them to provide excellence in education to their students.

Problem Resolution

In order to achieve excellence in supervision and perhaps education, collaboration with and receiving feedback from someone who has experience in their same content area was an important theme determined from the interview data. Sally, the high school librarian, craved an administrator who could provide both praise and suggestions to improve that were specific to her duties and responsibilities as a librarian. While it is a logistical challenge to hire administrators with advanced content knowledge for every faculty member's department, there are possible solutions to this dilemma.

A peer observation and coaching model from other educators in the district or neighboring districts holding similar positions to those of the non-classroom teachers may achieve the same positive evaluation experience as the teachers who benefitted from administrators from their content area's evaluations. Peer-to-peer collaboration for the purpose of professional development aligns with the systems thinking discipline of team learning (Isaacson & Bamburg, 1992, p. 44). When two educators with the same content knowledge background work together to improve pedagogy, excellence in education will likely come to fruition.

Another challenge in the supervisory system at FTSD is that for some positions, the job duties and hierarchy of supervision is unclear. Todd, Vanessa, and Sarah, the ESL Program Specialist, never had a clear description of their job duties and responsibilities and who they were to report to for guidance and support.

In "systems thinking schools" as Senge refers to them (2012, p. 46), even at a young age, students and their teachers reflect on how they spent time throughout the school days to "legitimize" learning. Even in traditional public schools such as FTHS, teachers might begin and end their lessons with learning intentions or objectives and a reflection on whether or not those intentions were met. This same practice should be applied to the supervision and evaluation process at FTHS in which all educators have a clear understanding of their essential role in providing excellence in education to each child. During the supervision process, educators can set specific and measurable goals from their job descriptions and work to make growth in identified areas of need.

Lessons Learned

Although it would be unusual to find teachers who say they love observation day, after speaking with the faculty members at FTHS, it seems as though they do want meaningful feedback regarding their on-the-job successes and failures. To be of greatest value, feedback should come from someone who is familiar with the content area and job description. Additionally, the PA-ETEP evaluation tool is a positive step in the supervision process for educators because it allows them to take ownership of their own evaluation and goals for improvement; however, this process would be more beneficial if accompanied with meaningful collaboration. Senge (2012) asserts that teaching is oftentimes one of the most individualized professions, with teachers believing that they operate independently within, "*their* courses, *their* skills, and *their* students" (p. 48). If schools like FTHS employ the use of a more collaborative supervision and evaluation process, the potential for more meaningful professional growth is more likely to increase and support the excellence in education motto the district boasts.

Conclusion

What is excellence in education or supervision? Are educators such as Amy, Todd, and Vanessa working toward it? According to systems thinking—yes! Their desire for collaboration and a more clear understanding of what their goals and objectives are show they are embracing values promoted by systems thinking. In fact, schools that pioneered as systems thinking institutions create time in teachers' work days for them to collaborate with other professionals, and they make teamwork to promote professional growth a daily practice (Senge, 2012, p. 48). Perhaps Amy, Todd, and Vanessa's approach can be the evidence they need to achieve "distinguished" on their yearly evaluations and showcase them as educators who live the school's motto.

Reflective Questions

- How should a public school district define excellence in education? What systems are in effect that could hinder or limit their ability to do so?

- How can building-level principals provide meaningful supervision and feedback to teachers whose content area is not in their range of expertise?
- Who should be responsible for peer collaboration and goal setting and evaluation in schools? How can teachers promote this strategy? How can school leaders?

References

Danielson, C. (2013). *The framework for teaching: Evaluation instrument* (2013 ed.). Danielson Group.

Edulink, Inc. (2020). *Electronic teacher evaluation portal (PA-ETEP) by Edulink Solutions*. Edulink. Retrieved September 14, 2020, from https://edulinksolutions.com/pa-etep/

Isaacson, N., & Bamburg, J. (1992). Can schools become learning organizations? *Educational Leadership* (November), 42–44.

Senge, P. M. (2012). Creating schools for the future, not the past for all students. *Leader to Leader, 2012*(65), 44–49. https://doi.org/10.1002/ltl.20035

20

COVID-19 FORCES MORE ENGAGED ONLINE LEARNING STRATEGIES

A Systems Thinking Approach for Successful Course Delivery (Higher Education)

Christina Gunther and Gail Samdperil

Introduction

The rapid emergence of Coronavirus Disease 2019 (COVID-19) forced an immediate shift in delivery of courses in higher education. The new learning environment required instruction to move swiftly to a virtual platform with faculty who were not necessarily prepared, nor who had the background, to teach online. The result on student learning has was been significant because the shifted course delivery was reactive in response to the global health crisis. Faculty were forced to engage online in new ways in order to meet the various cognitive and sensory representation needs of students (An & Carr, 2017). Senge (1990) suggests that any system that demands change must be viewed in a holistic manner. The entire system of learning must be evaluated in a process of interrelated parts to ultimately ensure success of the changes (Senge, 1990), particularly in a fast-paced transition such as this. An optimal system of learning had to be developed to meet the new landscape COVID-19 created. All key players had to quickly assess the process in order to achieve student success in the fluctuating and nascent climate. Due to the rapid nature of the transition, subsequent hurdles occurred despite the overall success of the change. The case study in this chapter describes the key players and interrelated system that contributed to the overall success and analyzes the challenges during the accelerated change.

System and Key Players

The system of learning in higher education and key players within that system include dynamic parts. Generally, key players in the university system include president, provost, deans, faculty, staff and students. The system is complex and

DOI: 10.4324/9781003028772-24

encompasses content delivery, assessment of learning, student engagement, and the adaptability of faculty which must all work together in an interrelated process. This interrelationship is critical particularly during times of forced change. All players must support and embrace the process for success to be achieved.

The key players in this case study include the same as those within any university system: the university provost, college of health professions' dean, faculty and students, as well as the college leadership team comprised of program directors and chairs. These individuals created the dynamic interrelationship in this case. The group formed a community, which established a collective process to transform learning.

Case Analysis

When COVID-19 reached crisis levels, higher education institutions had to quickly adapt to social distancing measures. The college was initially not prepared for the rapid change necessary. As a result, the shift to remote learning was in flux, decisions were reactive, and not all players were included in the dynamic decision-making process. When it became apparent that the situation would be ongoing, key players reassessed the system. At both the university and college level, the discussions shifted to using a framework to transform required changes in course delivery. Skills were not at the level initially required to make the complex transition successful, however. The process had to become intentional. Support was required within the system in order to prepare all players for the new and complex challenges of fully remote learning. At this point, instructional and informational technology personnel and college staff members were included in the system and discussions.

Universal design for learning (UDL) and the constructivist theory of learning provided a route to follow. Recruiting interest, a paradigm within the UDL, frames instruction to actively engage the learner by optimizing relevant information (CAST, 2018) and drawing student attention to the most pertinent learning material. Similarly, Bruner's (1966) constructivist learning theory posits that instructional methods should be designed to engage students while encouraging critical thinking skills. This was of importance to the group of key players during the implementation process. These parts of the framework were essential in order to create the learning community and maintain academic rigor within the system, as well as attend to all cognitive and sensory representations employed by various students.

The framework guided the system and players in adaptation of course materials in order to provide multiple representations that met all students' needs. Strategies were required that addressed sensory, cognitive, visual/spatial, and behavioral needs (An & Carr, 2017) in the college's online platform.

Problem Resolution

Various platforms were discussed in leadership team meetings and implemented in a pilot delivery program with the support of instructional and informational technology staff members. In order to increase the success of student learning outcomes, many instructional technology tools that activated multiple sensory representations for student engagement were employed, including online group discussions, PollEverywhere questions, interactive PowerPoints, and Jeopardy style games (An & Carr, 2017). These instructional methods lend themselves to deeper thinking and analysis because students are more "actively engaged in the learning process" (Oliva & Gordon, 2013, p. 271). Scaffolding techniques were also adopted, as these techniques reinforce multiple representations of engaged learning (Oliva & Gordon, 2013). For example, instruction for each learning objective was divided into units. Formative assessments were then matched to each scaffolded unit such as "check your knowledge" questions that were offered in both synchronous and asynchronous formats. Students could self-select the format desired based on their representational needs. Answers included feedback that provided a rationale for why the answer was right or wrong, delivering immediate evaluation regardless of delivery method. These types of activities allowed faculty to reframe online content delivery in order to maximize active and engaged learning based on the current learning environment and needs of each student.

Challenges persisted that again required the input from all players involved in the system. These challenges included faculty's lack of experience in online delivery, fluctuation in students' motivation and persistence, the support infrastructure of the college for both faculty and students, and limitations in technology. Each of these elements had to be re-addressed in an orchestrated manner in the holistic system. The systems thinking process enabled all players to overcome challenges and work together within an interrelated parts model (Senge, 1990) by looping in a reflective process. For example, the leadership team developed a check-in process for faculty and exchange of ideas to encourage student engagement. Through a continuous process of reflection, dysfunctional parts in the system could be addressed. Additionally, UDL and constructivist learning theory drove the engagement that often assisted with the prevailing challenges.

Lessons Learned

Throughout the process, success was achieved and failures were identified and often reconciled. Most faculty embraced the opportunity to change and develop their course infrastructure, which proved to be an invigorating challenge. This stemmed from a variety of professional development opportunities offered by instructional and information technology, which were necessary to meet the needs of student learning outcomes in the new environment. However, a select few chose not to engage in the new practice, which significantly impacted student engagement and learning outcomes. Student course evaluations reflected the success in learning for courses that were engaged in the process. A system of fragmentation was reflected in the evaluations for faculty who did not adopt the new course delivery.

The change to remote learning forced faculty to be reflective of their course engagement strategies regardless of platform and their overall course environment. Faculty began to examine delivery of their pedagogy. Through trial and error they were able to identify very interactive and engaging online activities that not only activated critical thinking skills but encouraged student online presence. For example, one faculty member discovered that encouraging students to share their personal space of learning fostered a more inviting climate. This resulted in students keeping video cameras on and being more participatory in their synchronous time online. The lesson here is that faculty must continue the more informal relationships with students in the online environment so that motivation for both the student and faculty can be enhanced and maintained. This discovery was shared with the leadership team so that it could become part of the reflective cycle and disseminated with others.

Initially, assumptions were made within the system about faculty and student motivation, skills, and abilities in an online learning environment. The COVID-19 pandemic also exposed students who were not internally motivated to learn online. Faculty who did not have the technological skills to create effective online learning environments saw student achievement failures. As faculty experienced this, they were required to invest a significant amount of time into retooling their teaching and technological skills so that they could be effective online educators. This resulted in feelings of overload and burnout, which were then addressed within the system through support from all players within the university.

The failure of the system was that it did not recognize the time and effort needed for faculty to invest in this endeavor initially. Leadership support developed in a learn-as-you-go manner, however, did not meet the needs of key players in the system in their entirety. Leadership support was reactive rather than proactive but developed with time. Leadership made assumptions about the level of technological skills of the faculty and students, assuming they were more skilled than they were. A lack of technological support and training occurred right at the onset of the transition, but was rectified through the reflective process of the system's feedback loop.

Once support and training were provided, most faculty were able to adjust. However, they were inundated with many different options. Because this part of the system was added after the first reflective cycle, the reaction was to provide support and training on every possible technological tool available. Faculty then had to sift through a plethora of options that absorbed much needed energy for teaching. As a result, faculty were left with an overwhelming feeling of "tech anxiety."

In the beginning of the transition, faculty adapted by simply transferring all in person course materials to synchronous Zoom sessions without adapting them to the platform. The result was this feeling of "Zoom fatigue." Many faculty continued in this fashion even after support and training on other options were available because the effort to sift through and then learn to operate the tools was overwhelming.

Conclusion

Prior to the COVID-19 pandemic, the university had not made the commitment to ensure all faculty were provided with the training and resources required to teach in alternative settings. Key players learned very quickly, though, how to adapt the entire system of learning. Although the overall process was successful, the few failures serve as lessons for the future.

The main lesson of this experience is that interrelationships of all key players is the essential part of a successfully functioning system. Because some key players did not adopt a cohesive path or align with others, the impact on learning was apparent. Recognizing this was occurring, a system adjustment was adopted. Ultimately, a measure for student remediation was implemented to allow students, who did not or could not, immediately and successfully adapt to the new learning environment succeed.

The entire situation exploited different types of learning representations and the need for adapted material in the online environment. The faculty who eventually adopted the UDL strategies were the most successful in creating an effective learning environment for all students, as highlighted by student outcomes and course evaluations.

Future initiatives must take into consideration the dynamic system in a holistic, interrelated process that includes an ongoing, reflective feedback loop to ensure the ability for rapid change if required. In doing so, obstacles to success can be averted. Establishing a system framework in a proactive manner allows for necessary reflection in advance of required change. Feedback loops should be reviewed continuously.

Reflective Questions

- How can university systems of learning anticipate rapid changes in a more globalized environment?
- How can all players' needs be anticipated in a learning system that support successful outcomes in a rapidly changing environment?
- What steps must be taken in order to recognize all representations of learning that may be evolving as new generations of students enter the world of higher education?

References

An, D., & Carr, M. (2017). Learning styles theory fails to explain learning and achievement: Recommendations for alternative approaches. *Personality and Individual Differences*, 116, 410–416.

Bruner, J. S. (1966). *Toward a Theory of Instruction* (Vol. 59). Harvard University Press.

Center for Applied Special Technology [CAST]. (2018). Recruiting interest. https://udlguidelines.cast.org/engagement/recruiting-interest

Oliva, P. & Gordon, W. (2013). *Developing the Curriculum* (8th ed.) Pearson.

Senge, P. (1990). *The Fifth Discipline, the Art and Practice of the Learning Organization*. Doubleday.

Senge, P. & Kim, D. (n.d.). From fragmentation to integration: Building learning communities. Retrieved from https://thesystemsthinker.com/from-fragmentation-to-integration-building-learning-communities/

21

INNOVATIVENESS

The Capacity for Building and Sustaining Educational Change (K-12)

Lynne Lieux

Introduction

In the 1980s, many schools introduced computers into their educational programs through computer labs and a handful of desktop computers. Some believed that computers would support the creation of constructivist learning environments (Means, 1994; Rogers & Price, 2007; Zhao et al., 2016), while others saw the introduction of computers into the classroom as a means of better preparing students for the knowledge-based workforce they would enter (Cuban, 2008, 2009a; Fullan, 2013; Sheninger, 2019; Warschauer, 2011). In 1997, Sophia Academy, a PK-12 school located in large urban area in the United States, began to seriously consider placing laptops in the hands of students and faculty, believing that true technology integration resulting in a more constructivist learning environment could only occur when each student had access to technology anytime, anywhere (Livingston, 2006).

For several decades, proponents of the integration of technology into schools have argued that 1:1 computing, students having 24/7 access to technology, could shift teaching and learning from a teacher-centered approach to a more student-centered approach. While some success has been achieved through this model, few schools have been able to sustain this educational reform for a significant amount of time. Fullan suggests that the success or failure of an educational reform is directly related to the capacity of individuals or schools to "put into practice" an innovation (Fullan, 2016, p. 6). Fullan describes this capacity of school communities to sustain educational change for continuous improvement as the *innovativeness* of the school community (Fullan, 2001, 2007, 2016). This case describes how systems thinking, with attention to the school as a whole and to the individual

DOI: 10.4324/9781003028772-25

stakeholders, as well as to the purpose or mission of the school, has allowed one school to implement and sustain 1:1 computing for more than 20 years.

System and Key Players

Sophia Academy is a PreK-12 independent school for girls. As a member of an international network of schools, it embraces a common mission consisting of five tenets: faith, intellectual values, service and an awareness of the global society, community, and the growth of the individual. When stakeholders were asked for reasons for the sustainability of the 1:1 program, the most frequent and consistent answer was that the program aligned with the school's mission.

In a learning organization, such as Sophia Academy, there are a variety of stakeholders: students, faculty, the technology director, current and former administrators, graduates and parents, board of trustees, and to some extent the organization (Network) which governs the school's adherence to its mission. At Sophia Academy, stakeholders ranged from trailblazers to staunch resistors. While the final decision to implement 1:1 computing rested with the board of trustees and the head of school, adjustments to the program were and continue to be made based upon input from all key players (see Table 21.1).

Case Analysis

In 1997, Sophia Academy began to seriously consider implementing 1:1 computing in the middle and upper schools. Prior to implementation, several meetings were held to present the program and hear concerns of faculty and parents. Despite the results of a survey of middle and upper school faculty, that indicated that approximately 90 percent of the faculty were in favor of the program, there were still resistors to the program. These individuals, in general, resisted the establishment of the 1:1 computing because they could not see how they could integrate the program into their practice. Faculty were given their devices eight months prior to the first students receiving them. The faculty survey revealed that while there was great support for the program, there was also great fear. This feedback helped to inform next steps in the implementation process.

Problem Resolution

To alleviate some of the concerns of the faculty, some individuals were sent to learn from other schools, establishing collegial resourceful relationships, and then returning to campus to share knowledge with others. The successes and failures of these schools informed the implementation at Sophia Academy. The technology director indicated that collaboration with other schools led to fewer mistakes, and, in turn, Sophia Academy has shared with other educators what it has learned from sustaining the program for more than 20 years.

TABLE 21.1 Key People and Responsibilities Pertaining to 1:1 Computing at Sophia Academy

Person and Role	*Responsibilities Pertaining to 1:1*
Head of School:	
• Former	Decision to implement; adherence to the school's mission; support of implementation; assuring that support and funding given to aspects of the program
• Current	Adherence to school's mission and continued support of program
Technology Director	Provided the passion, knowledge, and leadership that drove the implementation and sustainability
Division Heads	
• Former upper school heads	Support of implementation; ensuring that faculty are given sufficient time for professional development
• Current upper school head	Continued growth of program; hiring individuals who embrace the school's mission and the program
• Former middle school head	Support of implementation; ensuring that faculty are given sufficient time for professional development
• Current middle school head	Continued growth of program; hiring individuals who embrace the school's mission and the program
Faculty	
• Upper School Faculty	Integration of technology into curriculum and providing feedback about program
• Middle School Faculty	Integration of technology into curriculum and providing feedback about program
Students	
• Upper School Students	Educational use of technology in an ethical manner and providing feedback about program
• Middle School Students	Educational use of technology in an ethical manner and providing feedback about program
• Tech Support Students	Staffing of help desk; providing technical support to students, faculty, and staff
• Graduates	Providing feedback about long-term benefits of the program as well as difficulties
Parents	Purchasing devices for their children
Board of Trustees	Final approval of program; adherence to the mission of the school
Network	Ensuring the school's adherence to the mission

When the school surveyed the faculty about their needs in implementing the 1:1 program, overwhelmingly the faculty supported the establishment of a help desk to troubleshoot hardware and software issues. A student-staffed help desk has increased student knowledge and fluidity with technology and offered needed support to students and faculty. An environment in which faculty were not afraid to admit a lack of "know how" allowed students to play a key role as support to faculty and peers. The student support staff also provided continuous feedback to the technology director about who on the faculty needed more help and what was working and not working with the devices and the program.

While the resistance to educational reform by teachers was to be expected (Cuban, 1993, 1998, 2007, 2008, 2013a, 2013b, 2018), the school moved forward with the program. Some resistors were pulled along by the technology director and colleagues and through professional development, while others chose to seek different employment. New hires to the faculty had to be committed to integrating technology into their classes.

David Peter Stroh (2015) suggests that systems thinking helps a group of people sustain change by allowing them to meet four common challenges of change: motivation, collaboration, focus, and continuous learning. Being flexible about how and when change occurs, providing a safe environment for risk-taking, encouraging risk-taking, allowing failure to be a form of learning, and developing collegiality that supports collaboration helped to foster and sustain the change that occurred at Sophia Academy.

Motivation

Fullan (2007, 2016) recognizes that there are many agents of change within a school: the principal, faculty, students, parents, and the community beyond the school. The sense of shared leadership and ownership meant that no one person owned the success or failure of the program; most of the constituents shared in the efforts to change teaching and learning through the integration of technology and pedagogy. As indicated by the technology director, no one wanted it to fail. While it can be argued that the technology director played a primary role in the change efforts that occurred, there were others "who were also leading the charge." While some administrators have seen their role as that of nudging people forward, "believing the only way to motivate others was pushing and prodding them into action, overcoming their entropy by the sheer force of their own energy" (Wheatley, 2006, p. 77), others have recognized the evolutionary nature of change, where continuous feedback supports, motivates, and allows for corrections.

Collaboration

Stroh (2015) states that systems thinking *catalyzes collaboration* because people discern how their collective actions either bring about positive or negative change. From the beginning of the 1:1 program, there was a sense of the need to collaborate if the program was to succeed. Parent participation and input was essential since the 1:1 computing program was a large financial investment on their part. The Board of Trustees approved the initiation of the program and funding for infrastructure, faculty devices, and for scholarship devices. Administrators fostered a collaborative culture that supported mutual learning and the moral support necessary to embrace substantial change (Hargreave & Shirley, 2009). In this environment, faculty and students shared ideas and the leadership of the program. The student support staff were essential in solving technical issues for faculty and students and in providing input to the Technology Director regarding the program. Learning organizations in which opportunities for shared expertise are fostered are more likely to reflect positive educational change (Fullan, 2001). Teachers continued to guide what occurs in their classrooms, but with informal and formal input from colleagues and students. Change is more likely to be sustained in a culture in which silos are not the prominent form of dwelling.

Focus

From the beginning of the program, the primary focus was to ensure that the 1:1 computing program would improve the educational program. For this reason, the school focused its efforts and funds for professional development which would enhance the integration of technology into the curriculum. It can be argued that the success of the program was due in part because of the flexibility teachers were allowed in implementing 1:1 computing. Berman and McLaughlin (1976) found that the most successful educational reforms are those in which both the innovation and those implementing it have been allowed to mutually adapt for educational improvement. In classrooms in which the most constructivist learning seemed to be occurring, teachers had adapted the innovation and their style of teaching to best meet the needs of their students. In other classrooms, the innovation was coopted and/or lethally adapted in ways that suggested that future growth and sustainability might be hindered without an intentional focus on the practice of these teachers. Efforts to change how teachers teach in a 1:1 computing program, or any other education reform, need to be focused on the educational benefits for students and sustained and further developed through professional development activities and greater collaboration among faculty.

Continuous Learning

Professional development on the use of the laptops as well as the integration of technology into the curriculum was provided and continues to be a major reason for the sustainability of the program. Initially, professional development consisted of summer and after school programs that addressed a wide range of software, hardware, and programmatic issues. While faculty were expected to use the technology with their students, they were afforded a great deal of flexibility as to how and when to do so, as well as in which professional development activities to participate. Additional support staff was hired to work individually with faculty.

Continuous learning also occurred between teachers and teachers and between teachers and students. The implementation of 1:1 computing was viewed as a major shift in how education was occurring at Sophia Academy and to that end, everyone was expected to be continuously learning from each other as to how to best use technology for educational improvement. As mentioned earlier, students who operate the help desk play a key role in the learning of their teachers and peers.

Lessons Learned

Having a strong educational mission, a moral purpose, creates a *raison d'être* for change. Without a clear sense of mission, "organizations get tossed and turned by shifts in their environment" (Wheatley, 2006, p. 39). According to Peter Senge (2006), a shared vision or mission lacks a solid foundation without the practice of systems thinking. Sophia Academy's mission is a living force that is deeply embraced by all the parts of the learning organization, allowing it to be the impetus for change (Senge, 2006). If the individuals within an organization believe that the changes proposed will help achieve the goal(s) of their mission, they are more likely to embrace and sustain change.

Visits to schools that had previously implemented 1:1 computing and strong and numerous professional development opportunities helped to alleviate faculty concerns. The fact that faculty were allowed a great deal of flexibility in how and when they used technology in their classes also made the implementation of the program less stressful for faculty. Because faculty were willing to embrace risk-taking and learn from each other and from students, the program has become integral to the educational program at Sophia Academy. The student-staffed help desk also minimized technical issues and the need for faculty and students to be without their devices for a significant time while repairs occurred.

Conclusion

The school's mission formed the basis of the school culture, and it was within this culture that flexibility, risk-taking, and collegiality allowed 1:1 computing to be sustained. The school's mission supported a culture in which teaching and learning could be adapted, could become more constructivist, through the integration of technology into the curriculum. As Fullan (2005) notes, "sustainability is very much a matter of changes in culture: powerful strategies that enable people to question and alter certain values and beliefs as they create new forms of learning." Changes in beliefs and practices occurred because they were consistent with the mission. Using a systems approach, the administration sought continuous feedback from all constituents, especially those most impacted by the program, faculty and students. The school has been able to sustain the 1:1 program because the program continues to evolve. Using a lens of system thinking, the school has been able to sustain change through a program that motivates, promotes collaboration, and requires constituents to focus efforts and engage in continuous learning, while remaining true to its mission.

Reflective Questions

- How does systems thinking support educational change within your school? From whom is feedback solicited? How is this feedback used to sustain change?
- What factors contribute or hinder an evolutionary school culture in your school?
- What role does your school's mission play in decisions to adapt new program or to revise current programs?

Additional Resources

Banathy, B. H. (1968). *Instructional systems.* Fearon Publishers.

Cabrera, D., & Cabrera, L. (2015). *Systems thinking made simple: New hope for solving wicked problems* (2nd ed.). Plectica Publishing.

Lieux, M. L. (2018). Innovativeness: One School's Experience of Sustaining Educational Change. [Doctoral dissertation, University of New Orleans]. https://scholarworks.uno.edu/cgi/viewcontent.cgi?article=3639&context=td

Meadows, D. H. (2008). *Thinking in systems: A primer.* Chelsea Green Publishing.

Salisbury, D. F. (1996). *Five technologies for educational change: Systems thinking, systems design, quality science, change management, instructional technology.* Educational Technology.

Senge, P. M. (2014). *The fifth discipline fieldbook: Strategies and tools for building a learning organization.* Currency.

Senge, P. M., Cambron-McCabe, N., Lucas, T., Smith, B., & Dutton, J. (2012). *Schools that learn (updated and revised): A fifth discipline fieldbook for educators, parents, and everyone who cares about education.* Crown.

Shaked, H., Schechter, C., Ganon-Shilon, S., & Goldratt, M. (2017). *Systems thinking for school leaders.* Springer.

References

Berman, P., & McLaughlin, M. W. (1976). Implementation of educational innovation. *The Educational Forum 40*(3), 345–370. https://doi.org/10.1080/00131727609336469

Cuban, L. (1993). *How teachers taught: Constancy and change in American classrooms 1880–1990* (2nd ed.). Teachers College Press.

Cuban, L. (1998). How schools change reforms: Redefining reform success and failure. *Teachers College Record 99*(3), 453–477.

Cuban, L. (2007). Hugging the middle: Teaching in an era of testing and accountability, 1980–2005. *Education Policy Analysis Archives 15*(1). http://files.eric.ed.gov/fulltext/EJ800818.pdf

Cuban, L. (2008). *Frogs into princes: Writings on school reform.* Teachers College Press.

Cuban, L. (2009). *Hugging the middle: How teachers teach in an era of testing and accountability.* Teachers College Press.

Cuban, L. (2013a). *Inside the black box: Change without reform in American education*. Harvard Education Press.

Cuban, L. (2013b). Why so many structural changes in schools and so little reform in teaching practice. *Journal of Educational Administration 51*(2). 109–125. https://doi.org/10.1108/09578231311304661

Cuban, L. (2018). *The flight of a butterfly or the path of a bullet? Using technology to transform teaching and learning*. Harvard Education Press.

Fullan, M. (2001). *Leading in a culture of change*. Jossey-Bass.

Fullan, M. (2005). *Leadership and sustainability: Systems thinkers in action*. Corwin.

Fullan, M. (2007). *The new meaning of educational change* (3rd ed.). Teachers College Press.

Fullan, M. (2013). *Stratosphere: Integrating technology, pedagogy, and change knowledge*. Pearson Canada, Inc.

Fullan, M. (2016). *The new meaning of educational change* (5th ed.). Teachers College Press.

Hargreaves, A., & Shirley, D. (2009). *The fourth way: The inspiring future for educational change*. Corwin.

Livingston, P. (2006). *1-to-1 learning: Laptop programs that work*. International Society for Technology in Education (ISTE).

Means, B. (1994). Introduction: Using technology to advance educational goals. In B. Means (Ed.), *Technology and education reform: The reality behind the promise* (pp. 1–21). Jossey-Bass.

Rogers, Y., & Price, S. (2007). Using ubiquitous computing to extend and enhance learning experiences. In M. van't Hoof & K. Swan (Eds.), *Ubiquitous computing in education: Invisible technology, invisible impact* (pp. 329–347). Lawrence Erlbaum Associates.

Senge, P. M. (2006). *The fifth discipline: The art and practice of the learning organization*. Currency.

Sheninger, E. (2019). *Digital leadership: Changing paradigms for changing times* (2nd ed.). Corwin.

Stroh, D. P. (2015). *Systems thinking for social change: A practical guide to solving complex problems, avoiding unintended consequences, and achieving lasting results*. Chelsea Green Publishing.

Warschauer, M. (2011). *Learning in the cloud: How (and why) to transform schools with digital media*. Teachers College Press.

Wheatley, M. J. (2006). *Leadership and the new science: Learning about organization from an orderly universe* (3rd ed.). Berrett-Koehler Publishers, Inc.

Zhao, Y., Zhang, G., Lei, J., & Qiu, W. (2016). *Never send a human to do a machine's job: Correcting the top 5 edtech mistakes*. Corwin Press.

22

COMMUNITY-BASED ADULT ESOL INSTRUCTION

Challenges and Successes of Moving to Online Teaching (Education/International)

Ahoo Salem and M. Aaron Bond

Introduction

The outbreak of COVID-19 in March 2020 and the safety guidelines set by Virginia's governor resulted in cancelation of in-person services for nonprofits offering educational services. English for Speakers of Other Languages (ESOL) programs offered by Blue Ridge Literacy (BRL) were negatively affected, including the cancelation of daily contracted English literacy classes for newly arrived refugees, leveled ESOL classes offered twice a week at beginner, intermediate and advanced levels, and citizenship preparation programs addressing the English and Civics sections of the US naturalization test. Additionally, the closure of the Roanoke Public Libraries put a hold on BRL's one-on-one tutoring program, as meeting rooms of the city of Roanoke's six library branches were the primary meeting location for BRL's tutor and learner matches. BRL staff, instructors, and tutors faced an abrupt loss of contact with adult learners enrolled in ESOL classes and one-on-one tutoring programs. This loss was especially significant as BRL programs serve as a channel of information and a trusted social hub for many adult learners who have limited communication abilities and literacy skills.

To reduce the impact of cancelation of BRL's programs on adult learners, BRL staff implemented several strategies to remain connected with learners at a time of uncertainty and rapidly changing conditions. This chapter aims to describe the complexities of transitioning from face-to-face programs to online teaching through the perspective of a small nonprofit community-based literacy organization (CBLO) in Southwest Virginia. This case adopts a multilevel approach to reflect systems drivers and variables that influence and shape the range of abilities of BRL with consideration of the organization's learner base population, funding sources as well as staff and volunteer composition. These levels will be viewed in

DOI: 10.4324/9781003028772-26

the context of BRL's mission: helping adult learners reach their life goals through functional literacy skills and reflect how the organization changed to meet those needs in a time of crisis.

System and Key Players

A key component of any organizational system are the people working, serving as stakeholders, and learning within a system. Senge (2006) insists that one must consider the mental models of individuals in a system as a key to changing the larger system. There are several interactions at play in this scenario: the learners, the funding organizations, and the volunteers.

Learners

Blue Ridge Literacy was established in 1985 to address the basic literacy needs of American born adults in the area. By the 1990s the organization added ESOL programs to its services to address the English literacy needs of Roanoke's growing immigrant and refugee population. Currently, over 90 percent of BRL's learners are foreign-born adults seeking to improve their English literacy skills. Eyring (2014) notes that diversity is inherent to any adult ESOL program. Similarly, BRL students have a variety of educational backgrounds, skill sets, English proficiency levels, and differential level of access to resources. As indicated in Figure 22.1 in the 2019–2020 Fiscal Year, BRL served over 300 adult learners, representing over 50 countries including the US, through class programs and one-on-one tutoring services. The top five countries of origin of BRL learners were Afghanistan, Mexico, Democratic Republic of Congo (DCR), Haiti, and Sudan.

Besides being the "English School," BRL serves as a social hub where newcomers build networks and collect information while they acquire the functional language skills that are needed for self-sufficiency and survival in everyday settings. Exploration of any move to online learning has to consider the implications of digital divide for adult learners with different levels of English proficiency and literacy skills, exposure to digital spaces, and technology and internet accessibility issues (Cherewka, 2020; Ono & Zavondi, 2008; Pendell et al., 2013; Smith & Smith, 2010).

Funding Organizations

As a small nonprofit organization, BRL operates on an annual budget of under $200,000 a year. Funds are raised through charitable donations, grants, and contractual on-site and off-site services. It should be noted that some of BRL's funding sources have special contractual conditions about the delivery methods for instruction and a distrust of online delivery as an equitable or effective method. Successful program outcomes are an essential variable in securing continued

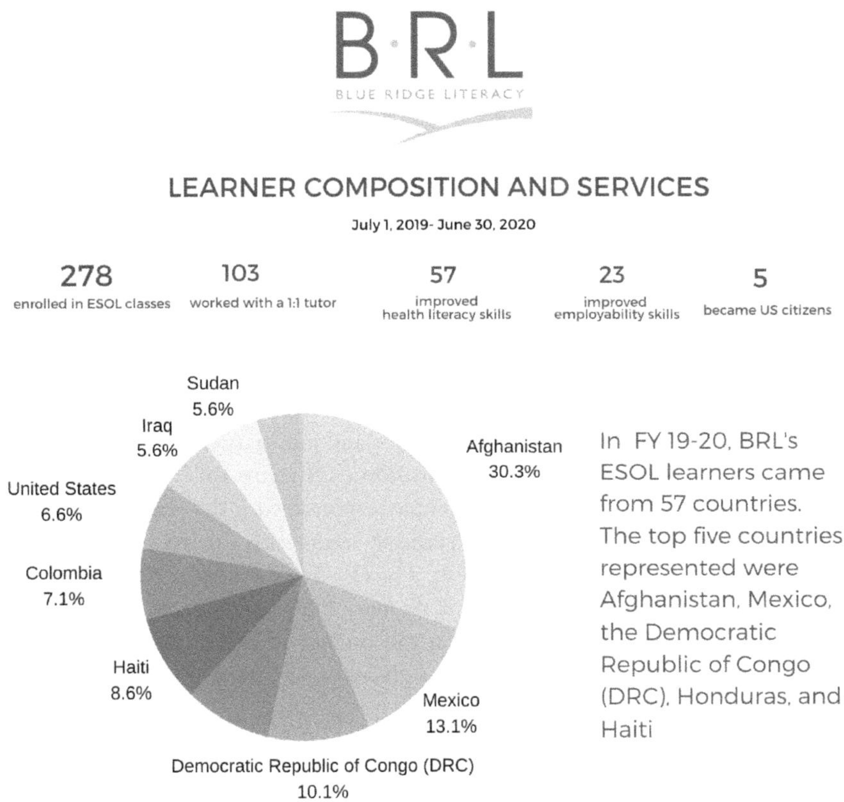

FIGURE 22.1 BRL's Learner Composition in 2019–2020 Fiscal Year

funding for the organization to maintain its existing programs and expand services to address the needs of the learners and community. For reporting purposes, BRL's program outcomes are commonly assessed through quantifiable indicators addressing learner enrollment, learner retention, and learner test scores.

Volunteers

Due to budget constraints, CBLOs rely heavily on volunteers to teach adult learners (Sanborn, 2012). BRL's volunteers, many of whom are retired individuals, serve as the organization's main resource for one-on-one tutoring services. Every year, the organization holds six training workshops to recruit and train new volunteers. BRL's guidelines require one-on-one matches to meet at a public space. COVID-19 presented unique challenges for the volunteers, as many of the volunteer tutors were not familiar or comfortable with distance learning technologies. Training and mentoring in order to use online technologies was required.

Case Analysis

As with any system BRL exists in a complex series of systems and subsystems. BLR's long history of providing ESL services and its central and easily accessible location in the city's main public library have made it a well-known and trusted resource to adult learners in the community. With a focus on functional literacy, BRL's programs aim to provide learners with the practical skills they need to read, write, and communicate real-life purposes, in order to ensure people can function effectively in their community. The stay-at-home order and cancelation of BRL's face-to-face programs suddenly eradicated BRL's accessibility at a time when adult learners most needed the skills for remaining connected with others, staying healthy, supporting school-aged children, and finding new employment. By suspending BRL's services, the stay-at-home order resulted in abrupt discontinuation of revenue from contractual services and put grant-funded programs at risk by negatively impacting projected outcomes. Systems thinking and change models are designed to allow time for people responsible for the change and those affected by the change to process and come to terms with a desired result (Stroh, 2015; Cabrera et al., 2018). In his book, *The Hot Sauce Principle: How to live and lead in a world where everything is urgent all the time* (2020), Brandon M. Smith posits that emergency situations often serve as the catalyst to drive change. COVID-19 prompted organizational change through an urgent need to adapt to a new instructional situation.

During this time period schools and educational institutions of all types and sizes were moving their instruction online. Adult literacy organizations have historically perceived this transition challenging due to complexities caused by adult learner's lower English and digital literacy skills (MacCalhahan, 2014). These conditions are even more pronounced in the case of immigrant and refugee women who make up 75 percent of BRL's foreign-born learners. Structural factors, role definitions, and family dynamics reduced women's access to technology tools, as well as skills and competences that were needed to use and navigate online resources (Antonio & Tuffley, 2014).

In addition to learners, BRL's tutor force also faced several challenges related to social distancing rules and cancelation of face-to-face programs. In the 2019–2020 Fiscal Year, BRL relied on a pool of over 100 active and on-hold tutors, 45 percent of whom were over the age of 60. A range of reasons, including lack of interest or familiarity with online teaching and being among the at-risk age group have reduced the availability of BRL's volunteers for one-on-one tutoring.

Employing systems thinking practices requires an analysis of the key players within the context of the system and with a lens seeking to understand how those players will be affected by the change (Senge, 2006). The way the BRL student population interacted with instructors, content, and their peers changed dramatically. To meet student needs and to continue the mission of BRL, an analysis of available technology resources, student learning needs, and learning environments was undertaken. A similar analysis was performed to understand the capabilities and capacities of the volunteer instructors. Finally, the expectations of the funding agencies required strategic management and communication.

Problem Resolution

Contacting the learners after cancelation of face-to-face programs was one of the initial challenges of resuming contact with learners and eventually moving to online teaching. At the time of registration, adult learners fill out an intake form and submit their contact information. Frequently, learners change their contact numbers without updating their contact information. It is also very common for learners to put down a family member's number, especially their husbands, as their primary mode of contact. Understanding the system in which the learners interacted outside of BRL, BRL staff used a variety of channels to continue to communicate with learners. BRL staff repeatedly called the numbers on file and left multiple text and voice messages. Facebook messages, for those learners who were on social media, were another useful tool for connecting with learners. By early April, BRL had created steady, albeit limited, communication channels with learners through WhatsApp groups. WhatsApp is one of the most commonly used messaging applications on smartphones (Montag et al., 2015) and is regularly used by BRL learners. The free and end-to-end encrypted messaging app allows for individual voice and video calls as well as group messaging and file sharing. In addition, word of mouth had always been an important tool for spreading news among BRL's learners. The first learners BRL reconnected with played an important role in encouraging and supporting other learners in their community to obtain phones, start using WhatsApp and eventually to join online classes.

BRL's experience of piloting online classes for a small group of learners showed that, despite initial concerns, online teaching was a viable option for our learner base population and also helped identify common barriers to learner participation. These findings shaped BRL's in-person and by appointment technical support services after re-opening of our offices in mid-August. The ability to address skill-based barriers increased the accessibility of BRL's online programs among adult learners. The majority of learners in online classes use their smartphones to join class. BRL is accepting donations of laptops and tablets to create a lending library for learners. These successful outcomes, along with considerations of health and safety of our community, helped shape the decision for a programming transition to mostly online services. An exception, however, is BRL's largest revenue-generating contractual service. The contractual conditions for this service do not consider online teaching as an acceptable delivery method for instruction. As a result, instructional services related to this contract are delivered in-person, with consideration of safety issues regarding COVID-19.

Currently, BRL offers a total of seven online leveled ESOL and citizenship preparation classes via Zoom, along with a limited number of small scales, in-person programs. Each class is supplemented with a WhatsApp group in order to replicate the classroom environment and to share class updates and Zoom links. By facilitating communication between learners and their instructors, WhatsApp groups have been extremely useful in increasing learner accountability and retention. At the end of each semester, learners are given the option to come into the BRL offices by appointment and take their final test. Instructors and BRL staff utilize the existing WhatsApp groups to send reminders to the learners about the final test and inquire about their preferred appointments for taking the test. Having the option of picking their test day has increased learners' participation in testing. In absence of in-person classes, the testing appointments create a suitable opportunity to register learners for the next semester and provide them with their learning material and study packet.

Online classes are rapidly becoming a popular option among BRL learners as they eliminate the need to commute or secure childcare. The ability to provide in-person and digital support has made BRL's programs more accessible to a larger group of learners. At the same time, there is a need to limit the number of learners in each class to ensure productivity. This situation has created a programming dilemma for BRL given its small budget, limited staff and high reliance on volunteers. BRL's leveled ESOL classes are managed enrollment programs, meaning that learners can join the program during a specific registration time before the start of the semester (Eyring, 2014). BRL is currently applying a cap of ten learners per online class. Learners who register after the ten-person cap is reached are put on a pre-registration list for the following semester of class. This approach increases the chances of learners losing interest while waiting and reduces overall retention rates. A suitable remedy for this situation is opening up more classes. This, however, requires an increase in resources for online teaching, namely instructors and Zoom Pro accounts. These are factors to be considered in planning BRL's 21–22 Fiscal Year budget.

To assist current volunteers with the transition to online teaching, BRL now offers individualized assistance with setting up Zoom and WhatsApp accounts and training on different features of these platforms. In the case of volunteer instructors, individual support is complemented with meetings for classroom instructors throughout the semester to address challenges and success stories and to share ideas and solutions. BRL's monthly newsletter now features a section entitled "Resources for Our Tutors and Volunteers" to share useful tips, tutorials and ideas to provide ongoing support and professional development. Nevertheless, many of BRL's tutors have opted to be on-hold until they can meet with their learners in-person again. As part of the 2021 Adult Education and Literacy Remix Conference, BRL and several other CBLOs are working on a joint project to create a road map for increasing diversity of their prospective volunteer forces. A common factor among all CBLOs involved in this project is the transition of their volunteer training workshops to online events. This strategy, so far, seems promising for attracting volunteers who are more open to the idea of online teaching and tutoring.

Lessons Learned

BRL's transition to online teaching has been a constant learning experience. As these online programs evolve and progress, they allow for a better understanding of how different key players interact with one another and shape the dynamics of BRL as a system. An interesting observation is that the same factors that account for success stories of online classes, namely the flexibility that comes with online interactions, have the likelihood of posing challenges.

BRL's incorporation of WhatsApp groups as the dominant mode of communication is a good example of this situation. WhatsApp groups are vibrant and interactive and allow for organic conversations among learners. As a result, they have quickly become an integral part of all BRL's programs, including face-to-face services. The ability to leave video and voice messages makes these groups especially useful for beginner level learners with limited writing abilities. At the same time, easy accessibility of the WhatsApp groups means that instructors and learners are connected at all times via their smartphones. This situation can create concerns about privacy and security, untimely messages, and use of inappropriate language for a classroom setting (Cetinkaya, 2017). A next step for ensuring continued success of these groups is creation and sharing of rules of conduct, especially regarding times of contact and content of topics discussed and shared through the WhatsApp groups.

By participating in online classes, adult learners share the experience of distance learning with their children. This provides an important avenue for family literacy and also shows the children, who are often second-generation immigrants, the agency of their parents in improving their language skills. At the same time, bringing the classroom to the living rooms of the learners requires a different set of classroom guidelines, including strategies for noise reduction and attentive participation during the class time. To address this challenge, BRL maintains regular communication with instructors and provides learners with easy-to-follow videos outlining classroom rules and step by step instructions for the use of video and microphone features on Zoom.

BRL's rapid transition to online teaching was in response to circumstances caused by the pandemic. This transition required a re-evaluation of modes of communication, methods of instruction, and provision of support. In absence of an emergency preparedness plan, the required shifts were planned and executed within the framework of BRL's existing resources and abilities. Going forward, it is critical for BRL's Board of Directors to outline a contingency plan to analyze the impact of potential crises and ensure appropriate arrangements are made to respond in a timely and effective way.

Conclusion

BRL's rapid transition to online classes started with assumptions about multi-level challenges that reflected the organization's existing systems and subsystems at the beginning of pandemic. Throughout the process of this transition, it became clear that, as a complex system, the key players at each level are adaptive and have the ability to self-organize and continually become better (Cabrera et al., 2018).

The pandemic highlighted the fact that our community faces an even more urgent need for literacy services. The ability to read, write, and communicate is key to remaining connected with others, accessing life-saving information, verifying the credibility of news sources and supporting children with school work. These factors play a crucial role in wellbeing of individuals, as well as collective resiliency and health of our community. Switching from in-person programs to remote teaching platforms has been a new adventure for our learners and instructors. It has also been a great reminder that when an adult learner joins our programs, they make an active choice to improve their literacy skills and create a better life for themselves and their families. This, in turn, is resonated in the support that our learners receive from their family members to cope with the challenges of online learning. Over the past months, we have witnessed how on days of class husbands leave their smartphones at home for their wives to access class, or how college-age children lend their tablets to their parents for a better learning experience. Nearly every class has a troop of young providers of digital support who make sure their parents are logged into class. As BRL's online services evolve, instructors and volunteers share ideas and suggestions for improving learning outcomes. As such, each online class is a collective effort to overcome the barriers of technology and adapt to a new learning environment.

Reflective Questions

Going ahead, it will be useful to reflect on the following questions:

- How can perceived limitations of a system's sub-set impact the dynamics of the system in short- and long-term scenarios?
- What is the relationship between a system and the context in which it operates and how can this larger picture increase the stability of the system under discussion?
- How do power hierarchies between different levels of a system shape the system's dynamics and how can stakeholders have a voice in decisions that impact other key players within a system?

Additional Resources

ProLiteracy, also known as ProLiteracy Worldwide, is an international nonprofit organization that supports literacy programs that help adults learn to read and write. Adult Literacy Education (ALE) is ProLiteracy's online, peer-reviewed, themed research journal which is published twice a year.

Virginia Adult Learning Resource Center (VALRC) provides adult education and literacy resources, publications, and training for adult education practitioners in Virginia. PROGRESS is Virginia's adult education and literacy newsletter.

Virginia Literacy Foundation (VLF) provides funding and technical support to private, volunteer literacy organizations throughout Virginia via challenge grants, training, and direct consultation.

References

Antonio, A., & Tuffley, D. (2014). The gender digital divide in developing countries. *Future Internet, 6*(4), 673–687. MDPI AG. Retrieved from http://dx.doi.org/10.3390/fi6040673

Cabrera D., Cabrera L., Powers E., Solin J., & Kushner J. (2018) Applying systems thinking models of organizational design and change in community operational research, *European Journal of Operational Research, 268*(3). https://doi.org/10.1016/j.ejor.2017.11.006

Cetinkaya, L. (2017). The impact of WhatsApp use on success in education process. *International Review of Research in Open and Distributed Learning, 18*(7). https://doi.org/10.19173/irrodl.v18i7.3279

Cherewka, A. (2020, September 03). *The digital divide hits U.S. immigrant households disproportionately during the Covid-19 pandemic.* Migration Policy Institute. www.migrationpolicy.org/article/digital-divide-hits-us-immigrant-households-during-covid-19

Eyring, J. L. (2014). Adult ESL Education in the US. *CATESOL Journal, 26*(1), 120–149.

McClanahan, L. (2014). Training using technology in the adult ESL classroom. *Journal of Adult Education, 43*(1), 22–27.

Montag, C., Błaszkiewicz, K., Sariyska, R., Lachmann, B., Andone, I., Trendafilov, B., … & Markowetz, A. (2015). Smartphone usage in the 21st century: who is active on WhatsApp?. *BMC research notes, 8*(1), 1–6. https://doi.org/10.1186/s13104-015-1280-z.

Ono, H., & Zavodny, M. (2008). Immigrants, English ability and the digital divide. *Social forces, 86*(4), 1455–1479. https://doi.org/10.1353/sof.0.0052

Pendell, K., Withers, E., Castek, J., & Reder, S. (2013). Tutor-facilitated adult digital literacy learning: Insights from a case study. *Internet Reference Services Quarterly, 18*(2), 105–125. https://doi.org/10.1080/10875301.2013.800013

Sanborn, V. G. (2012). Tutor training quality and student outcomes. *PROGRESS Newsletter, 24*(3), 3. www.valrc.org/about/issues/pdf/summer2012_a.pdf

Senge, P. (2006). *The Fifth Discipline: The art and practice of the learning organization.* Crown Business.

Stroh, D. P. (2015). *Systems thinking for social change: A practical guide to solving complex problems, avoiding unintended consequences, and achieving lasting results.* Chelsea Green Publishing.

Smith, B. M. (2020). *The hot sauce principle: How to live and lead in a world where everything is urgent all of the time.* Indie Books International.

Smith, M. C., & Smith, T. J. (2010). Adults' uses of computer technology: Associations with literacy tasks. *Journal of Educational Computing Research, 42*(4), 407–422. https://doi.org/10.2190%2FEC.42.4.c

23

CREATING A SUSTAINABLE AFTER-SCHOOL ELEMENTARY SCHOOL LITERACY PROGRAM IN PARTNERSHIP WITH A UNIVERSITY PRE-SERVICE TEACHER TECHNOLOGY COURSE (K-12)

Beth R. Sockman and Samantha J. Blevins

Introduction

This case describes how systems thinking and the systems heuristic of Purpose, Stakeholders, and Implementation (PSI) (Sockman et al., 2019) was used to support a mutually beneficial and sustainable partnership between an after-school literacy program at an elementary school and university using a technology integration course. According to the Children's Defense Fund, one in six children (www.childrensdefense.org/policy/resources/soac-2020-child-poverty/) live in poverty in the USA. In this case, the elementary school exceeded that number; over half, or 66 percent of the children received a free or reduced-cost lunch due to their poverty level. In an all-too-common scenario, many of this school's children were from underrepresented populations and did not meet literacy proficiency goals. The elementary school aimed to raise the academic achievement and support and the engagement of children. Two miles away was a university with the social capital of students that could benefit from volunteering.

System & Key Players

The university sought to create a service-learning experience for college students, which is considered a high-impact practice for higher education (Kuh, 2008; Celio, Durlak, & Dymnicki, 2011). Though service learning is a challenging pedagogy to implement, there are clear benefits such as increased student motivation, improved student confidence, and supporting students' sense of meaning in their

DOI: 10.4324/9781003028772-27

study (Bringle & Hatcher, 1996; Celio, et al. 2011; Sockman et al., 2018). Thus, the elementary school and university set out to build a mutually beneficial partnership with a clear sense of purpose.

According to Sockman et al. (2019) "Purpose" is the first step of the service-learning system's heuristic used to describe the important parts of service-learning pedagogy. A heuristic is an approach to solving a problem that follows a method or rules. The heuristic used in this case follows three steps: PSI which will be identified throughout the case study to explicate the systems thought.

The local university had an AmeriCorps worker called a VISTA, that stands for Volunteer in Service to America. It was the VISTA's responsibility to help with the partnership by implementing the literacy program, but the VISTA was only available for three years. They recruited college students, approximately 25 volunteers, to read with small groups of children from grades three to five at the elementary school once a week directly after school. The small reading groups encouraged children to value reading stories while teaching literacy skills. The college students and children were always excited to see each other, but the altruistic program was not sustainable. The time-intensive act of soliciting college students became too challenging to maintain since college students have fluctuating schedules and so volunteer attrition was high.

How can the elementary school–university partnership be sustained to support an after-school literacy program for a local elementary school in a mutually beneficial partnership?

Innovation That Was Eventually Implemented

An unlikely course, a *technology course* for pre-service teachers, used technology to create and implement a culturally relevant literacy program to select students in grades 3–5 during the elementary school's after-school program. Children received small group attention while engaging in lessons with technology delivered by college students. College students used technology to create literacy lessons based on diverse books, and integrated collaborative technologies to deliver meaningful lessons (Koehler et al., 2013).

The second part of the heuristic is stakeholders. A VISTA served as the program coordinator in a term that would end after three years. An advisory board was created that consisted of the principal, teacher liaison, parent, two professors, and a college student. The advisory board met once a semester, each representing their view. Even with multiple stakeholders bringing a wide array of perspectives and interests, their shared commitment provided members a deep sense of purpose (Cabrera & Cabrera, 2015; Stroh, 2015). The elementary school stakeholders, their respective roles, and perspectives are presented in Table 23.1. The university stakeholders, their respective roles, and perspectives are presented in Table 23.2.

TABLE 23.1 Local Elementary School Stakeholders

Person—Role	*Perspective—Primary Interest*
Principal: approves all programs; adheres and serves as a conduit of district policy; advisory board member **Teachers**: recommend students for the after-school program based on student need **Teacher Liaison**: present during the after-school program as monitor; helps the university professor answer questions about logistics and policy; advisory board member	• see the students enjoy the after-school program • increase literacy skills • support educational goals • children having fun within a controlled manner
Parents/Guardians of students in grades 3–5: gave permission for their child to participate in the after-school program; 1 parent—advisory board member	• see their child succeed in reading and writing • enjoy an after-school activity
Children in grades 3–5: children meet in small groups with the college student	• have fun • positive relationship with the college students

TABLE 23.2 Local University Stakeholders

Person—Role	*Perspective—Primary Interest*
Dean of the College of Education (COE): approves courses and acts as the conduit for the provost and university's policy	• strong community connections to show value of the university to the community
Chair of the Technology department: approves major course changes	• university students pleased with their courses • innovative courses within the departments to prove relevance
Professor of Reading: informs expertise in reading instruction	• university students become better at teaching reading • build a professional–friendly relationship with children
Professor of Technology Course: creates and implements instruction for the pre-service teachers; advisory board member	• university students see the cognitive benefits and challenges of technology use • university students engage elementary children in their work
University Students in the Technology Course: pre-service teachers; learning to write lessons and to use technology for learning	• elementary students like them • create and implement instruction for 3rd–5th graders that is engaging

Case Analysis

The third part of the heuristic is implementation (Bethany, 1973; Sockman et al., 2019). During implementation, there were many challenges to overcome. All the stakeholders could help determine the underlying causes of the problem and potential solutions. The after-school literacy program for elementary school students was successful in its first year because the VISTA persistently recruited college students to volunteer their time to read with elementary school students after their school day. After recruiting about 25 students, training began, and college students were paired with 3–5th grades. The pair forged a relationship through reading, talking, and playing. There was an enthusiastic beginning, but some college students would quit throughout the semester, and the children were disappointed as they were shuffled to a new college student. Then, some children also stopped attending and by the end of the semester, numbers dwindled. The model did not provide the consistency that children needed and it was labor-intensive to recruit and train college students. In addition, stakeholders' needs were not met.

Problem Resolution

Below are descriptions of complexities that served as underlying problems before finding a solution. Most of the complexities were inputs, which are structures or concepts that went into the system that were either static or dynamic, and affected how smoothly the program could operate. Below are the identified input complexities and how the problems were solved.

Input Complexity—Timing—Schedules

The school's and college's schedule were misaligned. An elementary school has a longer academic year than a university, with mostly predictable needs based on consistent scheduling. In contrast, the university has fluctuations, operating on a 15-week schedule. This particular university had little support for volunteer activities such as no staff dedicated to managing volunteerism. Given the limited resources, university partnerships were more likely to be sustained if embedded within an existing structure of academic courses that are 15-week cycles.

Input Complexity—Service Learning

There needed to be an easier way to get university students to work with elementary children. Courses provide a natural rhythm for college learning and within the course structure there are built-in support systems such as leadership, student social capital, time, and importantly, intentional learning goals. In addition, much research shows that service learning is highly beneficial to student learning objectives (Kuh, 2008; Sockman et al., 2018). Therefore, creating a sustainable partnership should be embedded in courses, ideally an elementary education course catering to literacy with elementary students. A course needed to be found that met from 3–5 pm, the "after-school hours" of the elementary school, and could work on literacy and social-emotional development.

Input Complexity—Finding the Right Course

The third input into the system was finding the right course. The education department already had partnerships and was unable to take anymore. The technology department taught a course for the elementary education majors that focused on technology integration for elementary school learning. The technology course would need to be substantially modified to accommodate going to the elementary school every week, meeting course goals, and supporting students in a real setting.

Integrating an on-site literacy program into a college technology course involved collaboration from elementary school and university stakeholders to reach a mutual agreement around goals and implementation. The VISTA brought together the professor, who taught the technology course for pre-service teachers, and the principal. After meeting to discuss the proposed program, the principal agreed that technology could be used for the after-school literacy program and would be attractive to the students. Both the principal and the professor needed to rally other stakeholders at their respective organizations. In addition, the professor had to redesign the course to incorporate literacy learning with technology integration.

Input Complexity—After-School Club Schedule

One of the easiest issues to solve was the schedule. The principal proposed the following scheduling idea to the elementary school teachers: after-school academic clubs on Mondays and Wednesdays, and Co-Curriculars on Tuesdays and Thursdays. Though distinct lines could be blurry between the two types of program offerings, the teachers quickly agreed that it would increase attendance to the different types of clubs.

Stakeholder Complexity – Getting Buy-In and Support

Getting stakeholder support from all the participants (Sockman et al., 2019; Stroh, 2015) encourages ownership and, thereby, cooperation for future development when needed. Since university students would be leaving campus regularly to participate in the after-school program, and participation in the program would become part of a course, the professor would need to seek support from the department chair and dean. First, the professor needed to devise a plan that fit into the course structure. Because the course met two days a week, it was determined that the students would go to the elementary school one day a week. The other class meeting day would take place at the university to encourage students to reflect on experiences and build theoretical knowledge. With this proposal, the professor sold the idea to the department chair and dean. Both quickly agreed that this would be a valuable program to meet students' learning goals and provide value to the community (Sockman et al., 2019).

The principal easily corralled buy-in from their teaching staff and secured the money needed to pay teachers from the elementary school to become a "club teacher," assisting and supervising as needed. The "club teacher" and principal ensured ongoing communication with the teachers and parents. In addition, the third grade through fifth grade teachers supplied a list of children struggling with reading or writing and forwarded their children's names to school administration. Admission sent permission letters to the parents, and children would take the after-school bus home or walk home.

Transformational Planning—Complexity—Course Redesign

The university course needed to be redesigned to meet the new purposes. Research shows that technology integration is best seen and understood in context, so the professor had a clear purpose to integrate technology and literacy. The technology professor worked with the reading professor to incorporate reading strategies that could be used with technology such as the use of anticipation guides and questioning techniques. They also identified picture books to accommodate semester themes such as courage, social action, or the environment. Picture books would need to change every semester to accommodate elementary students who were tutored the entire year.

Logistically, the technology course met twice a week, one day was a lecture, and the other included a two-hour lab, the days had set goals. On the lecture day, students stayed at the university and designed lessons that they would later implement at the elementary school. The university students chose picture books with a common theme, and then created Webquest about the books. Armed with lessons and Webquests, the university students taught the elementary school children on the two-hour lab day. After their lesson, the university students wrote a reflection about their experience, and pedagogical questions would be addressed when they returned for the lecture day. From the rotating process of creation, implementation, and reflection as feedback, revisions were made to the program. A visualization of the implementation systems flow is presented in Figure 23.1.

Summary—Complexities and Solution with Feedback

Addressing the complexities with schedules, finding a course, getting buy-in from all stakeholders, and then the curriculum redesign had its benefits. Given that the elementary school–university partnership began in 2013 and still continues

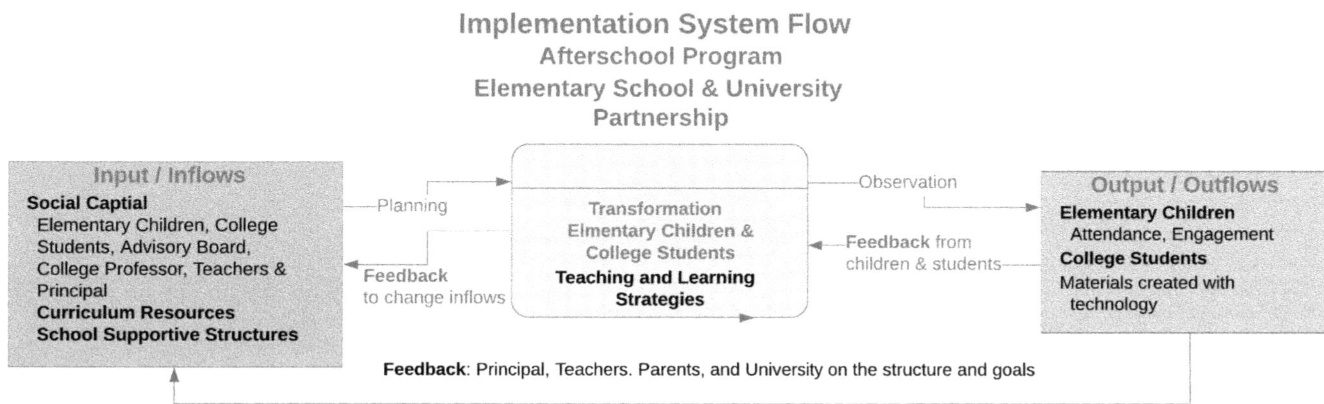

FIGURE 23.1 Implementation Systems Flow for Service Learning between the University and Elementary School

Note: This motion diagram conceptualizes the components that form the university course–elementary after-school program system; the various inputs are transformed through the learning experiences resulting in the outputs. Each process gives feedback in an iterative way. The feedback can be used to modify the system.

today, there is significant evidence that the systems approach used and discussed in this case study fostered a sustainable literacy program. Thirty-five to 50 children in the elementary school continue to participate each semester with consistent attendance. In addition, scheduling of academic-focused and co-curricular clubs on different days of the week increased attendance for all clubs.

Both elementary children and college students were surveyed after the second year. Twenty-seven of 40 elementary school children completed the informed consent protocol to complete a survey about engagement. Of the 27 who answered the indicator questions about engagement, 25 showed an increase in engagement (92.6 percent). The same percentage also indicated that they wanted to participate in a future reading-technology program. All 35 university students felt that the experience was beneficial for their learning and detailed the value of technology. A college student wrote: "Before, I knew that kids liked technology. When using it for tutoring, though, I was taken aback by the enthusiasm the students exhibited about using the iPads."

Problem Resolution

Creating a mutually beneficial, sustainable partnership was a challenge. After a year, the advisory board decided to revise the program since it was dependent on the VISTA partnership. The elementary school had a clear sense of purpose, and the university clarified its value based on service learning. The advisory board provided a central place to hear stakeholders' feedback that helped supply a common understanding of the perspectives that addressed complex obstacles and turn them into opportunistic inputs to address underlying problems. Using the lens of systems thinking, having a clear sense of purpose, involving all stakeholders, and providing continuous feedback helped determine the elements necessary for the successful implementation of a partnership that could be sustained and thrive.

Lessons Learned

The partnership between the school and university continued past the inaugural leadership that was originally conceived. Building a collaboration between two entities was key to representing different stakeholder groups and identifying the structures that enabled both to not only function, but to succeed. Teachers at the elementary school were encouraged that the university was supporting their students. College pre-service teachers were motivated to make strong lessons, since they had a sense of purpose, as well as real-time experience, using technology to build literacy with children.

There was an unanticipated challenge during the literacy program. One professor of the course was not seemingly suited to work within the school's culture. The failure resulted in the need to find a new professor. This misalignment in expectations demonstrates the need to have a strong match in vision, implementation, and participants that can complete the work.

Reflective Questions

- When partnerships between two parties ensue, both have systemic concerns that they need to address, structures that are not flexible, and processes that are flexible. With two educational systems working together, what are the systemic and structural constraints impacting how the two can work together to make both goals stronger?
- In partnerships, there are multiple parties that have different needs. When bringing in new people, how can clarity be increased, so newcomers to the partnership are aware of the parameters?
- The physical location of a university most often means there are local primary schools nearby. Universities also often have students that are eager to learn and grow into their chosen profession, or who are passionate about being civically engaged in the local community. How can schools leverage universities' social capital to help them create stronger learning systems for their students and create win-win relationships beyond traditional student teaching?

Additional Resources

- Compass Compact https://compact.org/initiatives/service-learning/ A national coalition of 1,000+ colleges and universities committed to democracy through civic education and community development. They have many resources including sample service-learning syllabi, grants applications, and professional development opportunities in the USA and some globally.
- George Lucas Educational Foundation on Service Learning www.edutopia.org/topic/service-learning
- Associations Dedicated to Experiential Learning: Service learning is considered experiential. Association for Experiential Education www.aee.org/ & National Society for Experiential Education www.nsee.org/

References

Banathy, B. H. (1973). *Developing a systems view of education: The systems model approach*. Fearon Publishers.

Bringle, R.G., & Hatcher, J.A. (1996). Implementing service-learning in higher education. *The Journal of Higher Education, 67*, 221–239.

Cabrera, D., & Cabrera, L. (2015). *Systems thinking made simple: New hope for solving wicked problems*. Odyssean Press.

Celio, C., I, Durlak, J., & Dymnicki, A. (2011). A meta-analysis of the impact of service-learning on students. *Journal of Experiential Education, 34*(2), 164–181. doi:10.5193/JEE34.2.164

Koehler, M. J., Mishra, P., Kereluik, K., Shin, T. S., & Graham, C. (2013). The technological pedagogical content knowledge framework. In J. M. Spector, J. Elen, & M. J. Bishop (Ed.), *Handbook of research on educational communications and technology* (4 ed., pp. 101–112). Springer.

Kuh, G. D. (2008). High impact educational practices: What they are, who has access to them and why they matter. In *Liberal Education and America's Promise* (p. 33). Association of American Colleges and Universities.

Sockman, B. R., Carducci, O. M., Clossey, L., Batson-Magnuson, L., White, G., Wehmeyer, A., Well, H., & Rauch, G. (2018). Service-learning experiences promote the university's strategic mission regardless of discipline or matriculation level. *Journal on Excellence in College Teaching, 29*(1), 75–117.

Sockman, B. R., Clossey, L., Carducci, O. M., Batson-Magnuson, L., Mazure, D., White, G., Wehmeyer, A., Green, B., & Wells, H. (2019). Systems thinking as a heuristic for the implementation of service-learning in a university In M. Spector, B. Lockee, & M. Childress (Eds.), *Learning, design, and technology*. Springer. https://doi.org/10.1007/978-3-319-17727-4_91-1

Stroh, D. P. (2015). *Systems thinking for social change: A practical guide to solving complex problems, avoiding unintended consequences, and achieving lasting results*. Chelsea Green Publishing.

PART V

Evaluating Change

24

REGISTRATION STRENGTHENING PROGRAM IN INDONESIA (HEALTH CARE/INTERNATIONAL)

Santi Kusumaningrum, Sri Andini Handayani, Widi Laras Sari, and Rahmadi Usman

Introduction

In Indonesia, a person can exist without ever being recognized by the state. People born in low-income families are less likely to be registered for birth certificates, without which they are less likely to continue education beyond primary school. Access to civil registration, therefore, can greatly skew an individual's economic opportunities. Once they turn 17, possessing an ID card will become even harder, requiring a family card subject to a person's registered birth. Without an ID card, people are at risk of being denied voting rights, legal protection, and access to public services. This atrocious cycle is, sadly, not a dramatization. As a result, millions of Indonesians are deprived of their fundamental rights, and the government lacks complete population data.

Responding to this situation, the government of Indonesia (GoI) prioritized birth registration strengthening in their National Mid-Term Development Plan (*RPJMN*) of 2015–2019, pledging to increase national birth registration coverage to 85 percent in 2019. The goal was ambitious, representing a 22 percent increase over five years; by contrast, during the previous RPJMN covering 2010–2014, Indonesia increased coverage by just 16 percent. To meet this ambition, the government—especially the Ministry of National Development Planning (Bappenas), the ministry charged with ensuring that state investments achieve their desired impact—welcomed collaboration with the Australian Government's governance facility KOMPAK and with PUSKAPA[1] in providing support through a Program named "Inclusive and Accountable Civil Registration and Vital Statistics (CRVS) System." To help the government achieve the national target, KOMPAK offered multi-year assistance to test and potentially replicate evidence-based vital registration solutions for the government to scale and replicate. KOMPAK

DOI: 10.4324/9781003028772-29

partnered with PUSKAPA in designing and piloting an initiative to strengthen vital event registration systems at the national and subnational levels.

This Program sought to demonstrate that strengthening birth registration would be contingent upon increased performance of the overall civil registration system, including death, marriage, divorce, migration, and adoption registrations. Moreover, an effective CRVS system would both fulfill people's right to legal identity documents that facilitate their access to basic services, and, at the same time, strengthen the government's ability to plan and deliver data-driven programming (see Figure 24.1).

This Program designed a multi-year comprehensive approach focused on bringing civil registration services closer to the community to reach the most vulnerable. It sought to facilitate civil registration processes through frontline services of health, education, and social assistance to record events at their first instance and improve the quality and utilization of vital statistics produced from the civil registry. This chapter describes the Program's first two years of implementation (2016–2018) in 16 districts in five provinces purposively selected by the government, KOMPAK, and PUSKAPA to allow for variation in governance, local laws

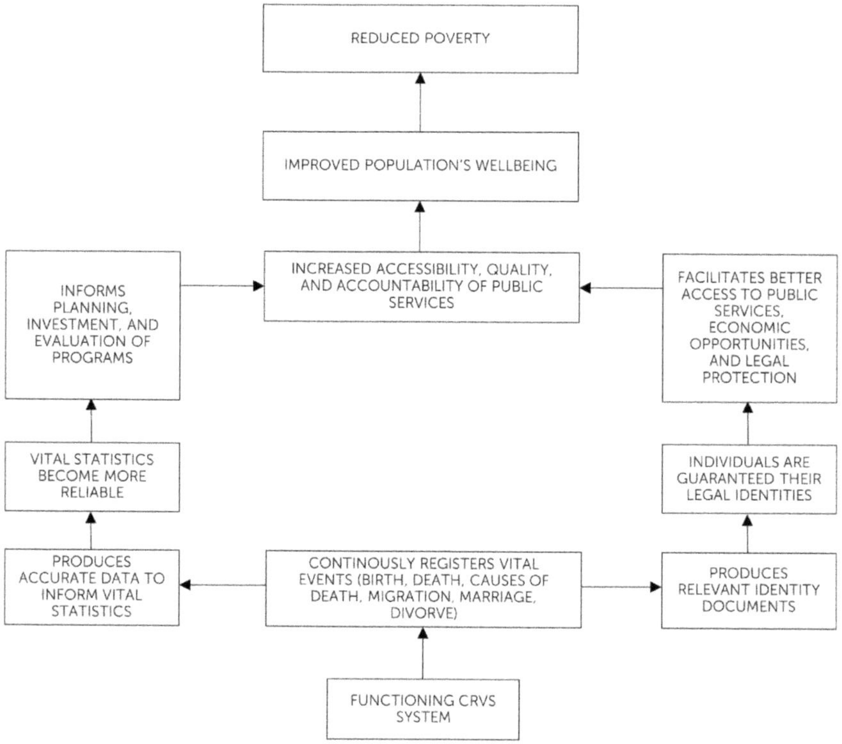

FIGURE 24.1 CRVS Strengthening Program Rationale

and regulations, legal identity coverage, cultural practices, and other contextual factors.

System and Key Players

CRVS describes national governments' continuous and universal registration systems for vital events throughout the lifecycle. Vital events include births, deaths, marriages, divorces, and migrations. In Indonesia, this system is mostly supported by Population Administration (*Adminduk*) and was established by Law No. 23 on Population Administration and Civil Registration in 2006.

CRVS System in Indonesian Governance

In Indonesia, the Ministry of Home Affairs (MOHA) holds the *Adminduk* mandate to register the population and vital events, as well as to manage population data and its utilization. Due to the points of service where vital events occur, CRVS in Indonesia relies on the interconnectivity of MOHA and the numerous others sectors, including health, education, social affairs, religious affairs, justice, law enforcement, and labor (see Figure 24.2).

Indonesia's CRVS in Practice and the Dynamic Among Key Actors

The intersectoral requirements of CRVS have not translated into integrated practice in Indonesia. Within MOHA, business processes between horizontal units (namely civil registration and population recording) and across different administrative levels (from central to village) are not streamlined (PUSKAPA, 2018). Existing collaboration between MOHA and other sectors may be present at some level but lack interoperability.

One source of disjuncture is that the MOHA unit that assigns an individual's unique identity number (NIK), recording individuals on a family card and later producing a national ID, is separate from another unit that registers life events and produces birth, marriage, and death certificates (Kusumaningrum et al., 2016). Moreover, the system has yet to support inter-district or inter-province registrations and updates. These detachments have caused discrepancies, or at least delays, in the data. At the level of basic service provision, they lead to data collection processes (PUSKAPA, 2018). Despite decentralization, local governments also still depend on *Adminduk* funding and procurement from the central government, while central funding has always been limited. This budgetary challenge has stalled local governments' efforts to bring services closer to communities (Kusumaningrum et al., 2016).

Although MOHA's responsibility to manage registration-based population data requires interconnectivity with sectoral data, each sector collects its data in a silo, again creating duplication of efforts and discrepancies (PUSKAPA, 2018).

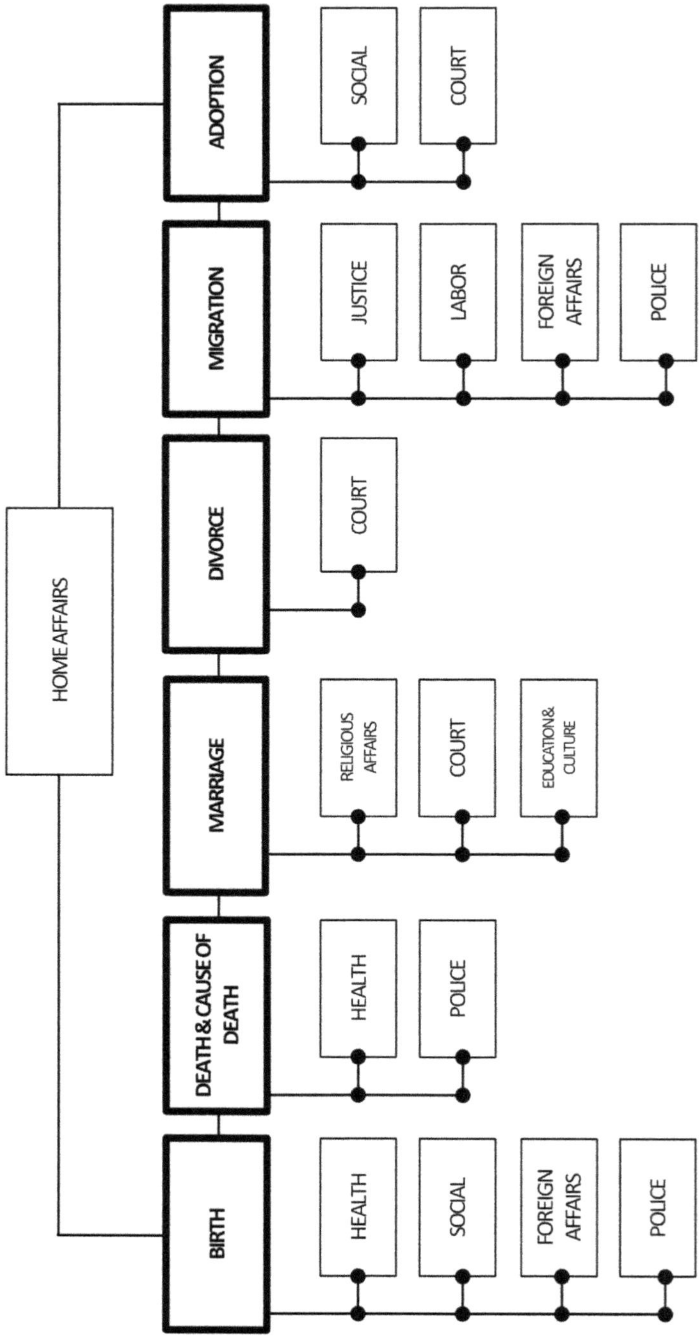

FIGURE 24.2 CRVS-Relevant Sectors in Indonesia

Consequently, the data stored in MOHA's information management system can differ from information systems of the sectors that capture the actual events occurring at points of service provision (PUSKAPA, 2018). Moreover, MOHA's efforts to digitize the backlogs for registrations previously done manually have been slow (Kusumaningrum et al., 2016). Last, the utilization of CRVS data for program planning and budgeting is low (PUSKAPA, 2018).

Case Analysis

An in-depth look into the 2015 national socioeconomic survey (Susenas), whose estimate of birth certificate ownership among 0–17 years served as a baseline for the CRVS Program, revealed structural issues in Indonesia's birth registration gap (Table 24.1). In addition to showing that poorer and more rural residents had less access to birth certificates, the survey also signaled a tendency to delay registration, as evidenced by lower birth certificate ownership rates for younger cohorts. The most commonly cited reasons for lacking a birth certificate suggested the problem was poverty-driven and logistical, with 45 percent reporting not being able to pay the associated costs, and 21 percent reporting that the government had not issued their birth certificates. Susenas also showed a geographical discrepancy in birth certificates coverage (see Figure 24.3).

TABLE 24.1 Birth Certificate Ownership in Indonesia

	Birth Certificate Ownership (%)
Wealth Distribution	
Bottom 40%	71.9
Upper 60%	87.0
Regional Status	
Urban	86.7
Rural	74.0
Age group	
Under-1	53.6
Under-5	72.9
Under-18	80.2
Reason for not having a birth certificate	
Hasn't been issued by the government	20.6
Don't have any money to pay	44.6
The registration office is too far	8.7
Don't know that a birth has to be registered	2
Don't know how to apply	10.1
Don't think it's necessary	8.6
Can't be bothered	5.5

Source: Authors' calculation based on the Indonesian Socio-economic Survey (SUSENAS), 2015.

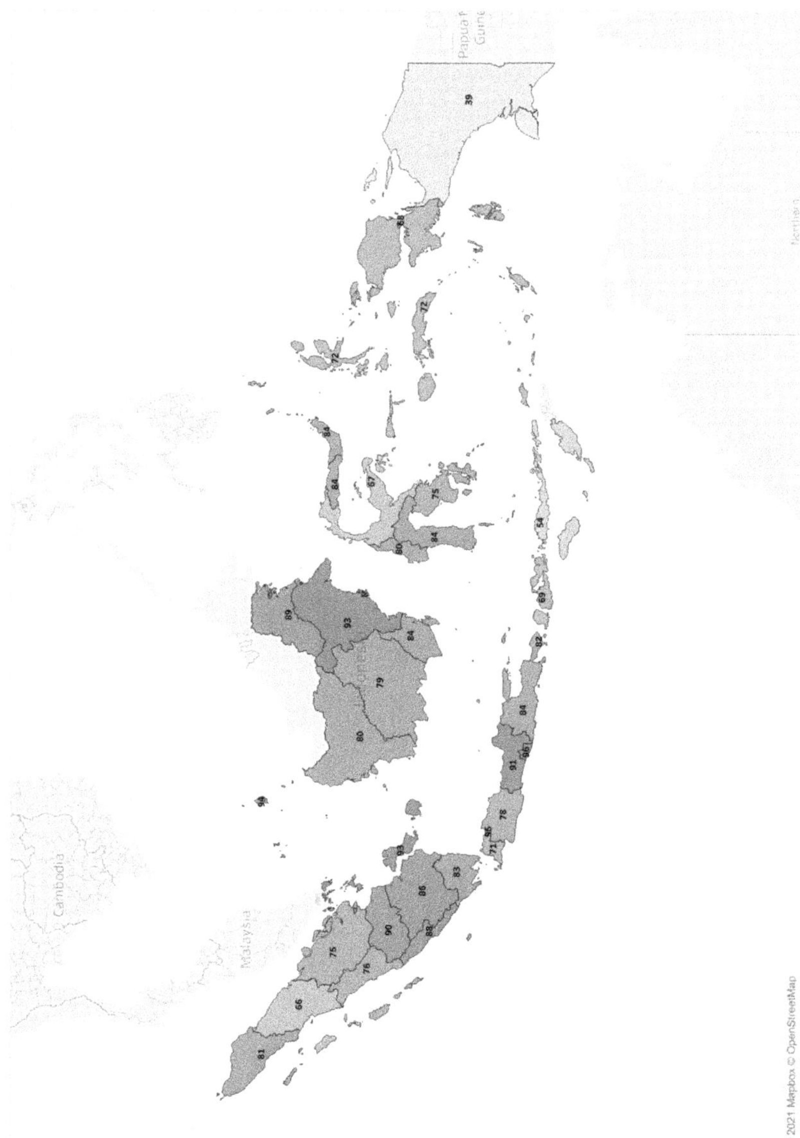

FIGURE 24.3 Proportion of Birth Certificate Ownership by Province

A cross-sectional survey conducted by PUSKAPA in 2013 offered additional insights (Sumner & Kusumaningrum, 2014). The 2013 study revealed inconsistencies between the number of live births and birth certificate ownership, which signaled a missing link between health facilities and civil registrars. The complexity of the birth registration process, in which an individual has to interact with several levels of government and judicial agencies, emerged as a key challenge.

Upon selecting the pilot areas for the CRVS strengthening pilot in early 2016, Bappenas with KOMPAK and PUSKAPA finalized a formative study looking at the bottlenecks, barriers, and opportunities in the birth and death registration systems in three sites in Indonesia. The report found that much work remained to achieve a stronger Indonesian CRVS system (Kusumaningrum et al., 2016). One in three children in the three study sites had no legal documentation of their birth. Two in five marriages were not registered, almost one in five adults could not produce an ID or family card with their name on it, and death certificates were almost non-existent. This study also found that civil registration services were challenging to reach and application procedures overly complicated; obtaining certificates involved informal fees and late registration fines, reducing the chance for the poorest to be registered. Although the late registration fines were abolished by the enactment of Law No. 24 of 2013, the study also found that the implementation varied across government bodies, whether horizontally (among sectors) or vertically (among different levels of administrations). Finally, limited staff capacity and training opportunities for civil registration officers were also reported to be bottlenecks in the provision of CRVS services.

Problem Resolution

This chapter employs the systems thinking framework synthesized by the World Health Organization (WHO) (2009) to illuminate problem identification and solution design in the Program strategy (see Figure 24.4). The systems thinking approach emphasizes understanding the context and connections among actors and systems building blocks; and deliberately identifying leverage points and developing mitigation strategies (Peters, 2014). Using this WHO framework, the Program analyzed the evidence (see Case Analysis) and diagrammed a problem diagnosis (see Figure 24.5).

First, the lack of understanding of the importance of legal identity documents and weak incentives for seeking them have contributed to the *passive demand side*. On the other side, the *supply side was also passive* and overly complex, which created high opportunity costs. Moreover, the horizontal and vertical disconnect within MOHA, and between MOHA and other relevant sectors, have led to *fragmented CRVS policies* and systemic inefficiencies. Finally, the *unreliability of the vital data*, coupled with the lack of data sharing protocols and interoperability, have contributed to the *low demand by other sectors for utilizing MOHA's data* in their policymaking, planning, and budgeting.

- **Self-organizing**. The building blocks of a system interact with each other and create the dynamic from within the system.
- **Constantly changing**. Systems can behave on their own, reacting differently to the same inputs because of the interaction with other parts in the system.
- **Tightly linked**. Due to the high interconnection in the system, a change in one sub-system affects another.
- **Governed by feedback**. A system adapts can moderate itself to the effects (positive or negative) that the system generates.
- **Non-linear**. The effects of system-level interventions can be disproportionally related to the intended outcomes.
- **History dependent.** Short-term effects of an intervention can be different from that of a long-term.
- **Counter-intuitive**. Some simple and effective interventions may work in one setting, but not in the other.
- **Resistant to change**. The complex interactions in the system may prevent seemingly obvious solutions from working.

Source: Savigny, D. and Adam, T. (Eds). *Systems thinking for health systems strengthening.* Alliance for Health Policy and Systems Research, WHO, 2009.

FIGURE 24.4 Systems Characteristics

Grounded in the systems thinking approach and informed by research, the Program developed a theory of change (TOC) to guide field intervention (see Figure 24.6). Despite its simplified representation, the Program noted the non-linearity of the CRVS system and interactions among the four building blocks, namely: *increasing demand for civil registration; improving supply of these services; enhancing the policy environment; and making data complete.* All four seek to create two CRVS-specific impact objectives: increased coverage of vital events being reported and recorded, and increased legal identity document ownership.

This Program worked through local civil society organizations (CSO) who were trained on the design and the technical aspects of CRVS strengthening. CSOs contributed to the four program outcomes. To increase legal identity seeking behavior (*Outcome 1*), they disseminated information and facilitated collective registrations to assist the communities in navigating the complex procedures. The premise of this strategy is empowering citizens to demand their rights to CRVS services, pressuring the government and service providers to deliver stronger civil registration/legal identity programs and services (*Outcome 2*).

Acknowledging that villages and sub-districts are critical subsystems that contribute toward the desired outcomes and impact, the Program developed three types of collective and integrated registration models (see Figure 24.7). On the ground, CSOs collaborated with health, education, and social workers to provide

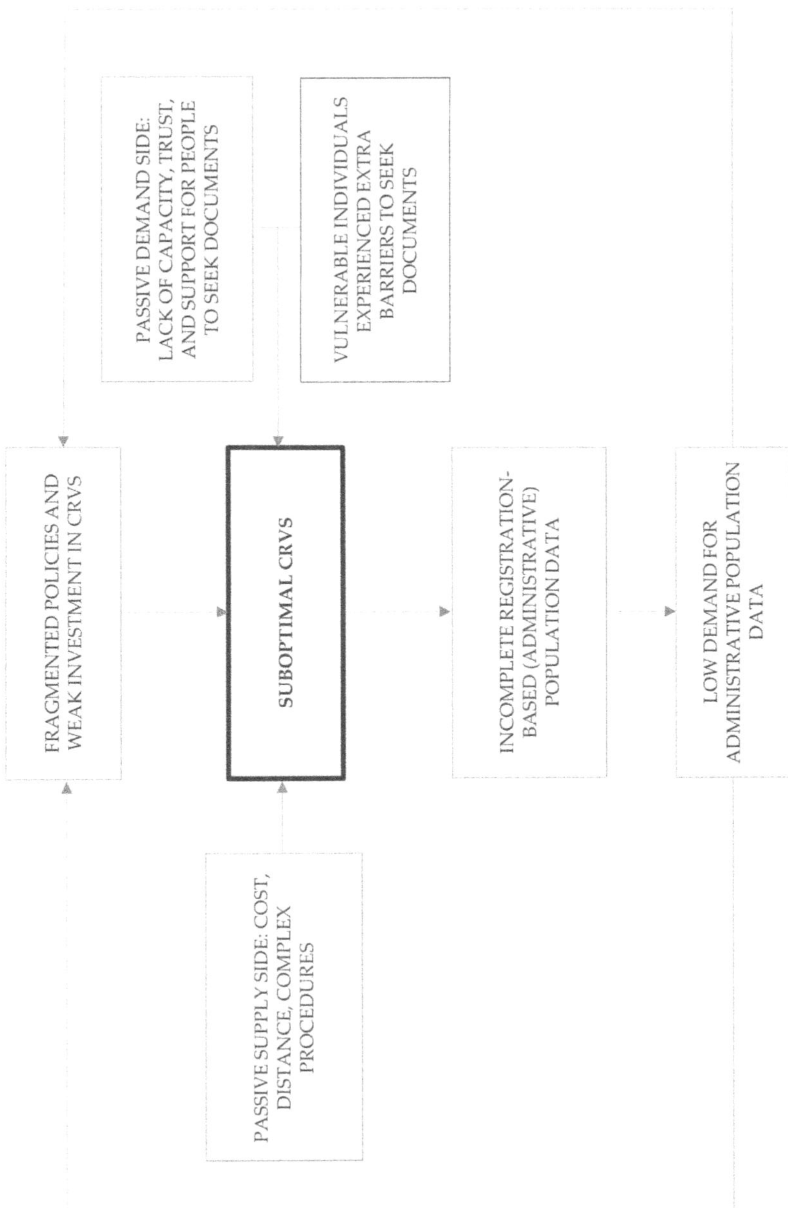

FIGURE 24.5 CRVS Problems in Indonesia

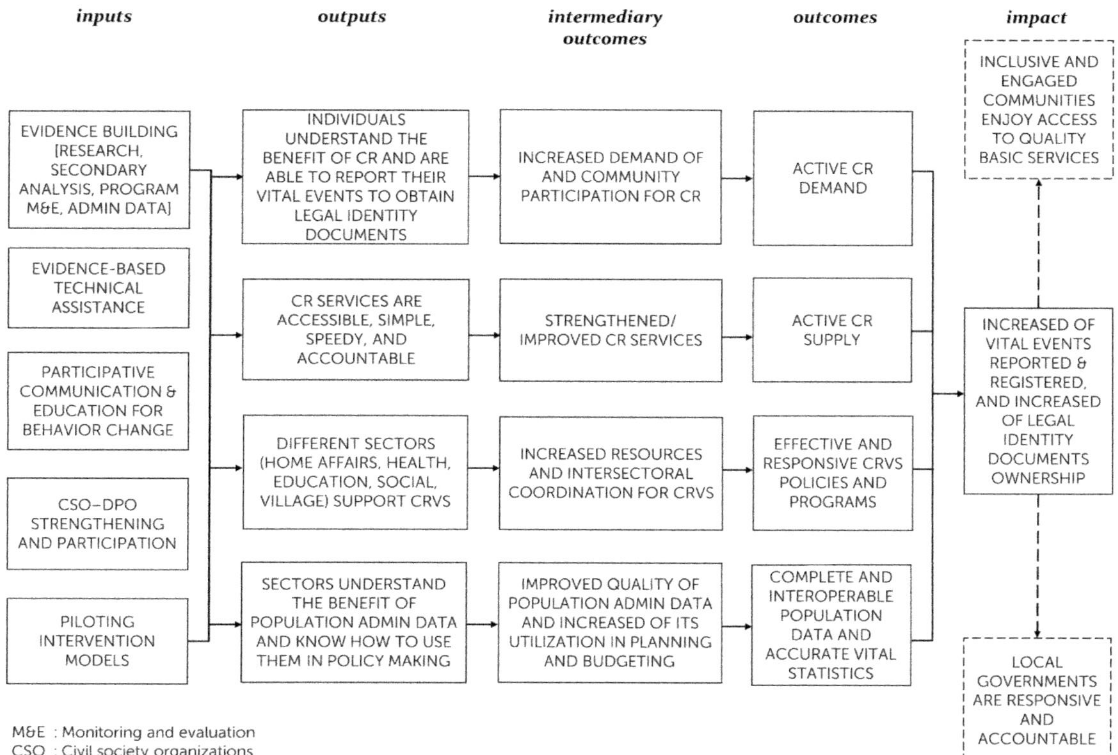

M&E : Monitoring and evaluation
CSO : Civil society organizations
DPO : Disabled persons' organizations
CR : Civil registration
CRVS: Civil registration and vital statistics

FIGURE 24.6 CRVS Strengthening Theory of Change

- **Acceleration model.** Targeting children who are already within SIAK, i.e., already owned a NIK, but without birth certificates and parents/couples without marriage certificates.
- **Prevention model.** Targeting children under-5 years old to prevent them from being unregistered by the time they enroll in school.
- **Outreach model**. Targeting remote areas and hidden population or socially excluded population, e.g., children born into a family who never registered them (due to disability or other factors); children born into unregistered family or parents (family or parents without NIK, National ID or family card due to migration status or being in nomadic indigenous communities); and children outside of the traditional household settings, e.g., orphanages, prison, halfway houses, homeless families.

FIGURE 24.7 Three Types of Collective and Integrative Models

relevant registration services as a benefit of accessing these services. It is important to note that these models did not promote the use of legal identity documents as a prerequisite to access basic services.

The Program's policy works has leveraged entry points in strengthening cross-sectoral collaboration, simplifying, and clarifying civil registration procedures to help fulfill citizens' rights to the legal identity.

Lessons Learned

In Program areas, communities became more active in seeking legal identity documents, and civil registration authorities in turn became more responsive in delivering services to meet demand

As the 2016 study found, not all community members appreciated the importance of legal identity documents or the value of having legal identity documents. Structural barriers and complex application processes also blocked community members from seeking legal identity documents. The implementing partners conducted a series of activities to disseminate information regarding the importance of legal identity, build the value of legal identity documents, improve access to several basic services, and facilitate the legal identity document application process. These processes meant that thousands of community members came to understand not only the importance of legal identity documents but also the processes of applying for them; tangible gains, such as orphans' access to government scholarships after receiving parental death certificates, made the value of these processes immediately visible.

From the supply side, the 2016 study found that CRVS services are performing poorly due to lethargic, bureaucratic service delivery. Addressing the situation, the program provided technical assistance to local governments in reaching the community by bringing the collective and integrated civil registration service models (see Figure 24.7) closer to the community. This approach resulted in 30 district-level regulations (such as memorandums of understanding and standard operating procedures) that institutionalized more efficient models, especially for the marginalized populations. Tens of thousands of legal identity document applications have been facilitated, including for people with disabilities in Aceh, Central Java, East Java, South Sulawesi, and West Nusa Tenggara. Working from the ground up, the program also provided technical assistance to MOHA to develop national SOPs based on lessons learned from the Program.

By April 2018, this Program had facilitated 93,555 vulnerable individuals obtaining their legal identity documents in the form of birth certificates, marriage certificates, family cards, national ID cards, and death certificates. Additionally, the models piloted in the 12 districts were institutionalized in a form of the appointment of village registrars who will continue to facilitate community legal identity applications.

Building on the Results in Subnational Level, this Program Contributed to Setting Up an Intersectoral National Strategy on CRVS

The exemplary work from the 12 pilot districts has resulted in an evidence-based policy proposal with which Bappenas convened MOHA and other key sectors to discuss ways to solve CRVS problems in the country. The policy proposal gained a strong buy-in from the key CRVS stakeholders, and together, they produced a national strategy on CRVS, which was adopted as Presidential Regulation Number 62 in 2019. The strategy highlights the importance of a more coordinated approach toward CRVS, aiming to bring a bigger and speedier impact for the millions of invisible children and adults. The strategy puts an emphasis on provision of collective and mobile legal identity services while making sure that programs work on an overall strengthening of the CRVS system. It also considers that people need to use their documents to access services so that people see the value of registration. The strategy promotes inclusive and constant registrations, accuracy of documents, and timely population data.

Conclusion

Informed by evidence, the Inclusive and Accountable CRVS Program was designed to increase the legal identity document ownership in Indonesia. During the first two years of implementation, this Program has reached close to a 100,000 unregistered individuals by closely working with the local governments, with, and in the communities. The systems thinking approach helped create a problem-solving oriented design to address a complex issue. Pilot interventions, despite being smaller in scale than national programs, served as a platform for exploring multifaceted and intersectoral solutions. The tangible results lent the Program's proof of concept credibility and maintained the stakeholders' commitment and participation. Last, the Program's investment in research and monitoring provided sound evidence for the political leadership of Bappenas and others to accelerate vertical and horizontal changes. This strategic blend of research, systems thinking design, human-centered activities, documentation of progress, and iterative adaptations has made this Program an example of how evidence can turn into actions that help vulnerable populations.

Reflective Questions

- *Service delivery model.* Migration and adoption were the least addressed in the Program because adoption and migration in the select areas were not recognized as the primary problems, albeit present. Simultaneously, migration and adoption have different scales and require separate models. *How would incorporating these two vital events affect our models implemented across the Program areas and what would be the best strategy to include them in CRVS strengthening?*
- *Technically sound and politically feasible program strategy.* The Program has employed a dual technical-political solution to create a system-wide change. And yet, Outcomes 3 and 4 are still the most challenging to achieve because of the involvement of a dozen ministries with competing interests. *Employing the political economy framework, what are the determining factors that drive the key stakeholders in maintaining the status quo? How do we balance between holding ourselves accountable to the outcomes and acknowledging that some factors beyond the Program's control may limit us from reaching these outcomes?*
- *Gender Equality and Social Inclusion (GESI) and outcome measurement.* During its implementation, the Program learned that GESI principles should avoid superficial approaches that stop at ensuring the participation of all genders and providing sex-disaggregated and relevant disability data. The Program found that exclusion happened to some community groups due to their social identities (i.e., religion, ethnicity, and gender and sexual identities beyond male and female binary definition). *How would similar programs incorporate granularity in their measurements so they capture the most hidden exclusions, hence, will be able to resolve them. Moreover, how to convince donors and governments to invest in*

GESI activities that might not satisfy the need for programs to reach a large number of marginalized people and rather address the depth and quality of the assistance provided for them?

- *Sustainability.* Institutionalization of vital registration at the village level and government budget allocation of outreach mechanisms are crucial for ensuring the sustainability and universality of services. *To what extent will this approach be sustainable in the context of ever-changing government structure? What other approaches should the Program explore to ensure the sustainability of the Program initiatives?*
- *Private sector role.* Budget constraints and bureaucracy limit the speed of CRVS service delivery innovations in the public sector. *What are the possible modalities for private sector engagement in service delivery innovation and how will these impact the system?*

Notes

1 PUSKAPA, an Indonesian abbreviation of Center on Child Protection and Wellbeing, is a think tank based at Universitas Indonesia that undertakes research, advocacy, capacity building, and program actions. The promotion of legal identity documents from birth is one of PUSKAPA's strategic priorities.

Additional Resources

Bennouna, C., Feldman, B., Usman, R., Adiputra, R., Kusumaningrum, S., & Stark, L. (2016). Using the three delays model to examine civil registration barriers in Indonesia. *PLOS ONE, 11*(12). https://doi.org/10.1371/journal.pone.0168405

Duff, P., Kusumaningrum, S., & Stark, L. (2016). Barriers to birth registration in Indonesia. *The Lancet Global Health, 4*(4). https://doi.org/10.1016/s2214-109x(15)00321-6

Siagian, C., Wandasari, W., Sahputra, F., & Kusumaningrum, S. (2019). Strategic yet delicate: The dilemma of involving health workers in facilitating birth registration in Indonesia. *BMC Health Services Research, 19*(1). https://doi.org/10.1186/s12913-019-4594-z

Williams, A., Kusumaningrum, S., Bennouna, C., Usman, R., Wandasari, W., & Stark, L. (2018). Using the theory of planned behaviour to understand motivation to register births in Lombok, Indonesia. *Children & Society, 32*(5), 368–380. https://doi.org/10.1111/chso.12262

References

Badan Pusat Statistik. (2020). *Survei Sosial Ekonomi Nasional (Susenas), 2015 Kor.* https://doi.org/10.7910/DVN/DGNKQ2, Harvard Dataverse, V2, UNF:6:20Lk8+WkpxjPj6Gi1Z7UvA== [fileUNF]

Kusumaningrum, S., Bennouna, C., Siagian, C., & Agastya, N.L.P.M. (2016). *Back to what counts: Birth and death in Indonesia.* Jakarta, Indonesia: The Center on Child Protection Universitas Indonesia (PUSKAPA) in collaboration with the Ministry of National Development Planning (BAPPENAS) and Kolaborasi Masyarakat dan Pelayanan untuk

Kesejahteraan (KOMPAK). www.cpcnetwork.org/wp-content/uploads/2016/09/CRVS-Research-Report.pdf

Peters, D.H. (2014). The application of systems thinking in health: why use systems thinking? *Health Research Policy and Systems, 12*(1). https://doi.org/10.1186/1478-4505-12-51

PUSKAPA (2018). *Collective Actions to Break the Cycle of Invisibility: 2015–2018 Program Report*. Internal report of Inclusive and Accountable CRVS Program, a collaboration between Center on Child Protection & Wellbeing Universitas Indonesia (PUSKAPA) with the Ministry of National Development Planning (BAPPENAS) and Kolaborasi Masyarakat dan Pelayanan untuk Kesejahteraan (KOMPAK).

Savigny, D., Adam, T. (2009). Systems thinking for health systems strengthening. WHO Library Cataloguing-in-Publication Data.

Sumner, C., & Kusumaningrum, S. (2014). *Indonesia's Missing Millions: A Baseline Study on Legal Identity*. Retrieved from Jakarta, Indonesia: Center on Child Protection & Wellbeing Universitas Indonesia (PUSKAPA) in collaboration with the Ministry of National Development Planning (BAPPENAS) and Australia-Indonesia Partnership for Justice (AIPJ). www.cpcnetwork.org/wp-content/uploads/2015/02/AIPJ-PUSKAPA-BASELINE-STUDY-ON-LEGAL-IDENTITY-Indonesia-2013.pdf

Appendix

Civil registration authorities (Dukcapil) administrative data on the coverage of birth certificates for children under 18 years of age in selected areas

Province	*Areas of Intervention (districts)*	*2015 as per December (%)*	*2016 as per December (%)*	*2017 as per June (%)*	*2015 to 2016 Changes (percent point)*	*2016 to mid-2017 Changes (percent point)*
Aceh Province	Aceh Barat	66.79	75.45	87.90	-7.66 pp	+13.45 pp
	Bireuen	42.72	54.61	72.43	+11.89 pp	+17.82 pp
	Bener Meriah	79.75	80.64	84.56	+0.89 pp	+3.92 pp
Central Java Province	Pekalongan	60.4	82.87	83.90	+21.81 pp	+1.03 pp
	Brebes	53.16	68.0	79.27	+6.25 pp	+2.44 pp
	Pemalang	52.39	55.22	79.55	+2.83 pp	+24.33 pp
East Java Province	Trenggalek	75.42	81.71	86.92	+6.29 pp	+5.21 pp
	Pacitan	40.91	75.36	66.61	+34.45 pp	-8.75 pp
	Bondowoso	84.34	92.24	95.03	+7.9 pp	+2.79 pp
	Lumajang	Data not available	64.44	64.89	Data not available	+0.45 pp
West Nusa Tenggara Province	Lombok Utara	61.05	82.87	87.17	+21.82 pp	+1.03 pp
	Lombok Timur	62.56	68.81	75.56	+6.25 pp	+6.75 pp
	Sumbawa	33.69	33.69	77.88	0 pp	+44.19 pp
	Bima	45.76	45.76	79.32	0 pp	+33.56 pp
South Sulawesi Province	Bantaeng	Data not available	Data not available	Data not available	Data not available	Data not available
	Pangkep	Data not available	Data not available	Data not available	Data not available	Data not available

Source: Program monitoring data compiled by PUSKAPA in collaboration with local partners.

Acknowledgments

This chapter drew from the data managed by the Center on Child Protection and Wellbeing at Universitas Indonesia (PUSKAPA). The program is funded by the Australia-Indonesia Partnership on Governance for Growth program (KOMPAK) under the coordination of the National Development Planning Ministry (Bappenas), the GoI. We would like to thank all KOMPAK and PUSKAPA program managers and their partners in all relevant districts, provinces, and the national level. We would also like to thank DFAT (Department of Foreign Affairs and Trade) at the Australian Embassy Jakarta for their support to the program. Last, we thank Mark Canavera for his review, inputs, and brilliant editing.

25

SCALING DOWN AND CHANGING UP

Leveraging Microlearning for Professional Development in the Pharmaceutical Industry (Healthcare)

Barbara B. Lockee

Introduction

Pharmaceutical and medical device training divisions have the large task of preparing their sales representatives to serve as a critical resource to physicians regarding company-specific products and related therapeutic treatments, as well as broader industry advancements in pharma research and development. In addition to their need to understand human physiology, pharmacology, disease states, and disease management, pharmaceutical representatives must also be cognizant of ever-changing healthcare regulations and the managed care landscape in which physicians and other medical stakeholders currently operate. Given the rapidly changing healthcare context, pharmaceutical sales personnel must be able to adapt and change course quickly, which necessitates the continuous updating of their training curriculum and content.

The goal of this case is to demonstrate how the evolving learning needs of pharmaceutical representatives have necessitated change in their professional development strategies to provide a more flexible and time-sensitive approach. The adoption of microlearning is one such method to accommodate the demand for more responsive, just-in-time learning experiences. Given the systemic nature of learning systems such as workplace learning in the pharmaceutical industry, a change to move away from standard e-learning courses toward smaller units of content and greater learner control prompts correlating changes within instructional design and delivery processes, as well as other systemic actions and considerations to facilitate adoption of this instructional innovation.

DOI: 10.4324/9781003028772-30

System and Key Players

Instructional design activities occur within the context of a system, so it is imperative that designers be aware of different aspects of the system and how they interact (Stefaniak, 2020). In this case, the instructional design intervention originates from CMR Institute (CMRI), a non-profit organization that has offered distance-delivered educational programming for the pharmaceutical industry for over 50 years. Their curricular offerings have evolved from print-based instruction to e-learning courses in order to make their instruction more accessible, current, and flexible. Even so, pharmaceutical representatives have struggled to find the time to complete online courses, even courses that are mandatory. In response to the changing learning context for their clients, CMRI's specific goal, based on their clients' needs, is to transition from a more time-intensive, course-based e-learning approach toward the provision of smaller, free-standing units of instruction that can be completed in a much more feasible and flexible manner.

Additional key players in this system include pharmaceutical sales representatives (the targeted learner group in this case), their sales managers, and training division leaders. Serving as an educational provider to pharmaceutical companies, CMRI personnel are stakeholders as well. Their employees include instructional designers who plan and produce e-learning solutions, client-facing sales and support personnel, marketing staff, and the organization's leadership—all members of the overall learning ecosystem.

Case Analysis

Perspective taking and understanding the different mental modes of all people within a given system can lead to successful change (Bui & Baruch, 2010; Senge, 1994). As key stakeholders in this case, pharmaceutical representatives have increasingly less time for formal training, which is a common theme across many current industry contexts (Hogle, 2021). For the past few years, these professionals have expressed a greater need for flexibility in terms of how to engage with their training experiences. In recent years, the training divisions of pharma companies have pursued strategies to give their representatives more manageable and engaging learning experiences. Pharmaceutical representatives are more overloaded with work than ever, and have demonstrated a great deal of difficulty in completing training requirements, even if they are offered online and asynchronously. Standard e-learning designs may include extensive amounts of content, leading to learner fatigue and disengagement in the learning experience for these busy professionals.

From a workforce perspective, generational characteristics are also influencing training demands. Many employees have now grown up with social media, the Internet, and ready access to information. These personnel have demonstrated expectations of having their immediate learning needs addressed just-in-time

(Hamilton, Hall, & Hamilton, 2021; Zhang & West, 2020). According to Leong, Sung, Au, & Blanchard, "In the workplace, people are used to having information at their fingertips, finding the answers they need within minutes. This has dramatically changed people's expectations of workplace learning" (2020, p. 89).

Pharmaceutical sales managers have indicated a need for change in how their representatives are prepared to effectively engage with physicians and medical personnel. This group of stakeholders have expressed the need to strike a balance between the provision of impactful learning experiences and instructional programming that minimizes the time out of the field for training, while also allowing for learning in the flow of work. Managers desire training strategies that facilitate sales representative completion of brief instructional events during moments of downtime, such as waiting for a client appointment, or engagement at the time of need, such as in preparation for a client conversation. Flexibility and access have emerged as important trends in the professional development needs for these employees.

CMRI leadership and customer support personnel have received feedback from pharmaceutical training division liaisons requesting assistance in addressing these changing learning needs and expectations for pharmaceutical representatives and their sales managers. In response, CMRI has been transitioning away from course-based delivery of e-learning programming to a microlearning strategy.

Problem Resolution

Microlearning benefits learners because it is designed to be completed in less time, due to the limited size of the lessons. "Microlearning focuses on one learning concept at a time and presents bite-sized bits information meant to be consumed in a short period of time through a technology-based medium" (Winger, 2018, p. 51). Learners can fit their learning experiences into their busy schedules and not have to worry about where they left off or recalling the concepts previously addressed in the lesson. Smaller units of instruction also benefit learners with their alignment with human memory capacity, reflecting evidence-based practices that address cognitive load requirements (Salas, 2017). From a motivational standpoint, learners are more apt to complete the training because it seems more approachable and feasible.

CMR Institute has engaged in the transition toward the design and deployment of microlearning as a key instructional delivery strategy, away from longer, more comprehensive e-learning modules and courses. The goal in this effort is to provide more flexible, accessible, and responsive learning opportunities, countering the need for long periods of seat time and a "one size fits all" learning approach.

The impact of this substantial change in the instructional delivery method toward a microlearning approach creates a ripple effect throughout the learning ecosystem and causes related changes on the part of the stakeholders, those internal to CMRI and external in the pharmaceutical industry. Following the directive of Cabrera and Cabrera, it is critically important to explicate the salient relationships that exist in any system under study (2019, p. 13). Describing the impacts of different members of the stakeholder community may serve to demonstrate the systemic nature of this change in learning content design and delivery.

CMRI's creation and deployment of a suite of microlearning offerings began with the internal instructional design team. Though the learning units are smaller in size and scope, the instructional design workflow has not shifted, as the same ID work is necessary to create effective educational experiences (Hogle, 2021). The ID team starts the process by analyzing the existing catalog of e-learning offerings to determine which content may be best suited to break into smaller units. A number of factors are considered, including the existing demand for the associated learning outcome, the ability of a unit to stand on its own, related assessment strategies, and how the content would fit into curricular pathways to address important skills and knowledge more broadly.

The team maintains a set of design assumptions in the microlearning development process. First, the units are designed to address a single learning outcome which serves as a basis for content. Also, learner completion of the unit should be possible within 5–7 minutes. The designers strive to incorporate interactivity with each piece of content as well, to maintain learner engagement.

For CMRI leadership and operations personnel, the shift toward a microlearning approach has prompted a change in the overall business model to devise pricing strategies for smaller units of content. Adding to the complexity is the variance in pharmaceutical training division needs. Some learning organizations want to fill a very specific need, for which CMRI will put together a specific pathway and design pull-through activities with correlating job aids. At the other end of the spectrum, some companies wish to make the entire library of CMRI content available to their sales personnel, allowing for complete access and learner self-directedness. In response to these differing strategies for adoption of microlearning content, CMRI devised a flexible business model to meet varying client needs.

In addition to changes in ID activities and business processes, the development and deployment of microlearning requires education of key stakeholders within the learning ecosystem. With the introduction of a significant change in instructional delivery strategy like microlearning, enhancing awareness of this approach and its systemic implications is critical for successful adoption and deployment in the workplace setting. Rogers (1995) diffusion of innovation theory contends that in order for an innovation (such as microlearning) to be successfully adopted, communication about the innovation is critical to bring about awareness of the new products or processes to all participants in the social system. As such, CMRI instructional designers provided guidance to internal colleagues in client-facing roles and marketing services so that these colleagues may effectively communicate about the new microlearning strategy and its implications. CMRI client support members then communicate with pharmaceutical training liaisons regarding the new approach and its pedagogical and technical implications. These learning leaders within pharma organizations are then prepared to educate pharmaceutical representatives and their sales managers about the shift in how they will engage in having their learning needs met in the flow of work.

Lessons Learned

As the process of microlearning design and development has been ongoing for three years, some lessons learned have emerged. First, one of the primary design benefits of microlearning, the ability to more easily revise and deploy instructional content, has proven to be a valuable advantage. Keeping content current is a priority for CMRI, with a goal of reflecting new developments within a five-day timeframe. The smaller scope of instructional units has supported this need to quickly revise content and make it available to learners in a timely way.

Making the entire repository of CMRI microlearning units openly available to pharma representatives is one option that many pharmaceutical training divisions have employed. While the provision of such access and learner control greatly enhances the flexibility of the learning experience, some learners struggle with the multitude of options. CMRI has responded by providing guidance in the form of recommended learning pathways to address specific learning needs and strategies for monitoring their learning progress within the more open system.

Not all content is well suited for a microlearning approach (Salas, 2017; Winger, 2018). In some instances, learning outcomes that target more complex skills and knowledge are challenging, if not impossible, to down-size into smaller units of instruction. As such, CMRI will maintain a core collection of e-learning modules in their library of offerings to address learning and development needs that cannot be effectively met through a microlearning strategy.

Conclusion

The systemic nature of workplace learning is apparent in the many factors and constituents which must be considered in the design and implementation of an instructional innovation such as microlearning. The instructional design process is but one component of creating flexible and engaging learning experiences that meet the professional development demands of busy pharmaceutical representative professionals. This case featuring the efforts of CMR Institute exemplifies the multifaceted process of responding to expressed workplace learning needs and the resulting actions that involve a myriad of stakeholders and considerations for effective uptake of a learning innovation.

Reflective Questions

- What design strategies can be used to repurpose existing instructional content into microlearning lessons?
- What factors should be considered when deciding how to organize and deliver microlearning offerings?
- How can designers effectively provide learner control related to microlearning content while ensuring that learners obtain necessary skills and knowledge?

Additional Resources

Cabrera, D., Cabrera L., Powers, E., Solin, J., & Kushner, J. (2018) Applying systems thinking models of organizational design and change in community operational research. *European Journal of Operational Research, 268*(3), 932–945.

Corbeil, J. R., Khan, B. H., & Corbeil, M. E. (Eds.). (2021). *Microlearning in the digital age: The design and delivery of learning in snippets*. Routledge.

Kapp, K. M., & Defelice, R. A. (2019). *Microlearning: Short and sweet.* Association for Talent Development.

Stroh, D. P. (2015). *Systems thinking for social change: A practical guide to solving complex problems, avoiding unintended consequences, and achieving lasting results.* Chelsea Green Publishing.

Torgerson, C., & Iannone, S. (2019). *Designing microlearning.* Association for Talent Development.

References

Bui, H., & Baruch, Y. (2010). Creating learning organizations in higher education: Applying a systems perspective. *The Learning Organization*, 17(3), 228–242. https://doi.org/10.1108/09696471011034928

Cabrera, D., & Cabrera, L. (2019). What is systems thinking? In J. M. Spector, B. B. Lockee, & M. D. Childress (Eds.), *Learning, design, and technology: An international compendium of theory, research, practice, and policy* (pp. 1–28). Springer. https://doi.org/10.1007/978-3-319-63880-5_2

Hamilton, J., Hall. D., & Hamilton, T. (2021). Microlearning in the workplace of the future. In J. R. Corbeil, B. H. Khan, & M. E. Corbeil (Eds.), *Microlearning in the digital age: The design and delivery of learning in snippets*. Routledge.

Hogle, P. S. (2021). Microlearning in corporate settings. In J. R. Corbeil, B. H. Khan, & M. E. Corbeil (Eds.), *Microlearning in the digital age: The design and delivery of learning in snippets.* Routledge.

Leong, K., Sung, A., Au, D., & Blanchard, C. (2020). A review of the trend of microlearning. *Journal of Work-Applied Management, 13*(1), 88–102.

Rogers, E. M. (1995) *Diffusion of innovations*. Free Press.

Salas, A. (2017). Microlearning: What it is not and what it should be. *Learning Solutions*. https://learningsolutionsmag.com/articles/2255/microlearning-what-it-is-not-and-what-it-should-be.

Senge, P. M. (1994). *The fifth discipline fieldbook: The art and practice of the learning organization.* Currency.

Stefaniak, J. (2020). The utility of design thinking to promote systemic instructional design practices in the workplace. *TechTrends, 64*(2), 202–210.

Winger, A. (2018). Supersized tips for implementing microlearning in macro ways. *Distance Learning, 15*(4), 51–55.

Zhang, J., & West, R. E. (2020). Designing microlearning instruction for professional development through a competency based approach. *TechTrends, 64*, 310–318. https://doi.org/10.1007/s11528-019-00449-4

26

FORTIFYING SYSTEMS THINKING AND CHANGE THROUGH NEEDS ASSESSMENT (INDUSTRY)

Tracey A. Regenold and Sheila E. Murphy

Introduction

Workforce development is a social system that includes private and public sector organizations working together to create opportunities for job seekers and employers. Approximately 525 workforce development local areas exist in the United States. Each has a volunteer board responsible for serving employers and job seekers while contributing to the larger community. This case study examines a needs assessment conducted within one local workforce development area. Needs assessment is defined as "the process of identifying needs, prioritizing them, making needs-based decisions, allocating resources, and implementing actions in organizations to resolve problems underlying important needs" (Altschuld & Kumar 2010, p. 20).

The overarching consulting project within which this needs assessment was situated involved the design of a strategic plan that would enhance workforce and economic development in a local area. Needs assessment is a useful tool when conducted as a standalone project (Jackson et al., 2018; Norman et al., 2018; Salinas-Miranda et al., 2015) or as support for larger endeavors (Careyva et al., 2018; Lundy et al., 2017). This needs assessment supported the larger endeavor of strategic planning and system design for a local area workforce development board.

The authors applied needs assessment through the lens of systems thinking. Change was anticipated once the needs assessment was complete and next actions were ready to be taken. The pivot point at which conscious change occurs is when a system is ready for (re)design (Gharajedaghi, 2011). During the needs assessment the authors sought to discover the extent to which board members connected with system stakeholders and providers. Of equal importance was the

DOI: 10.4324/9781003028772-31

quest to discover how board members and stakeholders perceived the purpose of the workforce system. The authors posed questions about the interconnection among board members and stakeholders and the directions perceived for the workforce development system.

System and Key Players

According to Ulrich (1977), a social system is a designed, purposeful system concerned with the actionable utility of information. As a social system, a local workforce development area contains several stakeholder organizations guided by a board. The Workforce Innovation and Opportunity Act of 2014 (WIOA) requires that each local board include business leaders representing industry sectors. Other board members include those representing education, vocational rehabilitation, and other designated areas of expertise. The key players involved in this social system also included staff to the board.

It is noteworthy that board members and stakeholders alike represented a range of world views. Diversity of thought among representatives of organizations could be perceived as an advantage while requiring considerable shaping to build common ground (Jones, 2014) toward setting a clear direction for all parts of the workforce system. Among the system dynamics are expectations concerning design and direction of workforce activities. The board is expected to design and direct, while staff and stakeholder providers are expected to deliver services with emphasis on innovation in service delivery.

Another issue within the system is the expansive knowledge base held by staff serving the board. Professional staff members have long-term knowledge and experience in the complex system of workforce development and understand more about workforce development law and requirements than individual board members. Staff's development of the board to achieve mutual stewardship in the local area, without overreliance or overstepping, presents a difficult and delicate balance.

Case Analysis

The fundamental challenge of the initiative was to carry out a needs assessment that would inform the board, staff to the board, partners, and service providers of opportunities for a strategic systems design. An effective systems design would direct workforce development efforts to support the economic development and quality of life in the local area. The needs assessment revealed complex challenges and underlying causes of the problem encountered in the local area.

There were several complexities involved with this case. Current workforce law (WIOA, 2014) emphasizes innovation in addition to compliance with regulations. The expectation of compliance and innovation adds a challenge to the work of the board and stakeholders alike. The sheer complexity of requirements necessitates an investment of time that can impede creative thinking. Serving two customers with workforce development services, namely employers and job seekers, also brought complexity to the initiative. Making best use of a volunteer board, including leaders in private companies and government leaders with knowledge of workforce development, further complicated the effort to find common ground (Jones, 2014) regarding a strategic focus for the board. Finally, the interests and agendas of each board member, their professional expertise and education, and their respective organizations' reporting and performance requirements added layers of complexity to this already elaborate system.

Underlying causes of the problem in this case study concerned the definition of a system and the board's awareness and understanding of the system. Two facets of system functioning—connection among parts and clearly focused system purpose (Checkland, 1999; Jones, 2014)—were found to be merely implicit. These two facets needed to be made explicit for the board to function effectively, and for board members to design a system that is both compliant and innovative. Although board members demonstrated strong commitment to workforce development and valued strong working relationships with fellow board members, the board itself was not sufficiently structured to connect with other system stakeholders. Further, the board was not structured to guide a central purpose. This lack of awareness and understanding by the board of what a system is and does challenged the board's effective functioning.

Problem Resolution

As Ulrich (1977) stated, "From a systems point of view, it is useful to consider problem solving as a process of *systems design*" (p. 1099, italics in original). The application of systems thinking to the needs assessment of the local area provided a useful framework for examining what the board and stakeholders wanted to design strategically. The authors consciously designed the needs assessment within the systems thinking perspective. Underlying these strategies was a fundamental question: How were system players positioned to design the future of workforce development? Was the board ready to challenge old assumptions, build consensus around a purpose, and design connectivity to fulfill that purpose?

Two strategies guided the approach. First, the authors designed needs assessment questions that emphasized properties of a social system. The questions sought to discover perceptions of the relationship between the board and system partners, the board and providers, and the level of understanding of the purpose and direction of the board and what that should be. Examples of questions are displayed in Table 26.1.

Gharajedaghi (2011) emphasized the importance of learning by social system members who optimally adjust their world view toward greater "collective, shared learning" (p. 62). A fluid organizational system benefits from building new ideas and approaches to the system's purpose. The needs assessment questions helped

TABLE 26.1 Examples of Questions Asked During Needs Assessment

1. How effective is the Workforce Development system in serving the City and Region?
2. How can the Board most directly influence workforce system performance?
3. How can the City and the Region distinguish themselves nationally as visionary leaders of a Workforce Development system that delivers?
4. What would the ideal workforce development system look like in the City and the Region? How would this differ from what is currently in place?
5. To what extent do you believe that the Board is positioned and has what it needs to bring the ideal system closer to reality?
6. Do the data show that businesses are satisfied when using the system? Are changes needed?

the authors discover the range of viewpoints about system connections, system purpose, and the potential for learning.

A second strategy was to analyze the findings of the needs assessment from a systems perspective. Themes of the needs assessment emerged within the systems framework. The authors engaged in dialogue with each other about system realities that emerged in the findings. This strategy guided the authors in discovering what board members and stakeholders considered important in the design of a workforce system. Emergent themes were determined, emphasizing structure, clarity of focus, outreach, and innovation.

Overall, the needs assessment revealed that system partners recognized the importance of designing a clear, consensus-based direction that would guide useful ways of connecting system partners. Interviewees indicated that relationships among stakeholders and the board would benefit from a purposeful direction and guide provider services and ultimately the outcomes directed by the board. System partners showed various levels of awareness regarding the roles that different agencies and individuals were performing or expected to perform. System roles clarified within a framework of systems thinking would strengthen the agreed-upon direction for the organizational system to perform. Guiding the use of federal and other funding, designing metrics, and building a strong economy through a capable workforce were also seen as key directions that would benefit from a systems design.

Lessons Learned

The needs assessment framed within systems thinking revealed subtle and powerful realities that guided the authors in their work with the board in designing a systems-based strategic plan. Lessons learned emphasized the world views of board members and stakeholders. These lessons shaped a deeper understanding about board members' thinking and its potential for shaping a new mode of building consensus toward purposeful connection among system parts.

Current organizational practices in public and private sector organizations reward linear thinking over systems thinking. Patterns of breaking down the parts and analyzing components for "small fixes" characterize organizational functioning. These patterns, while valuable at the process level of functioning, tend to work against seeing holistically.

The needs assessment revealed that many system partners thought linearly rather than from a systems view. The sheer complexity of workforce development law means that some board members expressed that "knowing more" would help them make stronger contributions to the board's work. However, placing emphasis on knowledge acquisition would support compliance at the expense of innovation. Knowledge that is gained linearly potentially leads to analytical, or compartmentalized, thinking. Holistic or systemic thinking guides the needed connection among parts of the system.

The human side of relationship reality proved relevant and worthy of notice. Given that relationship building is critically important to system functioning and strength, some ownership issues revealed themselves in this study. During the needs assessment phase, the authors became aware that some providers appeared to consider themselves as best qualified to design and deliver services without interference from the board or staff. Resentment of interference associated with quality assurance, a built-in practice that guides compliance, was revealed to be an issue for some providers.

Designing a solid and sustained governing structure emerged as important in the needs assessment. The system required a clear, understandable structure that would help focus the board and stakeholders on intentionally designed directions with supporting metrics and communication. Linkages among operating departments, stakeholders, and the board were seen as fundamental to an effective system. The authors learned that engaging the board in the design of a system that would support and sustain workforce development responsibilities would optimize the strategic plan while stimulating innovation that the current law (WIOA, 2014) encourages.

It became clear that a consciously designed, well-connected system capable of being sustained for the long term was key. Changes in the environment, in board membership, and in stakeholder participation were among anticipated shifts that the system must weather. The structure would be designed to address emergent needs presented within the local service area, and to provide one clear vision in fulfillment of a mandated mission through the orchestrated linkages among system partners.

Conclusion

The authors approached the needs assessment openly from a systems thinking framework that would guide design. Reflective thinking about needs assessment findings provided a creative and stimulating source of energy for the authors. The needs assessment offered a fluid opportunity to consider current system realities as resources that could be brought together to build a solid and flexible strategic plan.

The framing of the needs assessment within systems thinking fortified a foundation for change. The broad inclusion of relevant partners resulted in a comprehensive, focused strategic plan to serve the local workforce development area. This fortification of systems thinking and change was in accordance with Ulrich's (1987) assertion that his "Critical heuristics of social systems design" (p. 276) start with an understanding of the system itself. As he stated: "If an action system is not only to operate purposively, but also to act purposefully, it must know that, and why it is motivated to act" (Ulrich, 1977, p. 1105). Needs assessment is an ideal tool for such systems exploration and understanding.

The authors found needs assessment to be of great utility in strengthening our own systems understanding, as well as that of board members, staff, and stakeholders. Far more than a standalone utility, needs assessment revealed itself to represent a vital complement and support to systems and design thinking. Needs assessment strengthened the strategic design within a systems framework, developed in a collaborative manner, with confidence by the board, staff, and stakeholders.

Reflective Questions

- What is your organization's/system's purpose?
- Who are the stakeholders that should be included in identifying/supporting that purpose?
- How would you most effectively ensure that stakeholders (employees, customers, etc.) are working to fulfill the system's purpose?

Additional Resources

More information on Werner Ulrich's past and present work on systems thinking, Critical Systems Heuristics, professional practice, and planning can be found on his website: https://wulrich.com/.

References

Altschuld, J. W., & Kumar, D. D. (2010). *Needs assessment: An overview* (Vol. 1). Sage.

Careyva, B. A., Hamadani, R., Friel, T., & Coyne, C. A. (2018). A social needs assessment tool for an urban Latino population. *Journal of Community Health, 43*(1), 137–145. https://doi.org/10.1007/s10900-017-0396-6

Checkland, P. (1999). *Systems thinking, systems practice: Includes a 30-year retrospective.* Wiley & Sons.

Gharajedaghi, J. (2011). *Systems thinking: Managing chaos and complexity: A platform for designing business architecture* (3rd ed.). Elsevier.

Jackson, K. M., Pukys, S., Castro, A., Hermosura, L., Mendez, J., Vohra-Gupta, S., Padilla, Y., & Morales, G. (2018). Using the transformative paradigm to conduct a mixed methods needs assessment of a marginalized community: Methodological lessons and implications. *Evaluation and Program Planning, 66*, 111–119. https://doi.org/10.1016/j.evalprogplan.2017.09.010

Jones, P. (2014). Systemic design principles for complex social systems. In G. S. Metcalf (Ed.), *Social systems and design* (pp. 91–128, Vol. 1). Springer. https://doi.org/10.1007/978-4-431-54478-4_4

Lundy, E. L., Andresen, C. E., Freeman, S. A., Loy, D. D., & Gunn, P. J. (2017). Utilization of a modified Delphi method for needs assessment and curriculum revision of a senior-level beef systems management course. *NACTA Journal, 61*(3), 193–196. www.nactateachers.org/attachments/article/2632/7%20%20Lundy.pdf

Norman, C. C., McDonald, K., Schneider, A. E., Malinovsky, I., Goldmann, E., Blauschild, M. K., & Driver, C. (2018). The New York City Mental Health Needs Assessment Study (MHNAS): Objectives, design, and methods. *International Journal of Methods in Psychiatric Research*, 1–10. https://doi.org/10.1002/mpr.1606

Salinas-Miranda, A. A., Salemi, J. L., King, L. M., Baldwin, J. A., Berry, E., Austin, D. A., Scarborough, K., Spooner, K. K., Zoorob, R. J., & Salihu, H. M. (2015). Adverse childhood experiences and health-related quality of life in adulthood: Revelations from a community needs assessment. *Health and Quality of Life Outcomes, 13*, 1–12. https://doi.org/10.1186/s12955-015-0323-4

Ulrich, W. (1977). The design of problem-solving systems. *Management Science, 23*(10), 1099–1108. https://doi.org/10.1287/mnsc.23.10.1099

Ulrich, W. (1987). Critical heuristics of social systems design. *European Journal of Operational Research, 31*(3), 276–283. https://doi.org/10.1016/0377-2217(87)90036-1

Workforce Innovation and Opportunity Act of 2014, 29 U.S.C. § § 3101–3361 (2018). www.govinfo.gov/content/pkg/PLAW-113publ128/pdf/PLAW-113publ128.pdf

INDEX

For Product Safety Concerns and Information please contact our EU
representative GPSR@taylorandfrancis.com
Taylor & Francis Verlag GmbH, Kaufingerstraße 24, 80331 München, Germany

www.ingramcontent.com/pod-product-compliance
Ingram Content Group UK Ltd.
Pitfield, Milton Keynes, MK11 3LW, UK
UKHW022017180926
475701UK00005B/885
* 9 7 8 0 3 6 7 4 6 4 4 1 7 *